AF812619

De-essentializing Refugees: Perceptions, Experiences, and Becoming of Syrians in Türkiye

Umut Ozkaleli

De-essentializing Refugees: Perceptions, Experiences, and Becoming of Syrians in Türkiye

Springer

Umut Ozkaleli
School of Public and International Affairs
ADA University
Baku, Azerbaijan

ISBN 978-981-96-5518-2 ISBN 978-981-96-5519-9 (eBook)
https://doi.org/10.1007/978-981-96-5519-9

© The Editor(s) (if applicable) and The Author(s), under exclusive license to Springer Nature Singapore Pte Ltd. 2025

This work is subject to copyright. All rights are solely and exclusively licensed by the Publisher, whether the whole or part of the material is concerned, specifically the rights of translation, reprinting, reuse of illustrations, recitation, broadcasting, reproduction on microfilms or in any other physical way, and transmission or information storage and retrieval, electronic adaptation, computer software, or by similar or dissimilar methodology now known or hereafter developed.
The use of general descriptive names, registered names, trademarks, service marks, etc. in this publication does not imply, even in the absence of a specific statement, that such names are exempt from the relevant protective laws and regulations and therefore free for general use.
The publisher, the authors and the editors are safe to assume that the advice and information in this book are believed to be true and accurate at the date of publication. Neither the publisher nor the authors or the editors give a warranty, expressed or implied, with respect to the material contained herein or for any errors or omissions that may have been made. The publisher remains neutral with regard to jurisdictional claims in published maps and institutional affiliations.

This Springer imprint is published by the registered company Springer Nature Singapore Pte Ltd.
The registered company address is: 152 Beach Road, #21-01/04 Gateway East, Singapore 189721, Singapore

If disposing of this product, please recycle the paper.

To Hür, may your generation be better than ours at stopping wars that perish children

Acknowledgments

During the fieldwork, I met many people who shared their perspectives, ideas, and feelings with me. I thank each and every one of them. They made this research possible. They were eager to talk so people could learn their life stories and the meaning of war and displacement. Many made me promise to write about their experiences. I hope I have done these voices justice. There were a number of gatekeepers who trusted and endorsed me so I could reach the people who became interviewees. I am grateful for their support and trust. I am forever grateful to my interpreter for accepting a very low pay rate and for their long conversations with me about Syria in particular and war and loss in general. Hür developed skills of managing a parent who spent hours listening to experiences of war, loss, and displacement. I am blessed with his soothing presence. For endless hours, Murat listened to the field findings and read many versions of the manuscript with his keen and analytical mind. He never once doubted that I could complete this book and keep my promise to the participants of this study. This research has not benefited from any funding. I am thankful to these two guys who never complained about the use of family funds for this research. I thank Springer Nature and my editor, Anushangi Weerakoon, for giving a chance to human voices in war.

Competing Interests The author has no competing interests to declare that are relevant to the content of this manuscript.

About the Book

This book focuses on perceptions (Part I), experiences (Part II), and becoming (Part III) of Syrian refugees in Türkiye. The in-depth interviews with 79 Syrians are central to the analysis of the conflict and what it means to become a refugee. Part I analyzes Syrian refugees' perceptions of identities, actors, and causes of the conflict through conflict theories. An in-depth understanding of refugee perceptions about the conflict is timely, as a newly formulated governance in Syria is underway after the Asad regime was dismantled in December 2024. A considerable number of Syrians who were forced to leave were part of the uprising against the regime. Their agency will be part of the unfolding of a new Syria. Therefore, the book explores factors shaping refugee views and their possible expectations for the future of Syria to consider their role in the future of Syrian politics. The remainder of the book examines refugees in dual spatiality and multiple temporalities. The book investigates the transborder re-making of social interactions and refugee selves' articulation of agency in their everyday becoming. Refugees live with spatial duality and multiple temporalities, which shape their agency and becoming. Connections of past and future to the present in the narratives of refugees help explore the transformative impacts of dislocation and how they responded in different ways to reframe their identities. While Part II investigates lived experiences that formulate their expectations about the future, including return and aspirations in terms of the new socio-political structure for Syria, Part III focuses on refugee becomings, as a considerable number of Syrians continue living in Türkiye.

Contents

Chapter 1
Introduction

In the early days of moving to Gaziantep in 2013, my then nine-year-old son ran toward me in the playground and inquired, "What is a Syrian?" Children asked him this question before deciding whether they would play with him. The answer was perhaps the first symbolic articulation of this book: "A Syrian is not a *what* but a *who*." Sometime later, through the children's grapevine, I was *told* that "the Syrians poisoned the tap water." This misinformation was the second challenge that I symbolically located: "How can we avoid banal dehumanization that strips people of their complexities and humanity in societies that include many migrants and refugees?" After that dehumanizing depiction entered his mind, the child met many Syrian individuals whom he liked, loved, and saw as people just like himself. For me, as a social researcher, questions endured.

Syrians were either an "object" of anger and resentment or an "object" of sympathy. Additionally, their decisions to get married and have babies as refugees (particularly for the refugees in camps and urban refugees in poverty) were questioned and debated in everyday conversation. This brought a new set of realizations that class dimension was also part of the holistic creation and image of "the refugee." Such a reaction also provoked a chain of questions: Is there any guarantee for certainty and stability in the "normal," "routine" order of things? Who deserves to take the risk of building a family? Who is suitable to have children? Where does justification for continuing to build a life start or end? From another angle, and a more enduring one, how do people who are positioned as refugees feel when they get married in the middle of a war in an uncertain tomorrow? Who does not feel secure enough to get married (or have children), and what would that mean for them to put a hold on their life? What does it mean for them to be "refugees?" How does it feel to have the gaze of others upon them, and how does the gaze of others shape their actions? Questions were endless, yet through the reification of the term "refugee" that is applied to individuals, the experiences and lives of many different people are

© The Author(s), under exclusive license to Springer Nature Singapore Pte Ltd. 2025

U. Ozkaleli, *De-essentializing Refugees: Perceptions, Experiences, and Becoming of Syrians in Türkiye*, https://doi.org/10.1007/978-981-96-5519-9_1

reduced to simple forms, and their position in host communities is "frozen," which denies their agency (Ozkaleli and Ozkaleli 2024; Mahendran et al. 2019).

My field research and writing process departed from the premise that there is a need to understand Syrian people with diverse backgrounds and experiences from their own perspectives. An objectified perception of "the refugee" is not only happening in Gaziantep or Türkiye; this is a transnational, global problem, as refugee flows are the product of wars that are rooted in colonial histories. Not only refugees coming from one country but many coming from the Global South who are positioned as refugees are depicted with the singular colonial perspective that clusters them as "the Refugee." In connection with this transnational practice, there is a dominant gaze upon the "Syrian Refugee" in Gaziantep. The dominant gaze comes from the politically charged media images that are created every day about Syrians and the host community that is close in proximity but distant in interaction with Syrians in Gaziantep.

This research aims to discover the experiences and becoming of people who come from different social locations that would challenge such singular "Refugee" construction. For this, I focus on analyzing Syrian refugees' transborder re-making of everyday life in Gaziantep. Field explorations indicate that people do not experience themselves in a one-time framework. This means they lived in the present and continuously referred to the past, sometimes desiring to re-capture their past life. They could not live in the present without a clear image of what the future entails, either. Also, while living in Gaziantep, they constantly experienced spatial duality by physically traveling to Syria and recreating Syrian neighborhoods or imagining themselves in Syrian locations. Inevitably, the focus of the study intertwined with the multiplicity of time and space to understand how people experience themselves. Hence, this study is essentially built on the inquiry, "How is refugee 'becoming' experienced in dual spatiality and multiple temporalities?"

Individuals in the receiving community are "conceptually separated from the place where [they] originally belonged and displaced into a space unknown to [them], a space that already belongs to [others]. Being a refugee becomes a reflection of their non-being as they are placed into a land where they are considered not to belong" (Ozkaleli 2018, p. 17). They are *thrown into* it by force (Heidegger 1962). "Refugee" is an imposed term constructed by a rational-bureaucratic formation of the territorial nation-state's legalistic contours, which results in the invisibility of all personal differences (Ozkaleli 2018, p. 17). Not only are they stripped of their subjective experiences, but the refugee label that turns individuals into one-dimensional people also clusters them as a coherent whole, a group with the same values, attitudes, and behaviors (Crawley and Skleparis 2017; Zetter 1991; 2007). Nevertheless, through their journey from emplacement to displacement and re-placement, people develop multiple attachments, remembering and imagining the places (Malkki 1992, p. 38) they have experienced the self. To perceive refugees as visible actors with a *persona* (Harrell-Bond and Voutira 2007), their conceptualization of self needs to emerge in writings that center the life-world of refugees. Thus, such writings need to focus on individual stories, experiences, and standpoints (Malkki 1995; Zetter 1991). Transborder re-making of social interactions re-formulates refugee selves' articulation of agency in their everyday becoming. Connections of past, future, and present in the narratives of refugees help explore the transformative impacts of dislocation and how they responded in different ways to reframe their identities (Ozkaleli 2018). Departing from this point, my central research question can be refined as, "How is refugee 'becoming' experienced in dual spatiality and multiple temporalities?"

Chapter 1 starts with the methodology that guides this research. Chapter 2 briefly contextualizes Syrian history and the 2015–2016 socio-political context where Syrians experienced becoming refugees. The chapter follows with the theoretical framework of the study. The remaining chapters are presented in three sections, focusing on perceptions, experiences, and becoming of refugees. Part I, which includes Chaps. 3–6, uses conflict theories to analyze how Syrians in this study perceive identities, actors, and causes of the conflict. An in-depth understanding of perceptions about the conflict is relevant for today. The Asad regime was dismantled in December 2024. A newly formulated governance in Syria is underway. A considerable number of Syrians who were forced to leave were part of uprisings against the regime. Their agency will be part of the unfolding of a new Syria. Therefore, analyzing the way refugee views are shaped and their possible expectations for the future of Syria are important factors to consider for the future of Syrian politics. Part II, Chaps. 7 and 8 investigate experiences that formulate their expectations about the future, including return and aspirations in terms of the new socio-political structure for Syria. Both Parts II and III examine refugees in dual spatiality and multiple temporalities. While Parts II focuses on lived experience and their impact on future expectations, Part III focuses on refugee becomings, as a considerable number of Syrians continue living in Türkiye.

Methodology

Epistemology

Voices of Their Own

I see interviewing as a participatory process of meaning-making. Throughout the writing of this work, the voices of people who were part of the study are presented as meeting and conversing through the similar and different ideas they shared. This writing, therefore, is dialogical (Bakhtin 2010). In almost all sections, no "one" little segment represents and summarizes all others. Intentionally, extensive quotes are given from the voices of the people to create a conversation that has an intersubjective meaning. The conversation here does not refer to a writing style but rather a methodological approach, meaning that at points, voices are coming together for similar experiences, and at others, they are different, sometimes contradictory, and oppositional. The reader will also hear my voice and interpretation as my camera is inevitably positioned from a certain angle that shapes how I see (Ozkaleli and

Ozkaleli 2022). Hence, a blend of refugees' unique experiences and social interaction-based meaning-making surfaces in these pages as a dialogue that enriches our understanding of the multiple ways refugees experience themselves.

The real methodological challenge here is to be able to keep the genuine self-representations (Spivak 1988) of *each* interviewee while establishing a dialogical connection among them. Semi-structured interviews provided a beginning. A conscious effort had continuously been made to reach self-expressions and articulations of individuals to find answers to the following questions: "What was it like to be a Syrian in the pre-war era?" "What is to be a Syrian who experienced warring Syria?" "What is it to be a refugee"? "How does a Syrian individual feel now? What does s/he experience?" "How does a Syrian individual see the dominant culture?" "Where is s/he locating his/her self?" "What would s/he like others to know about his/her and his/her displacement experience?" "What is home?" "How does s/he see his/her past and envision the future?"

How I approach the field and interviewing needs to be elaborated here as it has direct relevance to my epistemological ground. In all my field works, I start the interview, regardless of the topic, with the same question: "Tell me about yourself." This question is not only to establish rapport with the participants but has a larger aim. Qualitative research is essentially about a deeper understanding of people's views, feelings, ideas, and experiences (Babbie 2009). Asking questions to the participants without contextualizing them as individuals leaves their answers hanging in the air. Moreover, without locating the individual in their larger context, elaborating on the questions, understanding in what ways they use symbols, and recognizing moments and topics to dive in deeper would not be possible.

Each person has a particular history. How participants define their "beginnings" is crucial for the researcher to understand this personal history. "Tell me about yourself" is intentionally broad and brings different reactions. Some start from birth, others from marriage, and still others the moment they leave home. Some ask directions, such as "You mean my age and where I am from, that sort of thing?" Some insist on a "specific question" to answer. All of these reactions are building blocks for me as the researcher to understand not only in what ways people will receive the questions but also give clues about what it is that they focus on, what they give importance in their life, what they are willing to share with an unknown person called the "researcher."

Another focal point in my interviews is to appreciate individuals in different temporalities and multiple spatial experiences. Each individual carries experiences s/he had in different spaces, and their past experiences inform their future expectations and present actions and thinking (Emirbayer and Mische 1998; Ozkaleli 2021). The interviews included questions from pre-war time to living in Türkiye. The spatial and temporal approach is important in two ways. First, as the researcher, I tuned in to the person as much as possible. This helped me see the individual in front of me as a person rather than an object of study. Where I started this research was the realization that "refugee" is a given, albeit undesired, position and did not "make" or even "define" individuals. Accordingly, I find asking participants about their self-definitions to be an effective method to learn about an individual's past, self-identification, and what makes them who they are. There is another reason for asking questions about different spatio-temporalities in people's lives. Without articulation of "before and after" in their life, the way individuals identify with different groups, important events that mark their view of the world, etc., it is challenging to work with the raw data of the interviews. The data can be interpreted in its natural richness only by meaningfully locating individuals in multiple spatio-temporalities. This approach, for me, is at the epistemological core of social research based on fieldwork and interviews.

Given the chance, individuals have impressive ways of articulating what they experience, how they experience it, and, in some instances, why they experience it. Using extensive quotes from the interview participants to provide a space for their voices is a conscious methodological act on my part. I do not "summarize" the quotes to avoid becoming the only one with a voice. If I summarize, this means my camera is the singular subject making the meaning; yet, interview participants, for me, are not the "bearers of meaning" but the "makers of meaning" (Mulvey 1975, pp. 6–18). Participants make sense of their own world, and this is where they are experts. As a trained researcher, my expertise is to see patterns and contradictions to find explanations of "why" the experience is the way it is when it is connected to others' lives. I bring explanations through theories. My emphasis on voice avoids a claim of "giving voice," which signals that they "do not have it" and that I am the one providing it. Individuals have a voice. Voices may have been silenced, muted, or deeply buried where people have not used them for long periods. I aim to recognize, surface, and bring these existing voices to the reader to explore them. Just because dominant groups turn it down does not mean the people cannot speak (Spivak 1988). This is the departure point of my epistemology. Within these existing voices, my position is to investigate and articulate individuals' patterns, deviations, and particularities. My interpretations and analysis, which are integrated with the social realities of interview participants, come from a multi-layer interaction; that is, my interaction with the interview participants, their textual conversation in the pages where I bring social research analysis, and the reader's exploration of the collective and intersubjective meaning that is created.

Author Positionality on the Field and Conceptual Meaning-Making

At the start of almost every interview, I was asked two common questions. "Who funds you?" and "Why are you interested in Syrians?" This research had no internal or external funding. When no funding agency is involved, the people's curiosity turns to "Why us?" Anthropologists argue that some researchers find a connection with the communities through relationality and a connection to their personal history (Navaro 2012). The core of my interest in social research emerged from a need to understand the effects of war on people, especially people who left their homes behind. The relationality for me is that I am an internally displaced Turkish Cypriot (from Limassol to Kyrenia) as a result of the 1974 war. Even though I was a newborn then, I grew up in this close yet distant home that I could not even visit for decades. Displacement was always expressed as yearning and loss by people who were the closest to me, and they never forgot this "other" home. Years later, as a trained social researcher, when I was driving to work in Gaziantep, I kept seeing the road sign that directed people to "*Halep*" (Aleppo), a little more than two-hour drive across the border. Just like the close but uncrossable border of my childhood, Aleppians saw that sign every single. Later, without any prompt, an interviewee talked to me about the difficulty of seeing that sign and not being able to go home. I saw many young Syrian parents with little children. In front of my eyes, in a different scale of displacement, these adults were experiencing what my parents' generation experienced. Nevertheless, for Syrians in Gaziantep, the challenge was even more complex as their displacement carried them to a country where their language and culture were different than theirs and where their positionality was not a "citizen." Therefore, when I was asked, "Why Syrians?" the answer became an icebreaker, a connection point between me as the interviewer and the interviewees when I told them, "In my country's history, I am your next generation, your children, and I would like to understand the first generation."

The interaction of different experiences is at the center of intersubjective meaning-making (Bourdieu and Wacquant 1992). The interaction of multiple human experiences and meaning-making can enhance making sense of the experience of war or the experience of growing up with a war background. Being in a dialogue with others who have had war experiences in different times and different places is the most effective way in this global (colonized) village (McLuhan and Powers 1989) to understand what has happened and what is happening to millions of us and how to locate the effects of war on individual lives. All the interviewees and gatekeepers I met in the field positively approached my reason, and we strived to communicate for a sense of understanding. I aspired for an empathetic connection and conversation where we met at a place within the destruction of war.

Inspired by standpoint theory and situated knowledge (Stoetzler and Yuval-Davis 2002; Harding 2004), my engagement with concepts starts with explorations of their meaning for the participants. Standpoint theory focuses on questions of power relations about who has access to producing knowledge and sees the oppressed people as the agents of knowledge production as subjects of research rather than objects (Harding 2004). Objectivity is aimed to be reached through situated knowledge as the object of knowledge is seen as an actor and agent. Seen as agents, they will not be examined via universal and transcendent criteria but will be understood within their limited location and their meanings (Haraway 2004). I focus on how people word and define concepts to grasp their meaning fully. Concepts and definitions that the researchers use are politically driven (Harding 2004), yet the mainstream often conceals the eye-camera behind the "dominant mode of vision," as it is positioned at the center (Akrivoulis 1999; Ozkaleli and Ozkaleli 2022). The mainstream language usually conceals political projects as "objective science." Standpoint theory aims for strong objectivity by arguing that the subjects of knowledge "are embodied and visible, because the lives from which thought has started are always present and visible in the results of thought" (Harding 2004, p. 132). I strive to reach objectivity through the surfacing of subjectivities, both the participants and mine. Any author, regardless of how covert it is, carries subjectivity as everyone has values, viewpoints, particular language, and ways of understanding past and present. The third-person omniscient writing style does not remove subjective meanings and ways of seeing but merely conceals them, leading to undiscovered bias. In other words, to avoid bias, subjectivities need to be surfaced in the analysis.

The concept of "revolution" is an example here, as it has been central to the participants' narrative. From the outset, regardless of their political positioning, let they be jihadists, seculars, "Westernists," moderates, Kurds, Turkmens, or Arabs, Syrian refugees in Gaziantep who were against the regime and actively participated in the demonstrations called the uprising a "revolution" at the time of my fieldwork which was done mostly in 2016. Even retrospectively, when they were critical of Islamist factions' domination of the uprising, the majority still kept referring to it as "revolution." As the author of this text, my approach is not to debate whether there was a Syrian revolution. Instead, I focus on people's usage of concepts such as revolution to inquire what these terms mean for different political groups, what is understood from a concept, how it is used, and what the participants' subjective meaning-making is. My main concern is to understand how people experience and perceive their world and what they name it. After this investigation, my position as the researcher is to investigate the implications of these meanings in people's past and future projections that decide their present assessments and possible outcomes. For example, many who perceived this event as a revolution ended up celebrating the collapse of Asad and the Ba'ath regime even though they may not be happy with the new power consolidation. Their deep resentment and opposition to the regime signaled that their first concern was to see Asad go.

My foremost task as a social researcher is to learn and understand "What is it like to be in that particular segment of society?" and "What are the ways people define themselves and experience their social location?" Such questions are also building blocks of my analysis and writing. This approach helps me to scrutinize other questions such as "In what ways do polarizations of host communities and refugees happen?", "In what ways are people positioned as refugees not seen in their becoming as much as the citizens?" Only then can we analyze how multiple ways of experiencing self in society can be achieved in constructive ways without dehumanizing or singularizing people under one category. The accuracy of answers to analytical questions depends on social researchers' understanding of social living from the position of the people they are investigating.

When I formed the interview questions, I used neither "government" nor "regime." I generally phrased it as "conflict" or "what is happening in Syria." After an interviewee chose a signifier, I continued with their usage for themselves in the remaining questions I asked. For example, after they made statements like "government," "regime," "revolution," or "war," I followed their realities to ask follow-up or further questions. I used a similar approach when interpreting and analyzing interviews. If they say "revolution," I mention it as such; if they call it "their so-called revolution," I point it out as such. If there is a contradiction in various participants' usage (revolution vs. their so-called revolution or Free Syrian Army vs. Free Army),

I stress it so the reader can follow the nuances and what they might mean. If, in this work, other than my general analysis, I present anything from *my own viewpoint*, that is where I use italics with a mention of *author-camera*. Methodologically, I see the interview as an interaction and my interpretations as an outcome of mutual meaning-making where I am also positioned as a subject and not a hidden one.

To achieve intersubjective meaning-making, this research distinctly aims to appreciate the diversity of voices. While participants are unique in their experiences, they belong to social groups that have an influence on their understanding of the events, their positionality, and the meaning of their social interactions. Individuals are not only shaped by their unique experiences and identity intersections that make them who they are, but they also reflect a discourse, a community's understanding that they are part of. Hence, when we hear one person, we also hear many who are articulating their ideas and thoughts. I also looked at intragroup differences and intergroup similarities in order to better understand the complex nature of social interactions. When I give their views on a given topic, I briefly present the intersecting identities of each and give a brief background in the first mention of a particular interviewee. Social research's challenge and necessity is to capture various ideas and experiences that travel through different people and groups. This is an endless cycle of action, reaction, interaction, and integration of people articulating their views, visions, expectations, and desires. It is important to understand people who are located differently spatially and temporally in various societies. Qualitative social research learns about patterns, not from one study and its limited number of participants, but it is cultivated through the comparison of many different studies in different places. This study aims to be part of such a collective by focusing on Syrian refugees in Gaziantep.

Author Eye-Camera in Writing

"Author eye-camera" is related to how I engage with my subjectivity and those of others. Whenever we look, let that be at people, countries, or words, we all look at a (metaphorical) camera. The epistemological base of the cinematographic apparatus (Baudry 1974) urges us to see the process of any knowledge production in terms of who positions the angle of the camera (operator—in this case, the field researcher), where/who this operator is looking/investigating (spectrum—in this case the interviewees within a temporal and spatial context), and when the operator positions its camera on the spectrum, who is expected to look at the results (spectator—in this case the text reader) (Barthes 1981; Ozkaleli and Ozkaleli 2022). Realization of the researcher's (operator's) subjective position may be used as a tool in writing, where interview participants' narrative becoming center stage could shift their position from the spectrum to the operator. When I, the researcher, listen to participants' words and namings, hear the ups and downs in their voices or tears or laughter in their eyes, become the spectator and shift from the operator position. In the end, I am the author of the text and inevitably have control of the decoupage (positioning the camera to narrate the story) and montage (cutting and adding that creates the final text as a product) (Baudry 1974, p. 40 in Ozkaleli and Ozkaleli 2022, p. 199). Hence, both I and the reader need to be conscious of I standing as a camera (perhaps, "the camera" as I/eye has the authorial power). It also encourages us to realize that every person who comes from intersections of many identities and interactions also positions themselves as a camera.

When reading this work, as a reader/spectator, if your lens is against conservatives, you will feel out of your comfort zone. If your lens resists Kurdish identity, you will feel out of your comfort zone when you are reading Kurdish voices. If you are from the regime-supporting lens (as someone once "advised" me to "talk to the 'real Syrians' in Syria to learn what 'really' is happening"), you will be in discomfort in the majority of this work, but there will be discomforting moments if you do not want to hear any regime-supporting voices as they are in these pages as well, even though much less than the opposing ones given the fact that majority of the Syrian refugees in Gaziantep were there because they were opposition to the regime. If you are reading perspectives, emotions, and experiences from people that you consider from your own group, and it does not represent you, you will have the daunting task of realizing that "your group" is not as coherent, wholesome sum that you make it out to be and intragroup differences are sometimes as acute as the intergroup differences (Tajfel 2010).

While challenging, my work aims to analyze and interpret people's life-world (how they experience themselves), make sense of their experiences, and what it means to be in that social location. Inevitably, my eye-camera has not only a particular positionality but also a lens transmitting colors of my understanding and shapes my interpretation. Still, I strive to take the participants' starting point as my departure point. I stand with the claim that objectivity can only be ensured by revealing one's political and subjective position (Harding 2004). Keeping with the spirit of standpoint theory, I am revealing relevant parts of my subjectivity so the reader can see how my interpretations are shaped: I am a secular, an anti-militarist, an anti-colonialist who argues for social justice for all individuals and groups who occupy the same social space. I am against war, and I am critical of the normalization of the state as a violent entity. My interpretation of what I see is influenced by the paradigms I have and the way I experience myself as a person and as a researcher. Recognition of subjectivity is a necessary starting point to move away from bias, but it is not sufficient. Let us discuss this in concrete terms. I am a Cypriot, coming from a colonized history, a minority in Cyprus in relation to Greek Cypriots who hold the recognized state and power. I come from a minority position in many parts of my identity, meaning that I am located on the less powerful side of the social structure, not only in terms of resource sharing but also in terms of being heard and recognized. I am of mixed heritage; part of my family ancestry is Black Cypriots, which makes me a minority of a minority. I am a female feminist scholar located in what is named "the global South." Almost everywhere "feminist-female" is mostly invisible or unwanted. I have lived most of my adult life as a "legal alien," not in places where I am recognized as a citizen. There is an obvious positionality where I can subjectively locate minority experiences. It makes me empathetic to minority positions, even though a minority position does not automatically instill empathy. I also hold power positions; I am in a comfortable level of middle class, I am educated, I have a respect-generating occupation, and my "immigrant" position is a "legal" one and often places me above the average living conditions of the locals, similar to European "expat" position rather than the negative connotations of "immigrant" or "refugee." While the former part of my identity position may lead me not only to empathize but also to depict people in minority positions always in a positive light, the latter part of my identity may normalize the stereotypes that are presented for the lower classes (also the dominant's power) or downplay the everyday challenges of living in a country without legal or underprivileged documentation. My awareness of my subjectivity leads me to create a dialogue among the participants, a dialogue between the participants and me, and a conversation among the reader, participants, and me. This is why contradictions, differences, and similarities are aspired to be shared to understand how people in different social locations feel, think, and experience. Methodically, I believe it is not enough to declare our positionality but to engage it with other subjectivities. Writing the text is done as a practice so that different experiences can find a space to meet. When the readers meet my work, they are asked to know the camera that dictates their seeing, others' seeing, and, of course, my seeing as the author of this text.

Eye-Camera Sorting the Data and the Analysis Process

The interviews were 85 h 18 min (5118 min) in total. Transcribing 79 interviews and sorting the data took considerable time. All of the interviews have been transcribed verbatim without skipping any parts. I did not use automatic transcription, professional transcription services, or research assistants to transcribe the interviews. I transcribed the recordings myself. While it may not be time efficient, I find the transcription and sorting of the data process a crucial part that leads up to analysis. When immersing yourself in the material you are working on, you capture many details where the true power of analysis lies. I do not transcribe only the most relevant parts of an interview but its entirety. This choice is connected to the temporal engagement of my interview questions. I ask people about their self-definitions, their life before and after the war, and becoming a refugee. Like this multidimensional temporal engagement, analyzing the entire interview is how I connect different parts of the person I conversed with. Whenever I am analyzing an answer they give, I look through the particularities of that person and how they define themselves throughout that text. It takes considerable time to go back and forth in the transcription. However, that transcription is a representation of a life where we cannot automatically crop from its holistic self. If I do not transcribe and listen to how they located themselves in their home country as a citizen, I cannot possibly get close to understanding what it means for them to be referred to as a number in contexts that position them as refugees. An example would make my point clearer. Depending on the social location different people held, their sense of belonging to their home country was varied, influencing their sense of integration into the receiving community. It is challenging to locate experiences in a new context without understanding the meaning of home and all its complexities. If people are asked about their experience in a place, it is not only that particular place and that particular time that decides the answer. For the analysis to be accurate, I needed to know as much as possible about the person's life journey. I could only do that with the engagement of the person's interview holistically all the time. This means continuous listening, transcribing, reading, writing, re-reading, and re-listening. Living a life is a multi-temporal experience, so it should be the sorting and analyzing of the transcription of the bits and pieces of that life that the interviewee is willing to share with the researcher.

I used MAXQDA software to sort and create categories and concepts (Saldaña 2013). In the first cycle, I used process coding, which provides access to action in the data and is an efficient coding strategy for capturing interaction and emotion (Saldaña 2013). "Processes are embedded within psychological concepts such as prejudice, identity, memory, and trust" (Willig 2008, in Saldaña 2013, p. 96), all of which are elements in the analysis of an individual's agency. In the second cycle, I used focused coding, which is categorized based on thematic or conceptual similarity (Saldaña 2013, p. 209 in Ozkaleli 2021). Focused coding is a step forward after initial codes to determine those that make the most analytical sense (Charmaz 2006, p. 57 in Ozkaleli 2021).

The Interview Participants

I conducted semi-structured, open-ended, in-depth interviews with 79 male and female refugees between November 2015 and June 2016 in Gaziantep, Türkiye, with urban Syrian refugees. Participant selection included purposive sampling based on gender, ethnicity, religion/belief/ideology, class, occupation, and age. Thirty-nine men and 40 women were interviewed, the youngest being 18 and the oldest 78 years of age. Syria has a very rich culture of people from different linguistic, religious, and ethnic backgrounds. In this study, only part of this colorful fabric is reflected, not including some, such as the Alawites, Êzîdî, and Armenian people. The study does not focus on Syrians in Syria and has a limited scope, covering the segments of Syrian society who fled to Antep. Each receiving state has its own policy regarding who they accept to their countries, and Türkiye accepted significantly fewer refugees from the remaining groups compared to the Sunni Muslim population. The minority position of refugees such as Alawite and Êzîdîs in Türkiye made them vulnerable and harder to identify. This made them even less accessible than Sunni Muslims as interviewees. Just like researchers face limitations with their language access, they are also limited with the populations they can reach. Even though there were few attempts to connect me with Alawite or Êzîdî people, I could not access anyone from these groups.

The majority of study participants identified as Sunni Muslim Arabs, and the remaining were Turkmen, Kurdish, and one Palestinian who grew up in Syria. Four identified themselves only as "Syrian" without any ethnic attachment, and one stated, "first Syrian, then Arab." One identified as both Turk and Arab, and the other preferred to be called Turk rather than Turkmen. Two (son and mother) said they were Kurds who were assimilated and Arabized and did not speak Kurdish. One had a Sunni Muslim and Christian parents. Ten people did not identify with any religion, calling themselves atheist, deist, non-believer, agnostic, or nonbeliever-atheist. One defined themselves as "anti-dictatorship," refusing any ethnic identity. Several people were raised in their early years in other Arabic countries like UAE or Saudi Arabia and returned to Syria later. Most participants were from Aleppo, and the remaining 30 were from various places such as Damascus, Idlib, Raqqa, Baniyas, Hama, Homs, Deir Ez Zor, and Latakia. Around 30 respondents were war widows, homemakers, urban lower-class refugees, or professionals who could not actively find a job, which led them to struggle financially, albeit at different levels. The remaining interviewees were NGO workers focusing on humanitarian aid to Syria and/or college students and some professionals who were also working in Türkiye. These include teachers, translators, and businesspeople. Religious-affiliated and secular participants were also interviewed as part of the field research. Given their refugee positionality, many of the participants were against the Asad regime. Still, two participants were openly supportive of the regime. One was not as opposed to the regime as the remaining participants in this study, and few of the interviewees implicitly stated that they favored the regime. The majority actively participated in demonstrations before the armed struggle started in Syria. While some were against armed struggle, others supported the armed groups.

There was only one focus group that included six Kurdish men, and they were interviewed in Urfa, which is another border city to Syria and a two-hour drive to Antep. There were several occasions when people preferred to talk in duos. Two married couples, one son-mother, a daughter-father, and two friends wanted to be interviewed together. While my preference is always one-on-one interviews, I do not refuse people's requests to talk together. Sometimes, one person may talk more than the other, and this issue limits reaching the participant in an in-depth manner; at times, duo interviews may contribute to enriching the interview process in terms of elaborating or surfacing different ideas and experiences during the conversation. Sometimes, I was invited to people's homes for the interview; at others, there was a meeting room in the community center, as in the case of the widowed women. Some interviews were held in my office with students or people's workplaces/offices. I met with others, mostly young NGO workers or students, in well-known coffee shops (I treated the coffee as an out-of-pocket expense for the study).

An oral consent of participants was sought at the beginning of interviews prior to recording. At the beginning of the interview, I introduced myself and my professional affiliation, and my interpreter, if she was present, informed people about the research topic. People were assured that their confidentiality was going to be preserved. I was transparent about my positionality as a researcher. While there was no funding attached to the research, and I deeply care about the vulnerabilities that war creates for people, which motivated me to do research on the topic, I was ethically bound to say that articles and a book publication were targeted, which was going to contribute to my career advancement. People were mostly concerned about their confidentiality when they heard about "appearing" in a book. I explained to them that I would avoid mentioning specifics that highlight their real identity.

Timeframe of Interviews

The interviews started at the end of 2015 (November and December); however, other than these first 15 interviews, most were held during late winter, spring, and early summer of 2016. The timing is important as it was at a turning point in the Syrian civil war. During the summer of 2015, the FSA (Free Syrian Army) was making progress toward Damascus, and the Asad regime was facing "military setbacks" (Stent 2016). Syrians in Türkiye believed that the regime was going to fall soon. This is reflected in their view of the "revolution" and their enthusiasm toward the demonstrations and the uprising. In October, Russia made it clear that it would intervene to support the Asad regime (Stent 2016). The end of 2015 brought a more observable transnational dimension to the forefront when Russian planes flew sorties for the benefit of the Asad regime, and the Western countries did not tilt the balance for the benefit of the Syrian opposition. Toward the end of Spring 2016, people who participated in my study had a considerable morale decline and questioned how much the uprising was for Syrians and how much of it was a tool for the powerful countries who were actively in Syria. Most of the study participants were against the regime and either were active in demonstrations as part of the youth groups or still actively supporting the opposition via humanitarian support to the "free" areas. The field results reflect the transition from a moment of belief that the war was going to overthrow the regime to the realization of an overstretched fighting with no transfer of power. Syrians from the Turkish border were looking from outside in and seeing only the increase of loss of human life, destruction of the neighborhoods and towns, and extension of being displaced from home for an unforeseeable time. Some of them were coming to the realization that they were not going back home in the foreseeable future.

"Horizontal Reach" to Interview Participants

Some studies reach participants vertically, meaning that heads of institutions like camps or refugee centers point out available participants. This study did not have participants from camps or particular refugee centers, which created a chance to meet people who were first-time interviewees. This means I did not face the issue of respondent "fatigue" where participants continuously answered different researchers. Many participants did not talk to any other researchers about Syria, which is a strength of this study in terms of bringing new voices to the literature. The few I met who talked to other researchers expressed surprise as they were not prepared for the experience-related questions.

I spent nearly 3 years building relations before deciding to get into the field to mostly avoid reaching participants vertically. It is not possible to completely wipe out power hierarchies, yet it is possible to put effort into minimizing it. I started with a few main gatekeepers who were Syrians living in Antep. I had access to different groups in the community which I consider as horizontal access to the field (my useage of vertical and horizontal is different than Geddes et al. 2017). Some were secular former students, and they were liked and respected by their peers. When they vouched for me, many young people, particularly students or NGO workers, were willing to talk to me. I also met gatekeepers who were affiliated with religious groups, which allowed me to reach people who wanted a Sunni religious state. Another gatekeeper had access to Kurdish men, who led to the focus group. In the end, I reached five clusters of people: students, NGO employees, and other professionals, female pious widows of the Syrian civil war, Kurdish men, and people of lower economic strata who were also struggling economically to survive in Türkiye. Other than the gatekeepers, I have reached participants through snowballing with the referral of my participants. During the process, I interviewed a considerable number of students. Many of these students were from different departments in the university I was teaching, but I had never met and never had the possibility of teaching a class; others were friends of my students from other universities. I had several students whom I had taught classes in previous semesters but were no longer my students at the time of the interview. Even though it was not my preference to interview students I taught, and I did not ask them, to my surprise, a couple of them approached me, stating that they had heard I was doing research with Syrians, and asked to be interviewed. I stated that I do not ask my students because I do not want them to feel obligated to accept. They said they wanted to talk. One of them, it turns out, was motivated to talk because they could not share a lot of their ideas with their friends. They did not agree with the uprising but could not freely express themselves and wanted their ideas to be known as well. I had many students I was teaching while I was on the field who asked me if I was "studying Syrians" and inquired what my research was about. I never asked them if they were interested in being interviewed, and they did not offer to talk. This way, to the best of my ability, I tried to avoid using my status to influence their choice.

Language and the Role of the Interpreter

Most of the fluent English-speaking participants were either students or professionals/NGO workers. Only two people who were Turkmen Syrians preferred interviewing in Turkish. The remaining interviews were conducted in Arabic, which means the interviews were mainly split between English and the use of a translator for Arabic. For the English speakers, other than small grammatical corrections, I tried to remain as loyal as possible to the original word choices of the interviewees, sometimes including odd usages, to keep the genuine meaning as they communicated them. In some of the segments, I draw the reader's attention to the sentence and interpret it, making it obvious that it is intentionally left sounding "odd" to the English reader. During the Arabic interviews, at some moments, I asked various questions about word choice or temporality. For example, one widow's words were translated as "I am married," and I asked the interpreter whether she used the present tense. Throughout the interview, it became apparent that she considered herself still married and never referred to herself as a widow. Interviews that were in Arabic transformed the interview into a dialogue between me and the interviewee and a three-way conversation that included my interpreter. Whether there is an interviewer and interviewee or an addition of an interpreter in the process, each interview is where meaning "is actively and communicatively assembled in the interview encounter" (Holstein and Gubrium 1995, p. 4). While the role of the interpreter might be seen as a limitation, it is also an enriching factor as a part of Bakhtinian dialogue, considering that it is the reality of people's everyday experience where the receiving community language is different from the refugees' native language.

Other than the focus group with 6 Kurdish men, I worked with the same interpreter. My interpreter was fluent in Arabic, English, and Turkish and had previously worked for different international organizations translating for Syrians. As I had other interviews in English and was planning to write the research results in English, I preferred that she translate from Arabic to English. However, her knowledge of Turkish was highly beneficial as sometimes she was able to translate certain sayings and idioms from Arabic to Turkish faster, and for certain words and sayings, she was able to tell me those words in Turkish briefly. This helped us to keep the flow and efficiency of the interview process, which was multi-lingual, flowing among three different languages, and it created an exploration of how to locate different expressions that the participants used. Even though we talked about her role during the interview, she was already equipped to carry an interpreter role and had a lot of experience. She was able to pose more in the background; she kept a notebook with herself during the interviews, made notes when she was listening, and then translated mostly without getting direct engagement with the participants. The way she positioned herself in the interview allowed the participants to focus on me and make eye contact with me when talking. We followed the research ethics guidelines and told the participant that she was also to follow confidentiality.

The next chapter will present the theoretical framework of this work. Conflict theories map how the participants perceive the conflict in different layers. This mapping is timely, as Syria is at the beginning of a new era after the Ba'ath regime was dismantled in December 2024. Conflict analysis formulated with participants' perceptions, who come from different segments of Syrian society, would bring insights into possibilities and challenges in the future of Syria as a new governing structure is emerging. After the conflict mapping and analysis, the theoretical framework of the remaining chapters focuses on relational pragmatics in examining refugees' agency by analyzing dual spatiality and multiple temporalities.

References

Akrivoulis DE (1999) Doing IR theory in the camera Obscura. Lecture. University of Kent, Canterbury, p 1

Babbie E (2009) The practice of social research, 12th edn. Wadsworth, Bedmont

Bakhtin MM (2010) The dialogic imagination: Four essays. University of Texas Press, Austin

Barthes R (1981) Camera Lucida: reflections on photography. Hill and Wang, New York

Baudry JL (1974) Ideological effects of the basic cinematographic apparatus. Williams A (trans). Film Quarterly 28(2):39–47

Bourdieu P, Wacquant LJD (1992) An invitation to reflexive sociology. University of Chicago Press

Charmaz K (2006) Constructing grounded theory: a practical guide through qualitative analysis. Sage Publications, London

Crawley H, Skleparis D (2017) Refugees, migrants, neither, both: Categorical fetishism and the politics of bounding in Europe's 'migration crisis.'. J Ethn Migr Stud 44(1):48–64

Emirbayer M, Mische A (1998) What is agency? Am J Sociol 103(4):962–1023

Geddes A, Parker C, Scott S (2017) When the snowball fails to roll and the use of 'horizontal' networking in qualitative social research. Int J Soc Res Meth 21(3):347–358

Haraway D (2004) Situated knowledge: the science question in feminism and the privilege of partial perspective. In: Harding SG (ed) The feminist standpoint theory reader: intellectual and political controversies. Psychology Press, East Sussex

Harding SG (2004) The feminist standpoint theory reader: intellectual and political controversies. Psychology Press, East Sussex

Harrell-Bond B, Voutira E (2007) In search of 'invisible' actors: barriers to access in refugee research. J Refug Stud 20(2):281–298

Heidegger M (1962) Being and time. Harpers & Row, New York

Holstein JA, Gubrium FF (1995) The active interview. Qualitative research method series, 37. Sage Publications, Thousand Oaks

Mahendran K, Magnussonb N, Howarth C, Scuzzarello S (2019) Reification and the refugee: using a counterposing dialogical analysis to unlock a frozen category. J Soc Polit Psychol 7(1):577–597. https://doi.org/10.5964/jspp.v7i1.656

Malkki LH (1992) National geographic: the rooting of peoples and the territorialization of National Identity among scholars and refugees. Cult Anthropol 7(1):24–44

Malkki LH (1995) Refugees and exile: from "refugee studies" to the national order of things. Annu Rev Anthropol 24:495–523

McLuhan M, Powers BR (1989) The global village: transformations in world life and media in the 21st century. Oxford University Press, Oxford

Mulvey L (1975) Visual pleasure and narrative cinema. Screen 16(3):6–18

Navaro-Yashin Y (2012) The make-believe space: affective geography in a postwar polity. University Press, Duke

Ozkaleli U (2018) Displaced selves, dislocated emotions and transforming identities: Syrian refugee women reinventing selves. Women's Stud Int Forum 70:17–23. https://doi.org/10.1016/j.wsif.2018.07.010

Ozkaleli U (2021) Agency in multiple temporalities: being Syrian women, becoming widows and refugees, remaining pious. Women's Stud Int Forum 89:102538. https://doi.org/10.1016/j.wsif.2021.102538

Ozkaleli FM, Ozkaleli U (2022) De-worlding IR theory. Postcolonial Stud 25(2):192–209

Ozkaleli U, Ozkaleli FM (2024) Panopticon, gaze, and rupture in the fantasy: the Syrian refugee experience in Turkey. Migration Stud 12(4):mnae033. https://doi.org/10.1093/migration/mnae033

Saldaña J (2013) The coding manual for qualitative researchers. Sage, Los Angeles

Spivak GC (1988) Can the subaltern speak? In: Nelson C, Grossberg L (eds) Marxism and the interpretation of culture. Macmillan, Basingstoke, pp 271–313

Stent A (2016) Putin's power play in Syria: how to respond to Russia's intervention. Foreign Aff 95:106

Stoetzler M, Yuval-Davis N (2002) Standpoint theory, situated knowledge and the situated imagination. Fem Theory 3(3):315–333

Tajfel H (2010) Introduction. In: Tajfel H (ed) Social identity and intergroup relations, vol 7. Cambridge University Press, Cambridge, pp 1–12

Willig C (2008) Discourse analysis. In: Smith JA (ed) Qualitative psychology: a practical guide to research methods. Sage Publications, London, pp 143–167

Zetter R (1991) Labelling refugees: forming and transforming a bureaucratic identity. J Refug Stud 4(1):39–62

Zetter R (2007) More labels, fewer refugees: Remaking the refugee label in an era of globalization. Journal of Refugee Studies 20(2):172–192

Chapter 2
Context and Theoretical Framework

Contextualizing Syrian History

Writing of historical context involves deciding what point to start a country's/conflict's history and what events and actors to focus on. Methodically, I aspired to stay within the commitment of the research to present the realities of a segment of Syrians who were positioned as refugees at a particular time in Gaziantep. No work can be comprehensive enough to write from every angle. Therefore, the extent of this review is limited to the focus of the interview participants. To achieve this, I read different works about Syria to locate my interviewees' accounts. Then, after sorting the data, I focused on the historical events that my participants mentioned and tied the events and history of "their" Syria to the rich historical accounts in the literature. The brief chronological review below is constructed by following the interviewees' narratives. This means the historical moments they prioritize as crucial regarding their identities and events that shaped their experiences were central in creating the historical context in this work.

Historical Place of French Mandatory Period (1918–1946) and Western Colonial Legacy The Sykes-Picot agreement (1916) between Great Britain and France, recognizing each other's right to establish direct control, the former on Basra region, Baghdad, and Palestine, the latter the coastal region of Syria and northern Iraq (Tejel 2009, p. 143). French and British ambitions resulted in the Peace Conference led by the King-Crane Allied Commission, which consisted of all American representatives to study the attitudes of the Levantine population (Tejel 2009, p. 14). The commission recognized "French privilege in military, administrative, and educational matters" (Tejel 2009, p. 14). The Syrian parliament declared independence in 1920. Nevertheless, France and Great Britain decided Syria's fate in San Remo despite the absence of Syrian representatives, and this agreement prevailed (Tejel 2009). The secret agreement of Sykes-Picot forcefully divided the country, yet this

© The Author(s), under exclusive license to Springer Nature Singapore Pte Ltd. 2025

U. Ozkaleli, *De-essentializing Refugees: Perceptions, Experiences, and Becoming of Syrians in Türkiye*, https://doi.org/10.1007/978-981-96-5519-9_2

was not accepted by Bolshevik Russia and the U.S. (Tejel 2009, p. 14). For Arab nationalists, colonial greed divided the Arab land into several states, and particularly "the Sykes-Picot Agreement cut up Arab land in such a manner as to place artificial obstacles in the way to Arab unity" (Chaitani 2007, p. 1). While the Sykes-Picot Agreement "rhetorically supported the creation of independent Arab states," its real intention is revealed in Article 2, which reads, "France and…Great Britain shall be allowed to establish such direct or indirect administration or control as they desire and as they may think fit to arrange with the Arab State or Confederation of Arab States" (Erlich 2014, p. 20). The French mandate divided the territory along sectarian lines. "Two separate states of Damascus and Aleppo contained Sunni Arab majorities and smaller Christian, Jewish, Shiite, and Ismaili religious communities, as well as distinct Turkmen, Armenian, Circassian, and Kurdish ethnic communities. The coastal Latakia region was designated a state for Alawites…who historically had been persecuted. The southeastern corner of Syria became a state for the heterodox ethnoreligious Druze religious minority" (Pearlman 2017, p. 23; for the historical development of ethnic and religious identities, also see Hinnebusch 2005, p. 19; Hokayem 2013, p. 17; Sorenson 2016, pp. 10–11). In 1925, secular leader Atrash led the Druze revolt against the French (Erlich 2014). "French authorities applied a policy of divide and rule by playing on the rivalry between the rural elites (tribal leaders and shaykhs) and the urban elites, between ethnic and religious minorities (local autonomy) and Sunni Arabs. At the same time, France relied on support from certain urban elites (Christian bourgeoisie and traditional elites in order to reinforce the Arab nationalist's isolation…Instead of looking for support from unified Sunni Arab nationalism, the French policy was based on the defense of non-Sunni communities, notably the Druzes, the Alawites, and the Christians. The French administration presented itself simply as being the arbitrator between the ethnic and religious minorities and the Sunni Muslim majority… For France, Syrian unity was nothing more than an Arab nationalist invention perceived as an artificial creation of the British to harm French interests in the Middle East and the result of Muslim fanaticism" (Tejel 2009, p. 16).

From Independence to the United Arab Republic (UAR) Independence from colonial rule marked struggles for democratic consolidation and trial of self-governance. The formation of the Ba'ath party started in the 1940s onward (Hinnebusch 2005, pp. 29–33). Integration of Syria into the United Arab Republic (1958) led by Nasser was seen as a triumph of Arab nationalism and Ba'ath domination (Tejel 2009, p. 47); Nasser abolished all political parties in Syria and put the Syrian army under Egyptian command (Tejel 2009, p. 47). Ba'ath rule started in 1963 *coup d'etat*. "Ba'athism is a variant of pan-Arab nationalism," and in Syria, "most of the constitution of the Ba'ath puts the emphasis on Arab nationalism" (Tejel 2009, p. 56). In its formation, Arab nationalism was embraced by "…peripheral minorities, the Druze, Isma'ilis and above all the Alawis…as a way both of integrating into the national community on an equal basis and contesting the power of the dominant Sunni elite" (Hinnebusch 2005, p. 4).

Ba'ath Dominance and Asad Rule 1963–70 was an era of the Ba'ath party military committee and Hafez Asad's rise to power from the Defense Minister (Hinnebusch 2005, pp. 45, 55). Arab-Israeli conflict and 1967 defeat "legitimated the creation of an authoritarian national security state" (Hinnebusch 2005, pp. 7, 12). Hafez Asad came to power in 1970 (see Hinnebusch 2005, pp. 7–8, about the political economy of power consolidation). Hafez al-Asad, born in 1930, was from a peasant Alawite family (Erlich 2014; Hinnebusch 2005, p. 64). Saturated in the Arab nationalist Ba'ath party, Asad's politics targeted land-poor, impoverished, and lower-class sectors that benefited the formation of a state-dominated economy (Hinnebusch 2005, p. 60). The regime "attempted to substitute legitimation through supra-state ideology (Pan-Arab or Islamic) and reliance on sub-state asabiya" (Hinnebusch 2005, pp. 8, 65). In its initiation, while dominantly Alawite, the "top elite remained a cross sectarian coalition...the top elite came to be shared by two dominant groups, the Alawi officers in the president's inner core and the Damascene Sunnis with their crucial connections to the Sunni business community" (66–7). Syria's Ba'ath early secularism was closer to the French system of *laicite* and later shifted toward a more Anglo-Saxon secular model (Khatib 2011). In intra-regime power struggles, *asabiya* (kinship and sectarian solidarity) was used to establish a patrimonial authority (Hinnebusch 2005, p. 5). In the 1970s, Asad faced challenges within the Alawite community, making him trust only a small section of the Alawite community from his family, tribe, or village (Van Dam 1996, p. 70 in Tejel 2009, p. 58), the Kalbiyya tribe (Tejel 2009, p. 58). *Mukhabarat* and the institutional culture of intelligence activities in Syria has its roots in the colonial legacy of the French Mandate as during that time, "the Intelligence Service...was the 'cornerstone of French administration in Syria serving as the link between the civilian regime and the military'" (Khoury 1987, p. 78 in Tejel 2009, p. 15). As the instruments of coercion, mukhabarat and the military used arbitrary arrest, imprisonment, and torture of dissidents (Hinnebusch 2005, pp. 5, 81) in both Asad periods. From the onset of the constitution, articles dictated that "[a]ll political and social groups established in the Arab fatherland which did not actively share the Arab national ideal were illegal" (Tejel 2009, p. 57). Asad also neutralized political movements by creating the Progressive National Front (1972), "which grouped together legal communist and Nasserite organizations into a political body that was formally represented in parliament and government" (Reilly 2018, p. 179). Civil society organizations beyond charitable organizations started to emerge after 2000, but there were restrictions on them (Abboud 2016; Khalaf 2015).

Concept of Syrianism "Syrianism" was introduced by the Syrian Social National Party as a direct rival of the Ba'ath, strongly secular and anti-leftist, rejected Arabism and targeted the educated middle class, members of the military, and minorities (Hinnebusch 2022). For some, the "origin of the term Syria" emphasized "distinctness from the term 'Araba,' denoting the birthplace of Arabs" and see people who came to the land as "Syrianized," which "distinguished them even from those with whom they shared linguistic and religious ties" (Talhami 2001, p. 1). For Syrocentric Arabism, see Ehteshami and Hinnebusch (2002) and Dawisha (2016, 32).

Muslim Brotherhood (al-Ikhwan) In the mid-1940s, the emergence of Syrian Ikhwan happened under the leadership of Mustafa Saba'i, who was against the French mandate (Hinnebusch 2005, p. 90; Van Dam 1996). Muslim Brotherhood was anti-imperial and Islamic conservative, focusing on colonialism's cultural and religious impact (Erlich 2014, p. 32) and had a continuous conflict with the Hafez al-Asad regime in terms of sectarian divergence (Van Dam 1996, for different aspects of the regime and Muslim Brotherhood clashes, see Khatib 2011).

Kurdish Identity and Experience in Syria The first Kurdish political party in Syria, established in 1957, experienced several divisions in the 1960s and 1970s, facing strong control by the Syrian state (Gunes 2021, p. 263, for the Kurdish Democratic Party, see Tejel (2009, pp. 48–49; 2021, p. 440, also see Tejel 2021, p. 440) about how demands for "Kurdistan" were oppressed). Repression of Kurdish identity, the politics surrounding Arabism [and Arabization] dates to the pre-Asad period as they were seen as a threat to Arab unity as a "non-Arab minority" and associated with "feudal chiefs" and the world of the "notables" that placed them in the position of power that authorities wished to eliminate (Tejel 2009, p. 48). "Under the UAR, recordings of Kurdish music were smashed in cafés. The publication and even the possession of books written in the Kurdish language were offenses punishable by imprisonment. Egyptian teachers were sent to Kurdish regions (Nemir 1992, p. 151 in Tejel 2009, p. 48). After the end of UAR, Syria was declared an "Arab Syrian Republic," and "repressive measures were applied to the Kurds, notably in Jazira" (Tejel 2009, p. 50). The teaching of Kurdish remained prohibited during Hafez al-Asad's time, despite the fact that "Armenians and Assyrians had private schools, clubs, and cultural associations where their respective languages could be taught" (Tejel 2009, p. 63). "The growing awareness of a separate Kurdish identity raised great suspicion among the Arab political elites who identified the Kurdish population as an obstacle to Syrian national construction, which was increasingly identified with Arabism" (13; see also Haklai 2000; Kienle 1995). Historically, "a large number of Kurds in Syria have been stripped of Syrian citizenship and described as 'foreign'" (Yildiz 2005, p. 92; see also Tejel 2009).

Hama Massacre (February 1982) The regime's creation of a new dominant class weakened its link to its mass constituency, and Sunni urban classes that fell outside of the regime's statism, rural and sectarian favoritism created political Islam as an alternative ideology that contested legitimacy of Ba'athist state (Hinnebusch 2005, p. 89). As surrounding villages were favored, Hama suffered economically, resulting in inner-city textile industries suffering as they could not compete with large state factories around Hama. Islamic Salvation Front was formed in 1980 to overthrow the regime for an Islamic government and prepare for an uprising. Fighting Vanguard, which the Brotherhood claimed was a splinter group, killed Aleppo Artillery School students in 1979 (Erlich 2014, p. 41). Security forces, led by Hafez al-Asad's brother Rifaat al-Asad's Defense Companies, besieged Hama that lasted with artillery and air strikes on the city (Reilly 2018, p. 185; also see Hinnebusch 2005, pp. 95–96), massacring not only Brotherhood fighters and members but other civilians that is estimated from 15,000 to 30,000 individuals (Reilly 2018, p. 185, for a detailed account of preceding conditions and events leading to Hama 1982, see Khatib 2011, pp. 213–232). Rifaat al-Assad was frequently in the narrative of study participants as he was feared by many for his brutality. He was considered responsible for many of the regime-initiated massacres. After an assassination attempt on Hafez al-Asad, his brother Rifaat massacred 550 Muslim Brotherhood political prisoners in Tadmur in 1980 (Reilly 2018, p. 185).

Dar'aa Incidents That Ignited the Uprising (March 2011) Dar'aa, located in southern Syria near the Jordanian border, is where the anti-governmental demonstrations began after police arrested, beat, and tortured preteen school children for writing anti-regime graffiti on walls of a school (Erlich 2014, p. 48; see also Reilly 2018, p. 222).

IS (Islamic State) ISIS (Islamic State of Iraq and al-Shams), ISIL (Islamic State of Iraq and the Levant), DAESH (the IS-*al Dawla al Islamiya fi al Iraq wa al-Sham* was the formal title but then became a pejorative term). The name chosen by itself is IS (Islamic State) (Sorenson 2016, p. ix). Fighters in Syria crossed into Iraq and joined other insurgents in Iraq (disaffected Iraqi Ba'ath, military, and generally disaffected Iraqi Sunni) to create the Islamic State (Sorenson 2016, pp. 3, 5). It is a group formed from the remnants of Al-Qaeda and re-emerged in 2011 and took the name ISIS in 2013 (see Wilson Center 2019 and Byman and Williams 2015 for a timeline of Islamic State on ISIS and Al-Qaeda). While at first, local people were supporters of the rebel forces, the threat became ISIS more than the regime. "ISIS killed and beheaded Alawites, forced hijab and gender segregation in public schools, and destroyed churches, making Christians flee the city. ISIS also launched a military assault against fellow rebel groups and jailed and tortured rebels who disagreed with its policies" (Erlich 2014, p. 66). IS "denounced everyone outside of its radical realm as apostates, worthy only of death" (Sorenson 2016, p. 3). ISIS was one of the most mentioned groups among the participants as a cause for them to leave Syria.

Contextualizing Türkiye and Gaziantep

The Syrian civil war erupted in 2011, and approximately 5.4 million Syrians became refugees who settled in neighboring countries such as Türkiye, Lebanon, Jordan, and Iraq. The first group arriving in Türkiye in 2011 was 252 people, reaching 14,000 and 224,000 by late 2012 (Erdoğan et al. 2021, pp. 5, 9). Syrians under temporary protection (SuTP) in Türkiye reached 3.2 million as of 2023, constituting 63% of the Syrian refugee population (UNHCR 2023). Türkiye houses the largest number of forcibly displaced people in the world (Özçürümez et al. 2021b; UNHCR 2020). The government's "open door" policy toward Syrian refugees resulted in most people moving out of camps and spreading to the country's major cities (Efe and Jacoby 2022). Approximately 2.4% live in the camps; the majority live in urban areas, of which over 64% live close to or below the poverty line (Karasapan 2019). Although there are approximately 2.1 million working-age Syrians in Türkiye, between 500,000 and one million Syrians are actively working. Most Syrians work in irregular and informal jobs, as only 65,000 work permits have been issued by the Turkish government (Kirisci and Kolasin 2019). Another estimate for work permits is around 30,000, arguing that permits are decreased due to the number of citizenships issued to Syrians along the process. The number of citizenships granted to Syrians is estimated to be 102,000 (Erdoğan 2019). Forty percent of Syrian refugee children remain out of school (Karasapan 2019). Studies on refugees show that unaccompanied women refugees are more vulnerable to poor living conditions and sexual violence (Özçürümez et al. 2021a; Şenses 2020). While there are 3.2 million Syrian refugees registered in Türkiye, constituting 4.5% of the total population, universal, institutionalized, and rights-based policies are missing because Syrians hold temporary protection status rather than refugee status (Lowndes and Polat 2020). As Syrians were received as "guests" and not given refugee status but only temporary protection, they face structural and ongoing problems along with a lack of planning for their long-term stay in Türkiye (Baban et al. 2017; Crawley and Skleparis 2017; Utku et al. 2017; Şenses 2016).

At the time of the interviews for this study (2015–2016), approximately 400,000 Syrians, which comprised 20% of the total city population, lived in Gaziantep (Erdogan et al. 2017). Before the nation-state borders were created between Syria and Türkiye after World War I, Ottoman Aleppo was considered the center and Gaziantep its periphery, which explains the similarity of the landscape and the familiar feel of the city for Syrians. People historically had relatives and economic relations on two sides of the border (Aras 2020). Many Syrians express closeness in culture with Türkiye, making them prefer to stay in Türkiye rather than go to Europe (Rottmann and Kaya 2021). The similarity, then, is not only religion but other factors that contribute to a sense of familiarity, such as landscape, cuisine, and cultural expressions like hospitality (Rottmann and Nimer 2021; Chatty 2017).

Different nation-building projects in Türkiye and Syria influenced the perception of Syrians and the receiving community about each other. On the one hand, Islam is a common denominator, but the historical distancing from Arabic and the development of Turkish in writing via the adaptation of the Latin alphabet not only created obvious linguistic and cultural differences but also positioned the two communities differently in terms of interpretation of religion. The majority of Syrians are Sunni Muslims who were controlled by the ruling Alawite regime, which ended in December 2024 when Bashar Asad fled the country. Therefore, the majority of Syrians in Türkiye are Sunni Muslims. Sunni Islam became an emphasized denominator with the majority of the Syrian refugees, especially by the Sunni Islamic ruling government, AKP (Justice and Development Party). As Arabic is the language of the Qur'an, Syrians feel empowered *vis-à-vis* the strongly religious segments of Gaziantep who value Islamic prayers and religious text reading. While Sunni Syrians' religion is a denominator with the dominant group in the receiving society, religion is expressed and practiced differently in different segments of society in Türkiye. This means in different cities and localities, while religion is a common ground, in some others, it is a point of divergence (Ayvazoğlu and Kunuroglu 2019). While the majority of the Turkish population is also Sunni, unlike the ruling power of Alawites in Syria, the Alevis of Türkiye are a minority, and the Sunni majority holds the governance power. Alevis of Türkiye are staunch seculars, and seculars in Türkiye as a whole group, Alevi or not, often have visible tensions with the Syrians. Secular groups do not want religious expressions to become dominant in the public sphere. Türkiye's secular group is resistant to Syrians, for they are perceived as religious and closely affiliated with the Sunni Islamist AKP government. Such perceptions make the secular group fearful of Arabization and Islamization of the urban space (Saraçoğlu and Bélanger 2019). While the pious welcome social expression of religion, this is not a unitary voice. There is a negative view of the Syrian female religious dress, *niqab* (black veil covering everything except eyes), or differently tied *hijab*, along with tensions about the way prayer is handled in mosques (Ozkaleli and Ozkaleli 2024). Additionally, there are ethnic (Turkish-Arabic) and sectarian tensions (Sunni-Alevi/Alawite). There is concern about demographic change being targeted by an increasing number of Sunni Muslims in majority Alevi cities in Türkiye and increasing sectarian tensions (Sandal 2019; Saraçoğlu and Bélanger 2019). Syrian regime forces were predominantly Alawite, while AKP is a strongly Islamist government, supporting Sunni militant groups in Syria and accepting mostly Sunni refugees to Türkiye (Sandal 2019; Saraçoğlu and Bélanger 2019).

Some other studies investigate conservative Sunni religious interaction and relations with Sunni Syrians regarding religious connection (Morgül and Savaskan 2022; Jacoby et al. 2019). Morgül and Savaşkan (2022, p. 1647) argue that while religious affiliation may play a role in reducing anti-refugee sentiments, economic concerns play a vital role in increasing prejudice and bias. Linguistic differences and distinctive cultural characteristics were not integrated in a systemic and planned manner. Even without Syrians being part of the analysis, there are structural problems in the labor market in Türkiye (Erdoğan et al. 2021, p. 23). In this regard, the steady decline in Türkiye's economy led many people to believe that Syrians were the main reason for it. Such prevalent sentiment among receiving community members increased anti-Syrian attitudes and hostility (Saraçoğlu and Bélanger 2019). This was further encouraged by the opposition parties and politicians using Syrian refugee othering as a central tool to attract votes and criticize the AKP government for its refugee policies (Kayaoğlu et al. 2022; Mencütek 2019, 2021; Yanaşmayan et al. 2019). Furthermore, the EU-Türkiye deal of 2016 shows Europe's stand on preventing Syrian refugees from crossing its borders (Almasri 2022), positioning Türkiye as a "shield" country, which was also criticized by the opposition.

In the early years of the civil war in Syria, both religious and secular segments of the receiving community were welcoming and compassionate toward forcibly displaced Syrians as a humanitarian duty (Narlı et al. 2020). As the number of Syrians and the duration that they were in Türkiye extended, so did the negative attitude and tensions (Lowndes and Polat 2020; Saraçoğlu and Bélanger 2019), declining the acceptance of living with Syrians in the same city from 72% in 2016 to 40% in 2019 (KONDA 2019 in Narlı et al. 2020). While the discourse created by calling them "guests" led to the receiving community expecting their stay in Türkiye to be temporary and short, on a systemic level, the temporary protection system denied Syrians rights under refugee status (Crawley and Skleparis 2017). In Türkiye, Syrians remained in temporary protection rather than international protection. International protection recognizes refugee status only for Europeans in Türkiye (Özçürümez et al. 2021b, p. 603; Şengül 2022; Almasri 2022). Giving refugee status to only Europeans signals the global endurance of colonial legacies. Still, some argue that even though there were eventual restrictions on Syrians, Türkiye's protection policy was based on nationality and religion that created hierarchies of protection, prioritizing (Sunni Muslim) Syrians for the award of temporary protection compared to other (non-European) asylum seekers (Almasri 2022). Still, the temporary status regime led to vulnerabilities and exploitation of people who are positioned as refugees (Kayaoğlu et al. 2022; Baban et al. 2017). In Türkiye, longer-term integration efforts for Syrian refugees came later (Akar and Erdogdu 2019). As the Turkish economy faced more challenges, tensions, hostility, and anti-Syrian sentiment increased along with the growing number of refugees in the country (Kirisci 2014; Lowndes and Polat 2020, p. 12; Saraçoglu and Bélanger 2019). Similar to Europe, refugees in Türkiye are seen as an economic burden and a source of unwanted cultural change. The interviews were held when the tide was turning against Syrians in Gaziantep, which was reflected in the experiences that Syrian participants shared. The pre-war era, the outbreak of the conflict, and Syrians in Türkiye will be presented through the narratives of study participants in the following chapters.

Conflict Analysis and Theorizing Refugee Agency

The cause of Syrians becoming "refugees" is a violent armed conflict. Various ethnic, religious, and political groups were involved in the conflict, and each received support from external actors. In Part I, I utilize conflict theories to map people's perceptions of the root causes of conflict. Chapter 3 starts with the formation of identities from the outside in, by beginning with external actors and the influence of colonial legacies to identify how participants approach identity divisions. Such analysis is crucial to show how people will approach living with others in the new governance and power-sharing structure of Syria. For example, if they perceive the identity divisions as a cause of primordial differences, it would signal a more challenging process for building peace than if they see these divisions as politically induced. Chapter 4 focuses on the major internal actors of the conflict: the regime, the FSA (Free Syrian Army), and different Syrian localities. What roles people attribute to different actors also gives insights into how they understand the conflict. Conflict mapping continues with Chapters 5 and 6, where the causes of the conflict are analyzed from the perspective of participants. Concepts of oppression, repression, and domination, along with stereotyping, prejudice, and discrimination, emerged from the field data analysis that are discussed in Chap. 5. Chapter 6 focuses on economic dimensions as the cause of the conflict.

As individuals are part of multiple social identity categories and belong to multiple social identity groups, Parts II and III investigate the importance of these concepts in terms of refugee experiences and becoming within a social structure. Individuals' social identity categories are imposed from the social structure at the macro level. They experience themselves at the meso level within social identity groups and at the micro level in their interactions with other individuals. Structurally, social identities have different access to power, which directly shape individuals' experiences. My discussion focuses on group membership through an intersectional lens to identity, given that people do not hold only one group membership, but they experience themselves within multiple social groups. In order to locate the experiences in these multiple embedded levels, spatial, temporal, and relational elements are incorporated in examining people's life-world.

While a person is positioned as a refugee by the dominant social structure, they have many different interactions that do not necessarily include their refugee position. This means how they experience their own self-conceptualization is not decided only by their refugee position. Thus, my aim is to discover refugees' subjective position by analyzing their agency through relational pragmatics. Relational pragmatics pays attention to how different social structures shape and influence individuals. Inevitably, structure is strongly related to space and time. Individuals have relationality to place and other people that are intertwined with their temporal situatedness. As relational pragmatics focuses on agentic processes with spatial and temporal elements, my main theoretical framework is built on the analysis of how refugee individuals emerge in their becoming.

My focus on the individual takes both the structurally born social categories and social groups as fundamental elements to understand how the self is experienced in the receiving community as a refugee. By doing so, I am not aspiring to reach *the ontological refugee self*. On the contrary, my field analysis involved seeing individuals thrown into *a "refugee" position* in these complex multidimensional identities where they develop a sense of self in multiple spaces that position them differently. This positioning influences all their interactions where power is distributed differently, which shapes their interactions in different layers of the structure. I investigate how people experience, articulate, and conceptualize their sense of self—how this shapes their perceptions, feelings, expectations, how they see the other, and how they experience their *being* and *becoming*.

Approach to Conflict Analysis

When looking at the Syrian conflict, the Conflict Analysis and Resolution (CAR) Field constituted the first lens of my eye-camera. At least partially, I prepared my interview questions through conflict mapping drawn by CAR approaches (Miall et al. 2000, p. 92, also see Wehr 2006). I use *Protracted Social Conflict* (PSC), named by Azar, who defined it as: "…[T]ype of ongoing and seemingly unresolvable conflict" (Azar 1985, p. 59). Protracted Social Conflicts are "hostile interactions extending over long periods of time with sporadic outbreaks of open warfare which fluctuate in frequency and intensity" (Azar and Farah 1981, p. 319). Such types of conflicts "immobili[z]e people and institutions. They retard the system and invite repression and exploitation of the economic and political resources available by those who favor the status quo" (Azar and Haddad 1986, p. 1341). Azar refuses to separate "levels of analysis" (Singer 1961) and sees connections between groups, states, and international linkages (Azar 1985). His perspective later developed into *International Social Conflicts* (ISC) and defined as "conflicts that are neither pure international (interstate) conflicts, nor pure social (domestic) conflicts, but sprawl somewhere between the two" (Miall et al. 2000, p. 77). Syrian conflict fits this definition with the involvement of superpowers (the U.S. and Russia) and neighboring states (Iran, Türkiye, Qatar, etc.). The conflict in Syria is not linear, and thus, dichotomous depictions such as Sunni vs. Shi'a or regime vs. rebel fail to capture its complex local, regional, and international dimensions (Abboud 2016). In sum, Syria faces a *protracted conflict* with an extended *stalemate* (Imady and Hinnebusch 2018, p. 330).

What led to the protracted conflict may be explained by structural violence, "*threat of physical violence* and indirect threat of mental violence that may even be characterized as some type of psychological violence… constrains human action" (Galtung 1969, p. 170). Structural violence is related not only to the central power in a country but also to a global system in which these governments are interlinked. Scheper-Hughes and Bourgois (2004) define structural violence as "chronic, historically entrenched political-economic oppression and social inequality, ranging from exploitative international terms trade to abusive local working conditions and high infant mortality rate" (426 in Abuelaish and Godoy-Ruiz 2020, p. 157). The state's ideological apparatus decides how different identities will be treated within the structure (Althusser 2006), and people have various experiences depending on their multiple social identities. For instance, the drought in Syria and unequal access to water were parts of the structural violence as they were important triggers of the conflict. Even though climate change and drought are often cited as a trigger, the focus should be on the consequences of the drought that were shaped by the policies (De Châtel 2014). The drought came after the market liberalization and mismanagement of agricultural resources and the Syrian government's lack of recognition of this mismanagement. Economic liberalization did not come with an economic reform that safeguarded the social safety that Syrians enjoyed (Lesch 2012, p. 62). Such changes victimized rural populations, which led to social unrest (De Châtel 2014). The state's treatment of differently located individuals and groups is important to realize the multi-dimensionality of conflicts and how complex intersectional identities experience conflicts.

The state is "the principal political unit in the international political system corresponding to a territory, a relatively permanent population, and a set of ruling institutions" (Barrington 1997, p. 713). Skocpol (1979) conceives the state as "administrative and coercive organizations - organizations that are potentially autonomous from (though of course conditioned by) socioeconomic interests and structures" without analytically collapsing state and society to one another and without reducing political and state actions to representations of socioeconomic forces and interests (14). All states involved in a conflict have a decisive and dominant role in how various groups and individuals will be treated and in what ways conflicts will be handled. The state has a considerable weight in the ways in which conflicts are going to be shaped either as constructive or destructive (Kriesberg 1998). Regardless of who and which groups hold the state power, at any given time, the state, through its institutions, is the major player in how conflicts are going to be handled. Azar approaches the post-colonial Westphalian state with a critical eye, seeing the state competing with identity groups for the individual's loyalty (Azar and Haddad 1986, p. 1338; Azar 1985; Miall et al. 2000, p. 84). When the state is a "highly centrali[z]ed political structure," it is argued to be "the source of conflict" (Azar 1986, pp. 33–34 in Ramsbotham 2005, p. 124). Further, what determines the precipitation or inhibition of the escalation of PSC is the "'governance and the state's role,' including the importance of perceived legitimacy" (Ramsbotham 2005, p. 124). In a similar token, some conflict analysis approaches argue that the government of the threatened state has the potential to prevent the starting of ethnic wars (Kaufman 2001, p. 13).

Problematizing "post-Westphalian state as more part of the problem than the solution" (Azar 1986, p. 32 in Miall et al. 2000, p. 85), Azar finds the sources of conflict within states and gives four different variables as preconditions where a conflict reaches high intensity (Miall et al. 2000, p. 72). The first is the identity group. "In many post-colonial-multi-communal societies the state machinery comes to be 'dominated by a single communal group or a coalition of a few communal groups that are unresponsive to the needs of other groups in the society,' which 'strains the social fabric and eventually breeds fragmentation and protracted social conflict'" (Azar 1990, p. 7 in Miall et al. 2000, p. 73). The second variable is the deprivation of basic human needs, which are "*security, distinctive identity, social recognition of identity,* and *effective participation* in the processes that determine conditions of security and identity, and other such developmental requirements" (Azar 1985, p. 60, emphasis in original. Also see Burton 2024 for Basic Human Needs). The third component is the state that lacks the ability to provide basic needs to the identity groups, and the last one is the political-economic dependency within the international system, which Azar identifies as "international linkages" (Miall et al. 2000, pp. 73–74). As the following chapters will show, participants touched upon all four sources of conflict identified by Azar, some focusing more on the deprivation of basic needs by the state, others focusing on identity groups, particularly religious and sectarian divisions, and yet others combining it with external actor interests guiding different sides of the conflict.

When I went to the field, my lens was already constructed with the above-mentioned approaches to analyzing conflicts. That is why my interview questions included "causes of conflict," "influential political groups," and "internal and external actors." However, there are some differences in my departure point from the above take-off, particularly in terms of units of analysis. Azar, while looking at the effects of group, state, and international links, argues that as the power rests on the identity group, it is the most useful unit of analysis in protracted social conflict situations (Azar 1985, p. 62). In this work, the unit of analysis, "the most elementary part of what is to be studied" (Babbie 2009, p. 99), is individuals. Individuals with intersecting identities fall into marginalized positions due to structural challenges they face, such as poverty and language barriers (Manuel 2007). In this work, structural violence and the role of the state are discussed in connection to their influence on the individual experience. There was an internationally recognized Syrian government under Asad's Ba'athist regime, which was, in Azar's terms, in competition with multiple identity groups. The conflict resulted in a huge number of people being pushed out of their country who became refugees.

Different individuals, in different ways, are located at a distance from the state (Ozkaleli 2015). This distance is decided by the state's treatment of their various identities. How individuals experience the state's perception and treatment of their various intersecting identity belongings is the way the state is analyzed in this work. States may play a significant role in "oppressing" large segments of society, where a selected few can be considered as the "winners" of the system, in the case of Syria, a particular segment of the Alawite. The majority suffer from a lack of "basic human needs" and "access to decisions and allocations" due to the oppressive structures created by the state (Azar 1990, p. 7 in Miall et al. 2000, p. 73). This has implications for individuals who are positioned in multiple identity groups, and it brings unique experiences for individuals as their constitutive identities decide how they experience multi-layer oppression. The state has competing actors who aspire to govern the state mechanism. Regardless of who holds power, the monopoly of violence and policies is carried out through the state mechanism. Hence, I investigate how individuals with their position at a given time, space, and context are experiencing themselves in connection to their distance from the state. Chapter 3 uses conflict theories and how individuals are positioned vis-à-vis the state by mostly focusing on primordial and instrumentalist division in the conflict literature. Within this framework, participants' perceptions of the conflict actors are analyzed.

Political Oppression, Repression, and Domination

This research created oppression, repression, and domination categories after careful analysis of people's narratives in Chap. 5. Oppression, referred to as *Zulm* in Arabic, is one of the most commonly used words among the participants to explain the state's behavior toward them. State repression is defined as "the actual or threatened use of physical sanctions against an individual or organization, within the territorial jurisdiction of the state, for the purpose of imposing a cost on the target as well as deterring specific activities and/or beliefs perceived to be challenging to government personnel, practices or institutions" (Goldstein 1978, p. xxvii in Davenport 2007, p. 2; Davenport and Inman 2012). People's experiences signal different types of state repression. One involves limits to freedom of speech, assembly, and press; the other includes government reprisal and obloquy toward beliefs and associations and suffering under criminal and civil penalties that prevent boycott, picket, or strike (Goldstein 1978, pp. xxx–xxxi in Davenport 2007, p. 3). The other type of state repression involves due process transgressions, which "involve violations of 'generally accepted standards of police action and judicial and administrative behavior related to the political beliefs of the person involved'" (Goldstein 1978, p. xxxi in Davenport 2007, p. 3). Repression, as outlined above, leaves out structurally experienced inequalities (Galtung 1969) that reflect on people's experiences from many different angles, such as the distribution of resources, lack of recognition of their economic, social, cultural, and human rights, and right to peace (Davenport 2007, p. 3). The latter part of the definition is important as study participants' narratives focus on structural inequalities in terms of economic, social, and cultural rights in Syria. The concepts of oppression and domination are necessary here to provide an interpretive explanation of the way many experienced themselves under the reflection of the state.

Oppression is defined as "a form of injustice that occurs when one social group is subordinated while another is privileged, and oppression is maintained by a variety of different mechanisms, including social norms, stereotypes, and institutional rules" (Taylor 2016, p. 520). In this regard, *Stereotypes and Prejudice*, as will be elaborated in Chap. 5, are closely related to oppression, as stereotypes and prejudices that travel from members of one social group to another are the product of institutional practices. There are several important elements of oppression. First, social institutions create harm through practices. Second, such harm is done to a social group; finally, such harmful institutional practices, while harming one group, benefit another (Taylor 2016, p. 522). Many participants stated that they indeed perceived their losses as others' gain.

Domination is yet another social condition that brings injustice (Young 1990). While closely linked, oppression and domination address different aspects. Domination, as a concept, focuses on "the institutional constraint on self-determination" (Young 1990, p. 37). In turn, oppression explains systemic institutional constraints on self-development, which "prevent some people from learning and using satisfying and expansive skills in socially recognized settings or institutionalized social processes which inhibit people's ability to play and communicate with others or to express their feelings and perspective on social life in contexts where others can listen" (Young 1990, pp. 37–39). As types of oppression include powerlessness, marginalization, exploitation, cultural imperialism, and violence (Young 1990), field data shows that people in Syria were systematically marginalized if they did not "fit" into the regime-induced identity. They were left without any decision-making power, and moreover, they were forced to act with the will of the governing structures which points to powerlessness and lack of access to their language or school rights. For example, Kurdish people bring forth the cultural imperialism, meaning that there is a "universalization of a dominant group's experience and culture, and its establishment as the norm" (Young 1990). While strongly interlinked with oppression, [d]omination consists of institutional conditions that inhibit or prevent people from participating in determining their actions or the conditions of their actions (Young 1990, p. 38). Stereotypes and prejudices create oppressive structures that prevent self-development, as glass ceilings exist for intersectionally situated individuals. Chapter 5 also focuses on how different types of stereotypes and prejudice are formed within the community.

Refugee as a Social Category

After exploring their past lives and perceptions of the Syrian conflict, this study follows the participants from Syria to Türkiye. In the remainder of the book, they are living in a different social structure and are located as "refugees." Their articulation of the past and expectations of the future are formulated within the new structure where their social position is shifted. Inevitably, this ties into the analysis of the implications of perceiving them as a group and how they position themselves within society. In this regard, important conceptual inquiries about "refugees" are necessary: Are "refugees" a group? Giving a more specific focus, do "Syrian refugees" constitute a group?

Large-scale categories like ethnicity, sex, and race are contextualized by the social relations between such categories (Hogg et al. 1995, p. 264). "Refugee" status, like race and gender, is based on structural divisions in society, and it is highly visible and relevant for persons across situations (Stets 2021, p. 295). While "refugee" is a structurally born and constructed social category, realizing that "refugee" is not a "social group" in a sociological sense is crucial. Social groups provide a "sense of belonging in which people feel accepted and valued" (Stets 2021, p. 295). "Refugees," even if they come from the same country, do not necessarily have the same sense of belonging. Clustering refugees as a "group" is problematic as it leads to essentializing "refugee" status. The structurally constructed identity category of "refugee" needs to be separated from social groups that refugees form or become part of in the receiving community. "Once in society, people derive their identity or sense of self largely from the social categories to which they belong. Each person, however, over the course of his or her personal history, is a member of a unique combination of social categories; therefore, the set of social identities making up that person's self-concept is unique" (Stets and Burke 2000, p. 226). The rigid one-dimensional approach to "refugee" category, however, strip people from their subjectivity when others gaze upon them as refugees which make their unique self-concept invisible (Ozkaleli and Ozkaleli 2024).

Goffman (1963), in his analysis of persons with stigma, mentions the conceptual confusion around "group" and "category." Even though people within a stigma category may refer to themselves as a "we" along with outsiders position them in group terms, "they will neither have a capacity for collective action, -nor a stable and embracing pattern of mutual interaction" (34). Goffman's assertion suggests that refugees constitute a *category* that may lead to the formation of groups, but in itself, refugees do not constitute a group. We may analytically consider refugees "a group" when they form associations, schools, or civil society organizations. For example, the locality is an important determinant for forming associations. While holding the overarching "Syrian" category, some participants in the field stated that outside of their locality (such as Aleppo, Damascus, Deir Ez Zor), they met people from other parts of Syria for the first time in Gaziantep. This further affirms Goffman's claim that "being a member of the category, an individual may have an increased probability of coming into contact with any other member, and even forming a relationship with him as a result. A category, then, can function to dispose its members to group-formation and relationships, but its total membership does not thereby constitute a group…" (35).

Refugees' group membership cannot be reduced to a single one, either, as their identities and groups are multiple and intersecting. This means that different constitutive identities would cause different experiences for individuals as power is not equally distributed among different identities within the social structure. When approached intersectionally, a person does not experience conflicts only through one identity, such as race or ethnicity, but how all other constituting identities shape their race/ethnicity experience. Constitutive take on identity focuses on how one identity takes its meaning from another in a relational manner (Crenshaw 1991; McCall 2005, Nash 2008, Samuels and Sheriff 2008, Shields 2008, p. 30). The new social structure shapes how these constitutive identities affect interactions. The "refugee" category forces a particular interaction with the dominant receiving community. Additionally, their relations within the family and with other people from their home country also shift. Gendered Geographies of Power (GGP) (Mahler and Pessar 2001) show how the geographic scale shapes people's experiences from intimate to transnational based on people's social locations (Chaudhuri et al. 2019, p. 371). Some of their other identities still continue in the new social structure; that is, if one is a Sunni Arab female in Syria, they are still a Sunni Arab female in the receiving community. Yet, the new structure has a different way of locating the "Sunni Arab female" than the home country's social structure. All of these constitutive identities are reshaped with the imposed refugee category in the new setting, which directly influences personal experience. Given the precarity of refugee legal status in Türkiye, how does a linguistically disadvantaged Arab woman experience life? How is a female identity as it is related to other identities that have shifted to a new structure now experienced? An Arab female in Türkiye finds herself in a setting where her native language and ethnicity are not the dominant ones, and refugee status influences all the other identities they hold. On an intimate level, such shifts in identity experience emerged in this field study. For example, a patriarch found himself jobless and lacked contextual knowledge to control the family. Parents ended up relying on the language translation of their middle school children, or women refugees, for the first time, found themselves as the sole parent leading their families. Some from rural parts of their country experienced poverty for the first time, and others learned that their money did not necessarily equate to affluence *vis-à-vis* the receiving community. Some experienced a sense of empowerment because of their multilingual status, which unexpectedly made them high-wage earners within the NGO market even if their age and education were not consistent with the earned income compared to more educated and experienced refugees who are denied access to their profession in the receiving community such as medical doctors, pharmacists, and engineers. This means "identity changes are not only endogenous or originate within individuals at the micro level, but they also are exogenous or develop outside of individuals at the micro, meso, and macro levels of society" (Stets 2021, pp. 286–287; Tajfel 2010).

Social structure, "patterned regularities that characterize most human interaction" (Stryker [1980] 2002, p. 65 in Stets 2021, p. 288), has to be analyzed by focusing on the concept of power. As different groups have different levels of access to power within societies, domains of power in macro, meso, and micro levels of social structure need to be visible. Refugees shift away from spaces that position them as "citizens" to places that perceive them as outsiders. This outsider and disempowered minority position carries the marks of racist, imperial, and neo-colonial global geopolitics (Alinia 2015). Power relations show differences within different nation-states, and there is domination of some over others that influences all aspects of social life (Collins 2019, p. 171). In my analysis, I am not taking an identity group as an exogenous, a priori entity; rather, I built my analysis on examining how each individual positions himself/herself in an identity group. Individuals create their meanings within multiple social identity groups. The analysis of refugees includes micro, meso, and macro levels and their engagement with power hierarchies. By discussing structural, disciplinary, interpersonal, and cultural domains of power at three different levels in the analysis (Collins and Bilge 2020), I aim to contribute to the refugee literature by urging the analysis to be on multiple levels.

The macro level is "institutions and the stratification system, [where] institutions provide the structural and cultural backbone of a society" (Stets 2021, pp. 289–290; Turner 2010a, b, 2012). The structural domain of power is defined as "public policies that organize and regulate social institutions" (Collins 2019, p. 175). Refugee selves are forced to re-learn their location in the structural domain, which often is burdensome and negative. Field data shows that policies directly affect not only the everyday quality of life of refugees but also their articulation and imagining of the future. Their status not as refugees but as temporary protection and restrictions to movement between cities are examples of the power of the structural domain.

Meso level addresses "groups, organizations, and communities that divide people along the distinctive lines of race/ethnicity, gender, education" (Stets 2021, pp. 289–290; Turner 2010a, b, 2012). Considering it with power relations indicates that rules will be applied differently to minoritized identities. "The disciplinary domain refers to how individuals use rules and regulations to create or challenge social hierarchies" (Collins 2019, p. 175). The field data presented in Chap. 9, for example, shows how government officers, NGO workers, police, etc., may become a source of disempowerment for refugees by use of their authority positions.

Micro-level interactions among individuals are embedded in meso and macro structures and culture (Stets 2021, pp. 289–290; Turner 2010a, b, 2012). This means the interpersonal domain of power draws attention to people's experiences with intersecting oppressions (Collins 2019, p. 175). The person may have multiple salient identities (political, religious, or gender/sexual identity) and experience them consciously, but they may suppress them to avoid persecution or discrimination. As will be highlighted in Chap. 10, one hijabi participant stated that wearing the hijab in "Syrian style" was creating othering, and some people preferred to use it in "Turkish style." Other examples could be found in hiding pro-Asad views.

Finally, the cultural domain of power points out "the hegemonic ideas that guide social institutions to justify social inequalities and counter-hegemonic ideas that critically approach unjust social relations" (Collins 2019, p. 176). The cultural domain of power influences all three domains. The choice of language of education for Syrian children is an example of an issue in the cultural domain. How refugees create meanings and articulate their past, future, and present happens within a certain cultural space while they also remember and carry another cultural experience.

Participants in this study expressed negative attitudes from the receiving community that felt different in their interactions with ordinary people compared to their interactions with officials within state institutions. For example, a negative attitude in public transport felt different than that of a state officer when acquiring official documents. The latter's negativity felt more severe regarding their sense of self. This does not mean that the interpersonal domain of power can be dismissed or trivialized, but its implications for refugees play a role in different layers. This is why different layers of structure are important to be integrated into the analysis, with power hierarchies located at the center of such analysis.

Multiple Spatiality and Temporality Shaping Agency

The self that constitutes multiple identities is not constructed in one moment. Self is never "done" and does not exist only in the "present moment." Self is an ongoing process, always in the making, in the making of looking back and forward in the moment. In this ongoing process, how do we locate a becoming self, particularly a traveling self like a refugee? How does abruptly shifting from one space to the other influence the becoming self? Space has "intersecting dimensions" as people are "shaped by their social, cultural, or geographical past, present, and future lives…" (Sniekers 2018, p. 1076; Ozkaleli 2021). For refugees, their relationship to space is complex as their becoming is shaped by dual (or multiple) geographies. Their previous social and cultural learning in a different geography meets a present that becomes part of their life, which shapes their future. Hence, space and time have complex connections. If we can find "the fundamental relation between the future and the past in the present" (Mead 1932, p. 37), how do we engage with refugee experiences within multiple temporal and spatial realms? Refugees' "articulation of 'home'…has become a space, a community created within the changing links between 'here' and 'there'" (Al-Ali and Koser 2002, p. 6; Ozkaleli 2018). In general, when we experience different places, are we "here" or "there"? If so, when we are "here," in what ways does "there" continue to be in us to be part of our becoming? Is the past already past us? Is the past already behind us? In what ways do we carry the past to envision our future? There is a "customary assumption that the past that determines us is *there*. The truth is that the past is there, in its certainty or probability, in the same sense that the setting of our problems is there" (Mead 1932, p. 3, emphasis in original). Do we solely live in the moment of now, or do we blend past happenings and future imaginings into that lived moment? In Mead's (1932) approach, "to see the past as past… is to see it when it is past, in relation to the present whose past it is" (Murphy 1932, p. xi).

The agency is related to multiple dimensions of people's temporal and spatial existence (Emirbayer and Mische 1998; Şahin-Mencütek et al. 2023, use temporality in terms of refugee governance). Multiple temporalities and spatial experiences modify refugees' perceptions, how they position their identity, and their sense of belonging. Social and relational aspects of agency are theorized with routine (past), purpose (future), and judgment (present) (Emirbayer and Mische 1998). Mead (1932, p. 76) argues that "as actors respond to changing environments, they must continually reconstruct their view of the past in an attempt to understand the causal conditioning of the emergent present while using this understanding to control and shape their responses in the arising future" (in Emirbayer and Mische 1998, pp. 968–969). "Chordal triad of agency" (Emirbayer and Mische 1998) is based on the dynamic interplay of three constitutive elements. These are (i) routine, where human agency is recognized to have habitual, repetitive practices through which actors selectively reactivate past patterns of thought and action (iteration); (ii) purpose, where there is goal-seeking and imaginative regeneration of possible future trajectories based on actors' hopes, fears, and desires (projectivity); and (iii) judgment, where humans use deliberation in evolving situations (practical evaluation) (Emirbayer and Mische 1998, pp. 963, 971, 972; see Ozkaleli 2021).

When individuals are generalized and stereotyped away from their *persona* (Harrell-Bond and Voutira 2007), they are thought of as not having agentic ability. As "refugees" are viewed by states and presented by media as "(problematic) aspects" of host societies (Malkki 1992, 1995a, b; Benezer and Zetter 2014), the possibility of realizing their agency is further limited. Taking multiple temporalities into account would help us see how the agency of refugees emerges. The following definition of agency is useful, as it would direct us to look at multiple temporalities of refugees, including their past in the home country and their future expectations that shape their experiences and actions today:

> *the temporally constructed engagement by actors of different structural environments-the temporal-relational contexts of action-which, through the interplay of habit, imagination, and judgment, both reproduces and transforms those structures in interactive response to the problems posed by changing historical situations.* (Emirbayer and Mische 1998, p. 970, emphasis in original)

Refugees simultaneously operate in at least two different habitus: the home habitus and the host habitus. If they relocate to a third country after the initial host country, they also carry traces of the previous host country's experiences. Interruption of their everyday practices in their home country does not mean a complete stop to their routine. In the new place, they blend home and host habitus. This means, "mentally, socially, and with all their interactions, refugees operate in multiple habitus, and the complexity of their experiences may be discerned by analyzing their experiences within different temporalities" (Ozkaleli 2021, p. 3). In order to comprehend individual experience, then, multiple temporalities approach would constantly drive us to see people not as playing one rigid social identity "category," meaning "refugee" in a given context, but to pull all the constituting identities which are engaged with past (habit), future (purpose), and present (judgment) that "play a role on ways actors engage with and experience their identities. Refugees' agency is conceptualized 'within the flow of time,' where actors, while they operate with complex transborder spatial interaction, are 'embedded within many such [past, future and present] temporalities at once' (Emirbayer and Mische 1998, pp. 963–964)… what aspects of their lives they will iterate or shift relate to possible future trajectories that decide their present judgments" (Ozkaleli 2021, p. 2).

Relational pragmatics analyzes multiple temporalities of past, future, and present within the life-course of individuals. Nevertheless, temporality operates in multiple ways for various refugees in different social locations. For example, pious individuals constantly refer not only to the life-course past but also to the past that is locked in/anchored to the scriptural past, where they aspire to reiterate the rules of prophetic and eternal future that are connected to their beliefs (Ozkaleli 2021, p. 2). Therefore, agency for pious refugees is shaped simultaneously within the past, future, and present temporalities in the life-course as well as their anchored scriptural pasts and eternal future. For refugees who are not driven by religious piety, the temporality is different, yet it can still be beyond their own past lives and future trajectories. Even if not guided by religion, they may be guided by tradition or a past political aspiration that they still follow and work for a future beyond their life cycle for the sake of future generations. In terms of the future, when refugees are concerned about their children's future, they consider their present actions in terms of their children's future, which shapes their imaginings beyond their own existence. For example, if they aspire to return to Syria, they desire a strong Arabic education so their children can easily return to their own society. If their future imaginings do not see a possibility of going back, and if they see a potential future in the receiving community, they look for ways to integrate their children linguistically into the receiving community. Similarly, if, in their becoming, refugees have a political agency where they articulate ideas and desires for the future of Syria, the temporality is still beyond the life-course, guiding their purpose, action, and commitment to a future even after their passing.

Human agency can exist within the social structure in which individuals operate. According to relational pragmatics, "interaction, perception, and cognition do not precede action but are phases of it, directed and redirected by changing situations and by the dialogical definition and redefinition of problems encountered in interaction … that may provide a solution or resolution to them" (Burkitt 2018). Emirbayer and Mische (1998) argue that actors show creativity in different situations by assessing their pasts, imagining their alternative future possibilities, and orienting their present through a practical evaluation (Burkitt 2018, p. 534; also see Ozkaleli 2021). As they have dual spatial experience in their home and host country and integrate different temporalities to locate their experiences and expectations, refugee positionality needs to be analyzed with these complexities.

"'Present' is the locus of reality," meaning that real exists "in relation to a present" (Murphy 1932, p. xvi). When I analyzed "the present" of the people in the field, their narratives led me to recognize the simultaneousness of multiple time and space in their life. People cannot look into their past life without its "relationship to what [they have] become" (Mead 1932, p. 31). Inevitably, I met with people in a particular context and space at a particular time. Yet, their narratives and positioning of the self, their understanding of themselves at the time of interviews, led me to look into the concept of self in shifting and multiple temporal and spatial analyses, which are developed in Parts II and III to show the complexity of dual spatiality and multiple temporalities in the lives of people who are positioned as refugees. Interviewee narratives were always connected to a time different than the present. It never was "hanging in the air" but always tied into a past or an envisioned future and connected to a different spatial experience (e.g., "back in Syria" or "if I can leave this place and go to…").

Life-worlds, the world of everyday lived experience (Van Manen 2016, p. 313), can be glimpsed through seeing the self that is constructed in different spaces and in different times as "the past 'in itself' is not a past at all – its relation to the present is the ground of its pastness" (Murphy 1932, p. xx). When we focus on people's experiences in the present, the past exists within the present, and "its presence is exhibited in memory" (Mead 1932, p. 17). When people remember past events, how they look into the past is closely intertwined with the temporal and spatial fluidity of the present and their expectations of the future. "Past, present, and future belong to a passage which attains temporal structure through the event" (Mead 1932, p. 24). Hence, as refugee experiences occur within social structure and culture, time, space, and relationality need to be central to the analysis. Overemphasis on the "refugee" category becomes a barrier to recognizing refugees' subjectivity and locating their agentic self. Stories that emerge in people's narratives show their agentic relationality to time and space; hence, the focus is not to "categorize" people but to "characterize" or locate them within relationships and life episodes (Somers 1994, p. 624).

Even individuals born and living in one locality have many intersecting identities that they develop intersubjectively with many people in various social identity categories. For refugees, capturing self-conceptualization requires understanding multiple spaces that produce different intersubjective meanings. Refugee selves are in an abyss between their home country and host country and between displacement and emplacement in the process of becoming (Heidegger 1962 in Lems 2016, pp. 322–327). Individuals' becoming is a continual process in human life (Benezer and Zetter 2014; Lems 2016; Ozkaleli 2018), and it is not linear. When spatial experiences become multiple, relationality to time also shifts. Refugee selves often go back to their past life in their home country in their imaginings. They often visit (envision) the future when they will be able to see their home country. People's narratives about their self-conceptualization are "constellations of *relationships* (connected parts) embedded in *time and space*" (Somers 1994, p. 616). In other words, narrative embeds identities in time and spatial relationships, making us understand that identity and the self are things one *becomes* (Somers 1994, p. 618). More importantly, one continues *becoming* rather than being (Hall 1996) as they are constructed continuously through time (Armbruster 2002; Hall 1996). When refugees are denied an emergence of their identities through their voices, they are no longer perceived as agents that are becoming. Even though refugees continue their becoming through the narratives that "*exist interpersonally in the course of social and structural interactions over time*" (Somers 1994, p. 816, emphasis in original), the outside gaze is unable to see this becoming; the gaze only sees a rigid "refugee" identity (Ozkaleli and Ozkaleli 2024). Such overlooking is possible as their power in the social structure is restricted and mostly silenced.

As argued extensively above, structurally enforced identities and categories in the existing social contexts and power structures (Mahmood 2001) produce inequalities and exclusions. Within these structures, the agency is exercised as an "interactional expectation" (Risman 2009); sometimes, it reshapes, while sometimes, it "undoes" those structures (Risman 2009 in Ozkaleli 2021). As refugees experience self in home and host societies, social structure is fluid and multiple. Across transnational spaces, how people are positioned within structures and their access to resources influence their agency as the level of access and social conditioning decides what they can imagine, plan, and strategize (Massey 1994 in Mahler and Pessar 2001, p. 447). Hence, the duality (or multiplicity in case refugees shift from one host society to another) of spatial experiences has to be evaluated. Space is closely related to the relational pragmatics understanding of agency as a "degree of creativity shown by actors in different situations … [relative] to various overlapping relational contexts" (Burkitt 2018, p. 534). In order to properly recognize people's agency, meanings created in home and host habitus need to be surfaced. In other words, spatial influence in their intersubjective meaning-making, along with articulation of self in multiple temporalities, need to be evaluated. Such a rich understanding can show us the agentic self, and only then can we distance individuals from a pre-defined rigid refugee identity.

References

Abboud SN (2016) Syria. Polity Press, Cambridge (e-book version)

Abuelaish I, Godoy-Ruiz P (2020) A holistic approach to addressing gender, violence, health, and peace. In: Byrne S, Matyók T, Scott IM, Senehi J (eds) Routledge companion to peace and conflict studies. Routledge, New York, pp 925–940

Akar S, Erdogdu, MM (2019) Syrian refugees in Turkey and integration problem ahead. J Int Migr and Integ 20:925–940

Al-Ali N, Koser K (2002) Transnationalism, international migration and home. In: Al-Ali N, Koser K (eds) New approaches to migration? Transnational communities and transformation of home. Routledge, London, pp 1–14

Alinia M (2015) On black feminist thought: thinking oppression and resistance through intersectional paradigm. Ethn Racial Stud 38(13):2334–2340. https://doi.org/10.1080/01419870.2015.1058492

Almasri S (2022) Why is Syria a war but not Afghanistan? Nationality-based aid and protection in Turkey's Syria refugee response. Refug Surv Q 42(1):29–54

Althusser L (2006) Ideology and ideological state apparatuses (notes towards an investigation). In: Sharma A, Gupta A (eds) The anthropology of the state: a reader. Blackwell Publishing, Hoboken, pp 86–98

Aras R (2020) Veiled memories: an ethnography of the single-party regime in Turkey. Middle East Stud 56(2):222–238

Armbruster H (2002) Homes in crisis: Syrian orthodox Christians in Turkey and Germany. In: Al-Ali N, Koser K (eds) New approaches to migration? Transnational communities and transformation of home. Routledge, London, pp 17–33

Ayvazoğlu AŞ, Kunuroglu F (2019) Being a Syrian university student in Turkey: intergroup relations, psychosocial issues, and boundary formation. Refug Surv Q 38(4):425–447

Azar EE (1985) Protracted international conflicts: ten propositions. Int Interactions Empirical Theoretical Res Int Relations 12(1):59–70. https://doi.org/10.1080/03050628508434647

Azar EE (1990) The management of protracted social conflict: theory and cases. Aldershot, Dartmouth

Azar EE, Farah N (1981) The structure of inequalities and protracted social conflict: a theoretical framework. Int Interactions Empirical Theoretical Res Int Relations 7(4):317–335. https://doi.org/10.1080/03050628108434558

Azar EE, Haddad RF (1986) Lebanon: an anomalous conflict? Third World Q 8(4):1337–1350

Baban F, Ilican S, Rygiel K (2017) Syrian refugees in Turkey: pathways to precarity, differential inclusion, and negotiated citizenship rights. J Ethn Migr Stud 43(1):41–57

Babbie E (2009) The practice of social research, 12th edn. Wadsworth, Bedmont

Barrington LW (1997) "Nation" and "nationalism": the misuse of key concepts in political science. Polit Sci Politics 30(4):712–716

Benezer G, Zetter R (2014) Searching for directions: conceptual and methodological challenges in researching refugee journeys. J Refug Stud 28(3):297–318

Burkitt I (2018) Relational agency. In: Depelteau F (ed) The Palgrave handbook of relational sociology. Palgrave Macmillan, Cham, pp 523–538

Burton JW (2024) Needs theory (1997). In: Dunn DJ, Brauch HG, Burton P (eds) John W. Burton: a pioneer in conflict analysis and resolution: key contributions on international relations, peace theory, world society, and human needs. Springer Nature, Cham, pp 307–315

Chaitani Y (2007) Post-colonial Syria and Lebanon: the decline of Arab nationalism and the triumph of the state. Bloomsbury Publishing, London

Chatty D (2017) The duty to be generous (Karam): alternatives to rights-based asylum in the Middle East. J Br Acad 5:177–199

Chaudhuri M, Thimm V, Mahler SJ (2019) Scaling educational policy and practice intersectionality: historical and contemporary cases from south and Southeast Asia. In: Hankivsky O, Jordan-Zachery JS (eds) The Palgrave handbook of Intersectionality in public policy. Palgrave Macmillan, Cham, pp 167–192

Collins PH (2019) The difference that power makes: Intersectionality and participatory democracy. In: Hankivsky O, Jordan-Zachery JS (eds) The Palgrave handbook of intersectionality in public policy. Palgrave Macmillan, Cham, pp 167–192

Collins PH, Bilge S (2020) Intersectionality. Polity Press, Cambridge

Crawley H, Skleparis D (2017) Refugees, migrants, neither, both: categorical fetishism and the politics of bounding in Europe's 'migration crisis.'. J Ethn Migr Stud 44(1):48–64

Crenshaw K (1991) Mapping the margins: Intersectionality, identity politics, and violence against women of color. Stanford Law Rev 43(6):1241–1299

Davenport C (2007) State repression and political order. Annu Rev Polit Sci 10:1–23

Davenport C, Inman M (2012) The state of state repression research since the 1990s. Terrorism Polit Violence 24(4):619–634

Dawisha A (2016) Arab nationalism in the twentieth century. Princeton University Press, Princeton

De Châtel F (2014) The role of drought and climate change in the Syrian uprising: untangling the triggers of the revolution. Middle East Stud 50(4):521–535

Efe İ, Jacoby T (2022) 'Making sense' of Turkey's refugee policy: the case of the directorate general of migration management. Migration Stud 10(1):62–81

Ehteshami A, Hinnebusch RA (2002) Syria and Iran: middle powers in a penetrated regional system. Routledge, London

Emirbayer M, Mische A (1998) What is agency? Am J Sociol 103(4):962–1023

Erdoğan M (2019) Syrian refugees in Turkey. Konrad–Adenauer-Stiftung Report

Erdogan M, Kavukcuer Y, Cetinkaya T (2017) Turkiye'de yasayan suriyeli multecilere yonelik medya algisi [Media perceptions towards Syrian refugees living in Turkey], Freedom Research Association. Retrieved from https://mmuraterdogan.files.wordpress.com/2016/06/oad_c2lgwsk.pdf

Erdoğan MM, Kirişci K, Uysal G (2021) Improving Syrian refugee inclusion in the Turkish economy: how can the international community help? World Refugee & Migration Council Research Report, (September) 2021, https://wrmcouncil.org/wp-content/uploads/2021/09/Turkey-Syrian-Refugees-WRMC-final.pdf

Erlich R (2014) Inside Syria. Prometheus Books, New York

Galtung J (1969) Violence, peace, and peace research. J Peace Res 6(3):167–191

Goffman E (1963) Stigma: notes on the management of spoiled identity. Penguin Books, New York

Goldstein RJ (1978) Political repression in modern America: from 1870 to the present. Schenkman, Cambridge

Gunes C (2021) Kurdish politics across the Middle East during the 1970. In: Bozarslan H, Gunes C, Yadirgi V (eds) The Cambridge history of the Kurds. Cambridge University Press, Cambridge, pp 250–268

Haklai O (2000) A minority rule over a hostile majority: the case of Syria. Nationalism Ethnic Polit 6(3):19–50

Hall S (1996) Introduction: who needs identity? In: Hall S, Du Gay P (eds) Questions of cultural identity. Sage Publications, London, pp 1–17

Harrell-Bond B, Voutira E (2007) In search of 'invisible' actors: barriers to access in refugee research. J Refug Stud 20(2):281–298

Heidegger M (1962) Being and time. Harpers & Row, New York

Hinnebusch R (2005) Syria: revolution from above. Routledge, London

Hinnebusch R (2022) Governance amidst civil war: From failing statehood to competitive regime reformation. In: Gani JK, Hinnebusch R (eds) Actors and dynamics in the Syrian conflict's middle phase. Routledge, London, pp 35–57

Hogg MA, Terry DJ, White KM (1995) A tale of two theories: a critical comparison of identity theory with social identity theory. Soc Psychol Q 58(4):255–269

Hokayem E (2013) Syria's uprising and the fracturing of the Levant. International Institute of Strategic Studies, Adelphi Series, London

Imady O, Hinnebusch R (2018) Conclusion: the early trajectory of the Syrian uprising: from agency to structure. In: Hinnebusch R, Imady O (eds) The Syrian uprising: domestic origins and early trajectory. Routledge, London, pp 329–335

Jacoby T, Mac Ginty R, Şenay B (2019) Islam, the state and Turkey's Syrian refugees: the Vaiz of Bursa. J Refug Stud 32(2):237–256

Karasapan O (2019) Turkey's Syrian refugees—the welcome fades (November 25). Brookings Institute. https://www.brookings.edu/blog/future-development/2019/11/25/turkeys-syrian-refugees-thewelcome- fades/

Kaufman SJ (2001) Modern hatreds: the symbolic politics of ethnic war. Cornell University Press, Ithaca

Kayaoğlu A, Şahin-Mencütek Z, Erdoğan MM (2022) Return aspirations of Syrian refugees in Turkey. J Immigr Refug Stud 20(4):561–583

Khalaf R (2015) Governance without government in Syria: civil society and state building during conflict. Syria Stud 7(3):37–72

Khatib L (2011) Islamic revivalism in Syria: the rise and fall of Ba'thist secularism. Routledge, New York (e-book version)

Khoury PS (1987) Syria and the French mandate. The politics of Arab nationalism, 1920–45. Princeton University Press, Princeton
Kienle E (1995) Arab unity schemes revisited: interest, identity and policy in Syria and Egypt. Int J Middle East Stud 27(1):53–67
Kirisci K (2014) Syrian refugees and Turkey's challenges: going beyond hospitality. Brookings, Washington D.C. Retrieved from http://madde14.org/english/images/0/0e/2014BrookingsSyriaKirisci.pdf. Accessed 2 Jan 2021
Kirisci K, Kolasin GU (2019) Order from chaos: Syrian refugees in Turkey need better access to formal jobs (July 18). Brookings Institute, Washington D.C. https://www.brookings.edu/blog/order-from-chaos/2019/07/18/syrian-refugees-in-turkey-need-better-access-to-formal-jobs/
KONDA (2019) Konda Barometresi Suriyeli Sıgınmacılara Bakıs [Konda barometer of looking at Syrian Refugees], https://konda.com.tr/tr/rapor/suriyeli-siginmacilara-bakis/
Kriesberg L (1998) Constructive conflicts: from escalation to resolution. Rowman & Littlefield Publishers, Oxford
Lems A (2016) Placing displacement: place-making in a world of movement. Ethnos 81(2):315–337
Lesch DW (2012) Syria: the fall of the house of Assad. Yale University Press, New Haven
Lowndes V, Polat RK (2020) How do local actors interpret, enact and contest policy? An analysis of local government responses to meeting the needs of Syrian refugees in Turkey. Local Gov Stud 48(3):546–569
Mahler SJ, Pessar PR (2001) Gendered geographies of power: analyzing gender across transnational spaces. Identities 7(4):441–459. https://doi.org/10.1080/1070289X.2001.9962675
Mahmood S (2001) Feminist theory, embodiment, and the docile agent: some reflections on the Egyptian Islamic revival. Cult Anthropol 16(2):202–236
Malkki LH (1992) National geographic: the rooting of peoples and the territorialization of National Identity among scholars and refugees. Cult Anthropol 7(1):24–44
Malkki LH (1995a) Purity and exile: violence, memory, and national cosmology among Hutu refugees in Tanzania. The University of Chicago Press, Chicago
Malkki LH (1995b) Refugees and exile: from "refugee studies" to the national order of things. Annu Rev Anthropol 24:495–523
Manuel T (2007) Envisioning the possibilities for a good life: exploring the public policy implications of intersectionality theory. J Women Politics Policy 28(3):173–203
Massey D (1994) Space, place and gender. University of Minnesota Press, Minneapolis
McCall L (2005) The complexity of intersectionality. Signs 30(3):1771–1800
Mead GH (1932) In: Murphy AE (ed) The philosophy of the present. The Open Court Company Publishers, London
Mencütek ZS (2019) Encouraging Syrian return: Turkey's fragmented approach. Forced Migr Rev 62:28–31
Mencütek ZS (2021) Governing practices and strategic narratives for the Syrian refugee returns. J Refug Stud 34(3):2804–2826
Miall H, Ramsbotham O, Woodhoulse T (2000) Contemporary conflict resolution. Polity Press, Oxford
Morgül K, Savaşkan O (2022) Identity or interests? Religious conservatives' attitudes toward Syrian refugees in Turkey. Migr Stud 9(4):1645–1672
Murphy AE (1932) Introduction. In: Murphy AE (ed) George Herbert Mead. The philosophy of the present. The Open Court Company Publishers, London
Narlı N, Özaşçılar M, Ipek IZT (2020) Turkish daily press framing and representation of Syrian women refugees and gender-based problems: implications for social integration. J Immigr Refug Stud 18(1):1–21
Nash JC (2008) Re-thinking intersectionality. Fem Rev 89(1):1–15
Nemir F (1992) La politique kurde de la Syrie. In: Hakim H (ed) Les Kurdes par-delà l'exode. L'Harmattan, Paris
Özçürümez S, Akyuz S, Bradby H (2021a) The conceptualization problem in research and responses to sexual and gender-based violence in forced migration. J Gend Stud 30(1):66–78

Özçürümez S, Hoxha J, İçduygu A (2021b) Does social cohesion solve forced migration riddles? Troubled concepts and constrained practices in Turkey. Migr Stud 9(3):597–616
Ozkaleli U (2015) State of the state in their minds: intersectional framework for women's citizenship in Turkey. Women's Stud Int Forum 48:93–102
Ozkaleli U (2018) Displaced selves, dislocated emotions and transforming identities: Syrian refugee women reinventing selves. Women's Stud Int Forum 70:17–23. https://doi.org/10.1016/j.wsif.2018.07.010
Ozkaleli U (2021) Agency in multiple temporalities: being Syrian women, becoming widows and refugees, remaining pious. Women's Stud Int Forum 89:102538. https://doi.org/10.1016/j.wsif.2021.102538
Ozkaleli U, Ozkaleli FM (2024) Panopticon, gaze, and rupture in the fantasy: the Syrian refugee experience in Turkey. Migr Stud 12(4):mnae033. https://doi.org/10.1093/migration/mnae033
Pearlman WR (2017) We crossed a bridge and it trembled: voices from Syria. Custom House (e-book version)
Ramsbotham O (2005) The analysis of protracted social conflict: a tribute to Edward Azar. Rev Int Stud 31:109126. https://doi.org/10.1017/S0260210505006327
Reilly JA (2018) Fragile nation, shattered land: the modern history of Syria. I.B. Tauris and Co, London (e-book version)
Risman BJ (2009) From doing to undoing: gender as we know it. Gend Soc 23(1):81–84
Rottmann S, Kaya A (2021) 'We can't integrate in Europe. We will pay a high price if we go there': culture, time and migration aspirations for Syrian refugees in Istanbul. J Refug Stud 34(1):474–490
Rottmann SB, Nimer M (2021) 'We always open our doors for visitors'—hospitality as homemaking strategy for refugee women in Istanbul. Migr Stud 9(3):1380–1398
Şahin-Mencütek Z, Gökalp-Aras NE, Kaya A, Rottmann SB (2023) Syrian refugees in Turkey: between reception and integration. Springer International Publishing, Cham
Samuels GM, Sheriff F (2008) Identity, oppression, and power: feminisms and intersectionality theory. Affilia 23(5):5–9
Sandal NA (2019) Solidarity theologies and the (re)definition of ethnoreligious identities: the case of the Alevis of Turkey and Alawites of Syria. Br J Middle Eastern Stud 48(3):473–491
Saraçoğlu C, Bélanger D (2019) Loss and xenophobia in the city: contextualizing anti-Syrian sentiments in Izmir, Turkey. Patterns Prejud 53(4):363–383
Scheper-Hughes N, Bourgois P (2004) Violence in war and peace: an anthology. Blackwell Publishing, Malden
Şengül I (2022) 'Syrian refugees' homemaking in Gaziantep: uncertainty, legality and temporality. Refug Surv Q 41(2):267–297
Şenses N (2016) Rethinking migration in the context of precarity: the case of Turkey. Crit Sociol 42(7–8):975–987
Şenses N (2020) Gender, women and precarity: examples from Turkey. In: Williams L, Coşkun E, Kaşka S (eds) Women, migration and asylum in Turkey. Migration, diasporas and citizenship. Palgrave Macmillan, Cham, pp 49–67
Shields S (2008) Gender: An Intersectionality perspective. Sex Roles 59(5):301–311
Singer JD (1961) The level-of-analysis problem. World Polit 10:2009557
Skocpol T (1979) States and social revolutions: a comparative analysis of France, Russia and China. Cambridge University Press, Cambridge
Sniekers M (2018) Defining dreams: Young mothers' agency in constructions of space. Soc Cult Geogr 19(8):1073–1096
Somers MR (1994) The narrative constitution of identity: a relational and network approach. Theory Soc 23(5):605–649
Sorenson DS (2016) Syria in ruins: the dynamics of the Syrian civil war. Praeger, Santa Barbara
Stets JE (2021) Micro, meso, and macro processes in identity change: the 2020 Cooley-Mead award address. Soc Psychol Q 84(4):286–308
Stets JE, Burke PJ (2000) Identity theory and social identity theory. Soc Psychol Q 63(3):224–237

Stryker S ([1980] 2002) Symbolic interactionism: a social structural version. The Blackburn Press, Caldwell
Tajfel H (2010) Introduction. In: Tajfel H (ed) Social identity and intergroup relations, vol 7. Cambridge University Press, Cambridge, pp 1–12
Talhami GH (2001) Syria and the Palestinians: the clash of nationalisms. University Press of Florida, Gainseville
Taylor E (2016) Groups and oppression. Hypatia 31(3):520–536
Tejel J (2009) Syria's Kurds: history, politics and society. Routledge, New York
Tejel J (2021) The Kurdish question in Syria. In: Bozarslan H, Gunes C, Yadirgi V (eds) The Cambridge history of the Kurds. Cambridge University Press, Cambridge, pp 436–457
Turner JH (2010a) Theoretical principles of sociology, volume 1: macrodynamics. Springer, New York
Turner JH (2010b) Theoretical principles of sociology, volume 2: microdynamics. Springer, New York
Turner JH (2012) Theoretical principles of sociology, volume 3: Mesodynamics. Springer, New York
UNHCR (2020) Syria emergency. https://www.unhcr.org/en-us/syria-emergency.html
UNHCR (2023) Operational data portal. Refugee situations: Syria regional refugee response. 7 September. https://data.unhcr.org/en/situations/syria
Utku DE, Unutulmaz KO, Sirkeci I (2017) Turkey's Syrians: today and tomorrow. Transnational Press, London
Van Dam N (1996) The struggle for power in Syria. Politics and society under Asad and the Ba'th party. I.B. Tauris, London
Van Manen M (2016) Phenomenology of practice: Meaning-giving methods in phenomenological research and writing. Routledge, London and New York
Wehr P (2006) Conflict mapping. https://www.beyondintractability.org/essay/conflict_mapping
Yanaşmayan Z, Üstübici A, Kaşli Z (2019) Under the shadow of civilizationist populist discourses. New Diversities 21(2):37–51
Yildiz K (2005) The Kurds in Syria: the forgotten people. Pluto Press, London
Young IM (1990) Justice and the politics of difference. Princeton University Press, Princeton

Part I
Perceptions of Syrian Refugees: Actors and Causes of the Conflict

Chapter 3
Formation of Identities in the Conflict

Internationally Intertwined Conflict

Syria is an example of multiparty "conflict complexes" as there are "multiple local, regional, extra-regional and global actors and…some thousand opposition groups," which result in the internationalization of ethnopolitical conflicts (Lounsbery and Pearson 2023, p. 39). The fighting in Syria spilled over to neighboring Iraq in the East, the Jordanian border in the West, and the border of Türkiye in the North, along with east and south Lebanon (Sorenson 2016). "'Competitive interference' by external powers and trans-state movements ratcheted up the unwillingness to compromise on both sides [the regime and the opposition]" (Imady and Hinnebusch 2018, p. 331). "From the very start, the Syrian uprising was marked by a complex interplay between domestic and regional factors, where rival international and regional actors supported various local 'proxies'" (Phillips and Valbjørn 2018, p. 415). Some of the reasons for this internationalization are to "promote 'regime change' or secession…border modifications or offsetting security threats or economic losses (Najafov 2017) [or] to promote ethnic integration or segregation" (Lounsbery and Pearson 2023, p. 39).

This complexity of the Syrian conflict is reflected in the participants' narratives. Some of the most mentioned religious groups were the Muslim Brotherhood (*al-Ikhwan*), Islamic State (ISIS, ISIL, or DAESH), and Al-Nusra Front.[1] International actors were Russia and Iran,[2] supporting the Asad regime, while the United States, Türkiye, and the Gulf Countries, specifically Iraq, Qatar, and Saudi Arabia, were seen as major players supporting different rebel factions. The roles of the U.S. and Russia were sometimes seen as ambiguous and confusing regarding who supported

[1] For information about Islamist armed groups, see Erlich (2014, pp. 53–57).

[2] For the Iran and Syria alliance, see Ehteshami and Hinnebusch (2002).

© The Author(s), under exclusive license to Springer Nature Singapore Pte Ltd. 2025
U. Ozkaleli, *De-essentializing Refugees: Perceptions, Experiences, and Becoming of Syrians in Türkiye*, https://doi.org/10.1007/978-981-96-5519-9_3

whom.[3] One common observation among participants was that groups were pitted against one another, and their inter-group conflicts served the interests of powerful states. Moreover, Syria was seen as a ground for international actors' conflicts with one another. Amir (21, from Latakia, agnostic) calls it a "proxy war"[4] between Russia and the U.S. in the Middle East. Many participants did not talk about one actor as the central one; rather, they viewed these actors as complexly intertwined. The most mentioned external actors are clustered in the following sub-sections: Arab States and ISIS, Russia-Iran, and the U.S. Seeing the contemporary violent conflict as a proxy war, along with the involvement of external actors, highlights how participants perceive the situation as an extension of Syria's colonial history in their collective memory. This section will, therefore, further examine the Sykes-Picot Agreement, as it serves as a critical reference point, both as a significant historical event and as a pertinent historical analogy. The examination of Sykes-Picot follows with the role contemporary international actors play to illustrate a critical view toward Western claims of prioritizing human rights.

Arab States and ISIS/DAESH

Amez, who actively worked in "conflict mapping" for European research agencies, was eager to talk about conflict parties. Amez counts Russia, Iran, and Hezbollah on the side of the Asad regime, placing the Kurdish YPG (People's Defense Unit) and PYD (Democratic Union Party)[5] independent from the regime. Amez sees the Muslim Brotherhood, the Turkish state, and the U.S. coalition from 2014 as the main supporters of the Free Syrian Army against the regime. He talks about regional and international involvement with Muslim factions in detail:

> …The Jordanian Intelligence plays a major role in Southern areas of Syria, such as Dar'aa. They influence the tribes there, and they are very connected, so the Jordanians are the inhabitants of Southern Syria. They have family relations. When the war against Iraq had started, the Iraqi government was the Ba'ath one. [After this war], all the Ba'athist senior officers were melted into the Islamic State of Iraq in 2006, and that played a major role in moving the conflict inside Syria itself when the events broke out. Then, you have the Saudis and the Qataris. Saudis forced Qatar to support Jabhat al-Nusra [Al-Nusra Front], and all these radical movements, mainly the Muslim Brotherhood, played a major role when they took Egypt. Their role decreased after the international community started rejecting them. Al Qaeda tried to commit to its project in South Syria, but it failed miserably at the beginning, so it had a major split with the Islamic State of Iraq and the Levant. Then the Jabhat al-Nusra is going there now. These are the major role players in Syrian events. Now, it is impossible to control the political flow. (Amez, 22, Kurdish, from Aleppo, non-believer, some college education)

[3] U.S.'s conflicting practices on Syria are detailed by Erlich (2014, pp. 64–65, 68).

[4] For different definitions and approaches to proxy wars, see Hughes (2014), Phillips and Valbjørn (2018) and Malmvig (2017).

[5] For PYD/YPG, see Savelsberg (2018).

It is important to note that some Syrians, like Amez, were deeply concerned about the actorship of the Islamist groups and the support they received from external actors as they shaped the conflict on religious grounds. Some, like Kamal (a 50-year-old Sunni Arab from Aleppo, religious), had a positive view about the involvement of Arab countries, arguing that despite the pressure they received from other countries, Arab countries gave Syria "humanitarian support." In contrast, others, like Noury, blamed these Arab countries for encouraging Syrians to join the war without properly backing the individual citizens.

Islamic State appeared as a major actor in the narrative. Participants from different identity groups all identified ISIS as working with others against their group. This signals that different groups were not allowed to form steady and lasting coalitions. While the other actors were mentioned in connection to each other and not by itself, ISIS was an exception, focused specifically as a dominating actor on the ground, at least for a time. Whether ISIS is an internal or external actor is a complex matter. In the literature, "the creation of the Islamic State (IS/ISIS) in Syria and Iraq in 2014" is seen as introducing "an unbridled global dimension to Jihadist terrorism" (Tschirgi 2020, p. 319). Consistent with the literature, some participants described ISIS as a multinational entity, having Syrian members along with members from other countries such as Tunisia, Morocco, France, the UK, and America [the U.S.]. Islamic State is also seen as connected to Iraq's Ba'athists. Many of the accounts about ISIS are consistent with the analysis that "one of the consequences of the Syrian civil war and the creation of ISIS has been the massive flood of refugees to neighboring Türkiye, Lebanon, and Jordan as well as to Europe…" (Tschirgi 2020, p. 319). Some participants suggested that ISIS had many members who were let out of the Asad regime's prisons and saw ISIS as connected to the Asad regime. A considerable number of study participants stated that after moving outside of regime areas, they did not plan to leave Syria, but facing ISIS was the reason for crossing the border. Camil, like others, also points out an obvious connection between the regime and ISIS and the endorsement of it by powerful world actors:

> What about countries that are investing ISIS? If the world wanted to defeat ISIS, they would have done it with a click of their fingers. Convoys of ISIS can travel from Syria to Iraq. Is it possible that no one sees it? They handed them cities in Syria and Iraq. They travel in 4x4 cars. Is there any rational person who understands that this happens without the superpowers of this world? Is there anyone who buys that ISIS exists without support? What about the oil? The whole world knows ISIS trades oil to the regime and Russia… (Camil, 35-year-old Sunni Arab from Aleppo)

Many believed that ISIS was used as a strategy by the Asad regime to steal and give ownership of the revolution. Kamal argued it was the product of the regime and international community to "kill the revolution." Similarly, Amal states:

> Asad played it cleverly. He put DAESH and Jabhat al-Nusra as big spots in the revolution, [had others] focused on them, and made the countries think only about these actors. There are civilians, honest, innocent people. The world does not think about this. The world only thinks about DAESH and how dangerous it is; yes, it is dangerous. Similarly, Jabhat al-Nusra, but there is another side. They must see it. Iran, Russia, and the USA support Asad. (Amal, divorced, graduate degree, 42, from Damascus, Arab-Sunni Muslim)

A Sunni Arab soldier who has fought battles against ISIS/DAESH and Hezbollah, Tawfik (age 50 from Aleppo), summarizes who has been internally used by the regime. He briefly mentions Iran's, Russia's, and even Iraq's support of the regime,[6] but focuses more on DAESH:

> The regime is the reason why the terrorist group DAESH is in our land. Everyone thinks that DAESH is against the regime, but they are helping the regime, and the regime supports them… The regime left a lot of storage of weapons for DAESH in military bases and airports. They are leaving the weapons there, pretending that the regime and DAESH are fighting with each other. Also, the regime is leaving the petrol [oil] in Deir Ez-Zor and not attacking these areas. Instead, they are buying petrol from ISIS, and they are giving them financial support.

Resonating with Tawfik, Ramez elaborates why DAESH is perceived to be under the Asad regime control:

> DAESH is the last intelligence center [unit] made by al-Asad but in a new outfit. They are (DAESH and Asad) not only connected, it is just like the boss and the worker, and it is about the father and the son…all the evidence is saying that. The leaders in DAESH were all in prison in Syria, on the regime side, and in Iraq. This is the first evidence. Second, anything that DAESH is doing is for the benefit of the regime… Third, it is not a coincidence that everyone whom the [Syrian] intelligence has wanted just got arrested by DAESH... Anyone thinking about these things can know that it is a center of al-Asad's regime… I experienced DAESH for two years in Syria. When DAESH enters an area, it uses three things to control it. The military, starvation of people, and the weakness of people's personalities. These three things make the unacceptable acceptable for the people who are starving and people who are dying, or people who are just afraid for their loved ones and their dignity. I imagine that DAESH will melt like salt after one week when al-Asad collapses. (Ramez, 40, male, from Aleppo)

It needs to be noted that Ramez's prediction of ISIS losing considerable power actualized when Asad was able to stay in power after 2016. However, with the collapse of the Asad regime in December 2024, the reemergence of ISIS has been receiving more attention from the media. It could be argued that in times of instability or re-order, groups like ISIS may be reactivated. This would signal the importance of analyzing ISIS with international linkages.

While many participants see DAESH and the regime in cooperation against the Free Syrian Army, Merwan (Kurdish, 60-year-old, from Raqqa) expressed that, at the start of it, ISIS was working with the FSA against the Kurdish but:

> Later, ISIS threw out everyone. ISIS followed us [Kurds] to Kobanî and destroyed and collapsed everything we built in Kobanî. (Merwan)

Avdel (age 35), who is a Kurd from Raqqa, included his personal story corroborating Merwan's assessment about earlier ISIS-FSA collaboration but also emphasizing the monetary gain that ISIS sought through kidnap and ransom:

> ISIS and FSA were together at the start of ISIS. When I was captured for 24 hours, ISIS did not let me sleep. They put me under the tap and opened the water, monitoring me. If they saw me sleeping, they shot a bullet and made me scared. In these ten days, they brought

[6] See Al-Salhy (2012).

food, but I could not eat it. I had a brother who negotiated with them. He collected money from all the family, and he paid them [ISIS]. (Avdel)

Other participants also reported ISIS kidnappings, which shows the micro-level hostility toward people.

Communal and urban-rural cleavages diluted cross-class mobilization, encouraging "pro-regime counter mobilization" (Imady and Hinnebusch 2018, p. 329) and ISIS, being a constant other, presented the conflict as a "war against religious extremism" (Reilly 2018, pp. 229–230). The regime's instrumentalization of sectarianism spread to the opposition and the grassroots level (Goldsmith 2018; Bartolmeni 2018; Rifai 2018 in Imady and Hinnebusch 2018, p. 331). The perceived threat by the minority groups was strongly constructed by the regime propaganda that claimed: "The rebellion was fueled by conservative Arab Gulf states' plotting to replace Syria's secular, multicultural character with an Islamic state" (Pearlman 2017, p. 32). Even though many people were not happy with the Syrian government's policies, the way the majority-minority positions were created forced people to pick a side.

Russia-Iran Coalition and the U.S.

Some participants, like Ziad (Turkmen, Sunni Muslim 28-year-old male newly married, postgraduate student), had concerns centered on Iran's strategic plans and influence on the Syrian government. Farah's (female, atheist, 27) attention to Iran's role includes economic interest, mentioning the dominance of Iranians as Arab shopmen in markets that spoke Persian. After the conflict, Iranians rented vacated places in Damascus. Nevertheless, Iran is not the only actor that is evaluated by commercial interests, particularly sales of weapons:

> It is all about the economy; if you look at this war from different angles, you will see that there are a lot of weapon sales, weapons deals, drugs, ruins, and smugglers. Russia, America, and every country in this war have sold Syria many weapons. This is all about trade and money. (Walid, 23, college graduate, single, entrepreneur, Arab-Sunni Muslim)

Russia and the U.S. were the focus of many. After Russian planes stopped the rebel forces, some only talked about Russia as the main actor. Others, like Kamal, find the U.S. as the sole influential actor allowing the regime to continue, hence, against the revolution. Russia and the U.S. were seen in contradictory light, sometimes being competitors and yet other times cooperators on the ground, creating question marks about the true intentions of two superpowers:

> I think I know that Russia and the U.S. are bombing the civilians and the FSA. They are not bombing the regime or the terrorist groups. So that is why I am very confused about it. I think Russia and the U.S. are fighting but are also very good with each other. (Ahlaam, 21, from Aleppo, NGO worker)

Who targets civilians perceived differently by Laila:

> The American strikes were precise; they did not harm many civilians, but we were scared of the regime and the Russians. The regime did not get to their target [fighters]. They only got the civilians who were living there. The Americans, it was rarely that they hit the civilians. The Russian side is not targeting DAESH but the civilians. (Laila, 30-year-old, Sunni Arab, from Deir-Ez-Zor, college-educated)

Most participants counted the Iran-Russia-U.S.-triad as the key external actors in the conflict, though each gave more focus on one of the three. These accounts indicate that external players sometimes appeared in coalition and sometimes in conflict with each other, leading to one result: endless destruction, countless loss of life, and millions becoming refugees. Participants' perspectives on external actors were shaped by their immediate observations and comprehension of the historical context regarding foreign influence in Syria. The most common historical trauma that informs their perception is the Sykes-Picot Agreement, which requires a thorough analysis to understand the participants' perceptions of external actors fully.

Colonial Past in Historical Memory: Sykes-Picot

The Sykes-Picot agreement (1916) between Great Britain and France had considerable importance in participant narratives as the historically chosen trauma (Volkan 2001). For interviewees from different ethno-religious identities, "1916" had a direct connection to their understanding of the contemporary external actors, particularly the way they positioned the "Western power role." As the historical analogy (Khong 1992), Sykes-Picot is prominent among participants, though each analyzes it from the angle of their identity group.

Sunni Arabs like Faysal (age 50, Businessmen from Aleppo) focused on Sykes-Picot as keeping the Sunni majority under control by giving opportunities to religious minorities by dividing the land. Ziad (28) focuses on the 1916 Sykes-Picot agreement as the event dividing up the Middle East on an unhappy note and connects it to today with his intersectional positionality of being Syrian Turkmen:

> In 1916, Europeans drew this map [and divided] Türkiye and Syria. In reality, if people think a bit, what does it matter [whether we are] Turkish people or Syrian people? In 2017, [Western powers] will draw a map again. Kurds want a state, and Alawite wants it, as well. We cannot do this ourselves [drawing a map]. America will come and do this for us. 1916-2016, this means we are still 100 years behind...We are making the same mistakes; we are not in 2017. We are in 1916.

Ziad, who carried Syrian and Turkmen identities, sees the drawing of borders as artificial and lacking the consent and decision-making power of the local people.

A Kurdish Syrian, 65-year-old Behram, who is a poet, calls himself a political and civilian activist, a defender of Kurdish women's rights, who was part of the 1969 Kurdish Freedom movement, places Sykes-Picot as:

> I should not be controlled by the ideologies of people who died 100 years ago. Each human should make a law for their time. Ask Kurds in Syria; they are victims. We are the victims of an agreement called Sykes-Picot. It is a 100-year-old agreement, and everyone who

> agreed to it died… I want to send a message to the Westerners. Without stability in the region, without giving rights to each minority, each person, educated or non-educated, you cannot win your investments. Put pressure on your allies and on your agents to find a solution for the Kurdish case. The Sykes-Picot agreement is unjust, and this is humiliation. We do not love war, but we will stay, we will keep asking our rights until our last breath, we won't give up…Do not put our people down. And do not make it again the [Algerian] tragedy of 1975. We are humans like you. We love democracy. (Behram)

Behram's narrative links external powers and their colonial legacies from the 1916 Sykes-Picot agreement to 1975 Algeria, where thousands of Moroccans were expelled (Lefèvre 2016), to the contemporary conflict in Syria. For Behram, Sykes-Picot is an "injustice and humiliation" that needs correction. Similar to Ziad, Behram identifies Western powers as the current decision-makers in Syria and over its people. The common ground in these voices is the claim that the Syrian people's political decision-making power has been eliminated since 1916.

Sykes-Picot left Syria under French colonial rule, and some participants, like Farah, believed that Syria could have become an industrial and self-sufficient country after independence from colonial rule. Nevertheless, a continuation of development was difficult because the way the French created the modern Syrian state "was practically designed to fail. France purposefully used tools of modern state building to perpetuate, if not deepen, pre-national and regional divisions and segmentation. Independent Syria was internally divided, a plaything for regional and international powers" (Reilly 2018, p. 242). Colonial legacies create hierarchies among colonized people through policies of divide and rule, where colonial powers stimulate the ethnic minority to seek political power and ensure that they access tools for claiming power (Haklai 2000, p. 25). As a point of reference in historical memory, the Sykes-Picot and what followed as independent Syria is why interviewees demonstrate a skeptical and critical view of Western claims of freedom and human rights, which will be examined next.

International Actors, Human Rights, and Arms

The participants perceived external actors to be encouraging the continuation of the civil war. Noury was critical to the role of Türkiye and the U.S., along with the Arab states:

> The conflict started in Dar'aa just as protesting. The regime started to fight, and these guys [opposition] started to fight... but who gave us the hope that it won't be a war? [It was] Recep Tayyip Erdogan [president of Türkiye] when he announced, "I do not want to make a new Halabja."[7] [Syrian] people were encouraged by these words that we have our ally who

[7]The 1988 use of chemical weapons in the Kurdish city of Halabja in northern Iraq by Saddam Hussein's forces massacred thousands (Hiltermann 2007; Kelly 2008). Erdogan's speech about Halabja was delivered in 2013 on the 25th anniversary of the attack. He commemorated the dead, and mentioned the war in Syria, stating that Türkiye opened its doors to Syrian people who faced oppression just like it did to Kurds in Iraq (Bianet 2013).

> will support us. Also, Obama [the U.S. president at the time] encouraged us, [along with] the king of Saudi Arabia, the previous King Abdullah, and the Jordanian king [encouraged us].[8] So, everybody just encouraged and left us alone when we got involved. (Noury, 22-year-old male student from Aleppo)

While Noury does not elaborate on the reasons for encouragement, Camil sees the war as an economic gain for outsiders. Regardless of the certainty of outcome, Camil believes that different actors get involved in the Syria war:

> All over the world, parties in the conflict are gambling on Syria. Some will be injured, and some will be losing, but all these parties who are seemingly against each other get along with each other because politics is an interest, and all the actors say, let's invest, let's gamble. We [other states] have nothing to lose, and they [Syrians] do. (Camil, 35-year-old Sunni Arab from Aleppo)

The "gambling" metaphor, with its conceptualization of war (Chilton and Lakoff 2005) "as an arena for winners and losers," shows the objectification of Syria as a commodity in a capitalistic, competitive notion of "interest." The timing of the interviews is crucial and must be incorporated into the analysis. During the last phase of interviews in 2016, the Free Syrian Army was on the verge of reaching Damascus but was halted by Russian airstrikes without a significant response from the United States. Syrians in Türkiye consequently not only lost their faith in the revolution but also felt betrayed and exploited, as they perceived international actors used Syrians as bargaining chips for their bid in an ongoing war gamble.

The feeling of betrayal extended to other spheres, as participants came to believe that international actors had both encouraged and profited from the war in Syria. As their perception of support for overthrowing Assad diminished, their trust in the Western narratives of human rights and freedom also began to erode. Salah (49, Arab-Sunni Muslim, married, engineer) argues that the cause of the conflict is international policy lacking humanitarianism as countries who are supposed to support democracy and human rights are silent to the documented crimes of the regime. The expectation of respect for rights, freedoms, and dignity from Western countries is very low among the participants:

> The revolution was about people who wanted equality, rights, freedom, justice, and dignity. [It was] between these people and a regime that thinks the whole country is for him. Then, the Syrian revolution against the regime turned into an international war in which the Syrians were fighting against bigger liars and international aggressors… I want to talk about the oppression that is applied to the Syrian people…The cause of the refugee wave and people leaving their countries is because of the extremists and the ones who are hitting the cities and doing strikes on civilians. The international community lies to us and says they want to solve this problem, but they do not see the cause of it. They are just putting a pinkie solution for this. The proof of this is people dying at the sea. Every country or state has a different purpose in Syria. (Rashid, 33, male, from Latakia, college-educated)

[8] A field study suggests that some members of the Free Syrian Army "acted religious," i.e., growing beards and praying five times a day to get funding from Saudi Arabia and other Gulf States (Erlich 2014, p. 11).

When people locate powerful states as having strong control over how the Syrian conflict evolved, they look into global arms trades and commonly known imperial policies. They also have local information about how people's attitudes and behavior are shaped through the influence of outside actors. Aykut's analysis of Syria just before the demonstrations provides an example of local knowledge about influential external actors and their reasons for distrusting freedom and rights language of the West:

> Before the opposition was given arms, they were instilled with this idea. Some people are devoted to freedom. Civil people. They wanted this movement to be done in democratic ways. Some people did not want a single drop of blood to be wasted. Some people who started the uprising were enlightened people sitting in coffee shops full of ideas. Nevertheless, their biggest dream was to announce a free newspaper or gather together in a free manner. These people have already received financial support. Some Western countries send them money monthly. For example, the entire salary of someone in Damascus is twenty-five thousand Syrian lira. In those times, each dollar was 50 liras. Thus, it was like $500.[9] Westerners told them, 'Here is $1000 for you. This money is for you only to express your ideas and concepts freely. We support you.' They also told them that if they build more networks, they will be given smaller amounts like $100, $200, or $300. This idea has continued from then until now, and these people have now become the significant people of the opposition. They instilled the idea of getting armed. Even though some of them now say, 'We wish there were no arms,' I know that they instilled this idea of getting armed in Dar'aa, Homs, and Hama. The other group that instilled the idea of getting armed was the Muslim Brotherhood. Why? Because in Hama in the 1980s, they wanted to do an uprising. Who did they use? They used children. Before the 1980s uprising, well-known names went to Gulf countries and some to Europe. The regime was bombing the mosques, and people were dying in Hama. These influential names from the Arab countries or Europe were condemning the regime. How they got radicalized is a very complicated situation. I do not think a normal citizen would easily become radical. There are other elements and reasons for people becoming radical. However, getting armed was an idea that was instilled in the society by two groups: people who use religion as a tool for politics and some, indeed Westernists, enlightened people. (Aykut, Turkmen from Damascus, age 40)

The literature is consistent with Aykut's observations that radicalization is a complex process. Under repressive structures where ordinary career people witness atrocities done to their villages, they get radicalized and turn into militants (Gettleman 2018; Nossiter 2016 in Pearson and Lounsbery 2020, p. 82). Aykut goes a step further to explain the complexities of the structure by positioning external actors' roles in imagining and actualizing violence. The comparative similarity between the religious and Westernist elite is important to note here. The continuation of external influence in a similar manner is also located by comparing the preceding periods of the 1982 Hama massacre to contemporary conflict. Western influence and responsibility are positioned along with the Arab states and the responsibility of internal actors who utilized these discourses within Syria. Aykut's focus on the continuity of Western actors is apt as "the [French] mandatory period [1918-46] also perpetuated the triangular relationship between European powers,

[9] This interview was in 2016. Erlich (2014) also reports that one dollar was 50 Syrian pounds [lira], and in 2013, it was 142.

the local states, and 'minorities'...which have continued up to the present day" (Khoury and Méouchy 2007, pp. 20–1 in Tejel 2009, p. 3). The resemblance between the regime strategy and French colonial practices is worth further analyzing. In 1925 the Druze-led revolt against the French depicted rebels as backward and anti-Christian against progressive French; the similarity led some Syrians to argue that Asad followed the same strategy (Erlich 2014, p. 31). "Assad managed to mobilise key social groups by equating his regime's survival with the security and standing of Alawite and other minorities, as well as by portraying the opposition as armed, radical, Islamist, foreign-backed and seeking to change the very fabric of Syrian society" (Hokayem 2013, p. 16). The regime's indiscriminate violence to depopulate Sunni areas, Alawite dominance of the military, and its backing of Hezbollah and Iran allowed Sunni militants to frame the issue as a Shi'a war on Sunnis (Imady and Hinnebusch 2018, p. 331), making arguments about armed struggle persuasive.

Aykut's narrative points to specific strategies to embed ideas that violent armed struggle would be needed for resistance. Spreading the idea of violence became an income-generating activity. The local actors' agency has an intertwined relationship with the outside actors regarding the actualization of violence. Kaufman's study confirms that foreign countries "can provide money, advice, and propaganda support to help extremist elites mobilize politically and promote ethnic hostility as well as arms to enable chauvinist elites to initiate violence" (2001, p. 33). Following Azar's formulation of seeing protracted social conflicts as having linkages among groups, states, and international actors, the chapter now examines ascriptive identities to seek answers about how internal actors are perceived.

Perception of Ascriptive Identities

During the fieldwork, I broadly asked people how they identify themselves. The general pattern was that Kurds and Turkmens immediately identified their ethnicity. If ethnicity and religion were not mentioned, I asked about each. A considerable number of Arab participants asked, "What do you mean by ethnicity?" adding once more that they are "Sunni Muslim." When I further elaborated, "whether they were Arab, Kurd, Turkmen…" they nodded immediately and said, "Of course, Arab." The only exception to this pattern of being puzzled by ethnicity questions was Sunni Muslim Arab participants who interacted with ethnically diverse people and immediately located themselves as Arabs. Generally, minoritized identities are underlined, while the majority consider it a given. Arabs did not see the need to stress their Arab-ness, unlike Kurds and Turkmens, whose ethnic identity was suppressed. In contrast, Arabs stressed their sectarian identity, Sunni, even if they were politically secular, as they felt minorizes *vis-à-vis* Alawites.

A crucial identity expression emerged when it came to being Syrian. For example, Obadiah (21), who identified as Sunni Muslim, thought identifying with any ethnicity was pointless. Despite its historic political existence, "Syrianism" or being

"Syrian" was not something that appeared as a common sentiment. At the same time, many talked about politics and being away from the country in terms of "Syria." "Syrian" was much less stated as an identity. Rouaa (37, female, engineer from Aleppo), who identified as Sunni Muslim, was among the few who identified as "Syrian." Four male participants used "Syrian" as their identity; one of them, the youngest of the participants, 18-year-old Anas (male), initially said Syrian and then added "Arab." Naser stated he is Arab but called himself "Syrian." Noury, calling himself "Syrian," said he believed he came from a mix of different "races" and said he was not sure whether he was Arab, Turk, Kurd, or a mix of these identities. Tawfik, who was a member of the Free Syrian Army, stated that he had strong feelings for the "Syrian" identity.

Syrian conflict is referred to as an ethnic-religious-sectarian or ethno-sectarian conflict (United Nations 2012; Phillips 2015) or considered to be "a large extent ethnic in nature" (Kaufman 2023, p. 17). Ethnic group members "share a common name, a believed common descent, elements of a shared culture (most often language or religion), common historical memories and attachment to a particular territory" (Kaufman 2023, p. 18; Smith 1986). Race, religion, sect, and ethnicity are "primarily ascriptive" (Kaufman 2023, p. 18).

One view sees ethnicity as primordial and argues that primordial attachments (Shils 1957) are givens of social existence as one is born into a particular religious or linguistic community that follows particular social practices (Geertz 1963; Smith 1996). One is bound to the community, not because of personal affection but because the bond is *ipso facto*, meaning the tie creates the bond to the community (Geertz 1963, p. 109). Primordial bonds may differ from person to person, but "for virtually every person…some attachment seem to flow more from a sense of natural - some would say spiritual - affinity than from social interaction" (Geertz 1963, p. 110). When ethno-religious clashes happen, primordialists perceive this to be "ancient hatreds" (Kaufman 2001). Some study participants believed that the root cause of the conflict was directly related to these ethno-religious differences. Therefore, identity differences are treated as the direct result of ethnic resentment, and there is a firm belief that the other side wants to eliminate or disempower the group just because of its identity, which I call *primordial divided identities*.

Another view argues that nations, as political communities are constructed, invented traditions (Hobsbawm 1983) that, through state apparatuses (Althusser 2006), shape people's ethnic identities. These identity constructs in the hands of internal and external elites could turn into political instruments (Hardin 1995; Brass 1997). From this perspective, ethnic identities may not be rooted in "ancient times," ethnic groups may not necessarily be "primordial," and at different points in time, religious diversity and co-existence have been experienced (Kaufman 2001, p. 5). Some study participants focus on ethno-religious identities as a tool that was used for pitting groups against one another, which I call *politically divided identities*.

The following sections in this chapter will examine the meaning people place on ethnicity, whether it is seen as primordial or political, and its implications for their understanding of the root causes of the conflict. Participants focused more on localities than on an overarching Syrian identity in Syria and learned about people in other parts of Syria after becoming refugees. These findings will also be examined in terms of its political implications for the future of Syria.

Primordial Divided Identities: Latent to Manifest

Religious and ethnic symbolisms are preexisting historical myths. When people carry such myths unquestioningly, it may renew hatred and othering in new generations (Kaufman 2001, p. 11). This section shows that some participants argued that while primordial identities may have been latent, armed conflict made their reality apparent. Noury, while he questions ethnic purity, depicts the Syrian social fabric from the angle of severe religious and ethnic divides. Unlike some others who claim that before the conflict, they did not experience any clashes among different groups, Noury claims that "conflict was always there, but it needed to be ignited to start." The narrative also emphasizes the rich multicultural fabric of Syria:

> Many Syrians try to say to the media that we were living in harmony and elegance, but no, the situation was like in Türkiye between the Turks and Kurds. Inside all Syrians, there was [an understanding that] this is Sunni, this is Alawite, this is Kurdish, this is Circassian, this is Druze/Durzi. We have ethnicities: Arabs, Kurdish, Turkmen, Circassians, Armenians, Êzîdî; we have religious groups Sunnis, Shi'a Twelvers, Alawites, Ismailis, Druze, Christians, Assyrians, Orthodox, we have Roman and Greek Orthodox, and we have Protestant, Catholic, and others. We have Jews in Syria in Aleppo and Damascus, but they flee after the conflict…Let's keep it a secret: I am an atheist. We have many atheists, but they are beneath [the surface], invisible. We cannot be loud. Ethnic and religious identities were not in conflict, but it was like an invisible conflict. For example, Christians just married Christians, and Christians just bought from Christian people; they were afraid of us [Sunni Muslims] as the majority. When you see Christians in the old times, they were afraid of us. I do not know why, as we are a nation good at hiding things about the past. The Kurds hated us, and they hated the regime for not letting them learn their language and teach it. When [Kurds] were in the army, [Alewites] sent them to serve the officers and cook. It was hard for them; they were part of the nation, but they were not part of the nation in real life. Circassians were good people, but I do not know why we had a bad idea about them. Their girls were beautiful, but most people did not marry them. Armenians were the newcomers after the genocide. They came to us; they are smart and good people, but actually, they are like the man who is not opening his door to others. The newcomers are not communicating with us. Even though Armenians are Christians, our Arab Christians hate Armenians. (Noury)

Author eye-camera: When ethnic and religious identities are mentioned with "one hating the other," we need to do multiple things simultaneously. We need to remember that people have a camera to look at the world. We also immediately need to realize that many people in these identities may not express their feelings to one another as "hate" and, hence, not necessarily accept this statement as the "truth" of people in different identity groups. Another immediate realization is that while these views belong to one person, their camera and how they understand these identities are a product of social interactions and identities. While this may not be a "truth" statement for all, such individual statements are born from meaning-making through social interactions that cannot only be attributed to one individual. As a social researcher, I struggle when I write about expressions of "hate" as I feel the responsibility of not reproducing it. Still, when we look at the civilian death toll (casualty somewhat seems a euphemism), it is estimated to be between 300 thousand people (UN 2022*) and more than 600,000 (SOHR* 2021*), these perceptions in the everyday construction of individuals become important to locate.*

Noury's narrative reveals that, at least in some parts of society, the interaction of groups in terms of marriage and sharing of neighborhood is very low. While some opportunities exist for people to mix in school, schools mostly cater to religious or linguistic groups. On the one hand, having schools of different religious and linguistic groups is an advantage in creating opportunities for people to educate their children in their cultural and linguistic backgrounds. On the other hand, the separation of neighborhoods reduces inter-ethnic-religious social interaction. Mariam (mix of Christian-Muslim heritage, 23, female), who lived in a Christian neighborhood, gives a similar account regarding the lack of interaction between different identity groups by contextualizing everyday life. She argues that they largely lived within their neighborhoods, where they had schools, supermarkets, and even car mechanics, stressing the solidarity along ethno-religious lines. Even though some other participants had very different experiences of meaningful interaction as neighbors or business partners with other identity groups, their perceptions shifted when the armed conflict started. For example, Haya and Zeinab focus on primordial identities more after the start of the violent conflict that led to the trauma of seeing neighbors killing neighbors. This means violent conflicts make people perceive identities more primordially than before the war began. Haya's experiences and observations led her to question the deep-rootedness of identity clashes:

> When I first saw the interview about the woman who worked for the *Mukhabarat [Syrian intelligence/secret police]* who reported over four hundred people, including her brother-in-law and eighteen girls who got raped under custody, I was shocked. Did we have these kinds of people living among us? We lived with these people; they were our friends, neighbors, and families; we partnered in jobs, and we had relationships somehow. At one point, you realize we did not actually [have these relationships]. We were living in a dream. They were not our neighbors, and we trusted the wrong people. You can be against my opinion; you may not follow me, but that does not give you the right to kill me, to humiliate me, to underestimate my powers, my position, my religion, my thoughts. Just say you do not agree with them. Just being Alawite or being Sunni supporting the regime does not give you the right to do what you are doing. You can keep telling yourself that Alawites and Sunnis love each other and Sunnis and Christians love each other, but that is a lie. We all had these tensions with each other… People used to ask your name and how old you are. Now, the first question they ask you is, what religion and which sect are you? Do you support the regime or not? These are the important questions. They become your friend only after these questions [are answered]. Whenever you meet someone, you ask "*maa'na-aa'lena*" (with us or against us). If he is against the regime or supports the regime. (Haya, 23 years old, married female student with strong Sunni religious affiliation from Damascus)

It is important to see that Noury and Haya's experiences slightly differ. After seeing the violent conflict, Haya started questioning the authenticity of the relations. Noury's explanations signal "ancient hatreds," but the experience of business partnerships, marriage, and friendship negates this argument. Haya's explanation shows that political alignment in a violent context causes deep divides in people's perceptions of one another. New experiences shift past beliefs and experiences, leading her to argue that tensions were always there and that primordial identities were becoming manifest.

Zeinab's memory of the past friendships and tolerance of different groups merge with the post-conflict situation where primordial identity divides emerge as embedded realities in war-torn societies:

> In Aleppo, there are neighborhoods for Kurdish; they are not mixed. However, in Raqqa province and Bakka, there are residents from all the cities in Syria, housing Muslims, Kurdish, Alawite, and Sunnis, living like one family... My father had many Alawite friends in Latakia and Tartus. We visited and stayed in each other's homes. Sometimes, when I look at the picture from outside, I cannot believe these are the same people we were living with. But the regime tried to change this atmosphere between people; it was Assad's game. Feelings are not the same. I do not belong to a village where people are killed by the Alawite neighbors. There are crimes in some places that I cannot believe. People's neighbors who were like a family [committed the crimes]. You were my neighbor, we ate together; our kids were friends. A mother's worst [nightmare] comes when the knife of this neighbor kills her daughter, and they know the murderers. Who knows how they will deal with such a thing? (Zeinab, 50, Arab female with leftist political views)

While Zainab explains the shift in relationships with destructive politics, similar to Haya, Zeinab's story illustrates that although various identity groups in Syria had friendships in their daily lives, when people witnessed terrible acts committed by neighbors and people who knew one another, they started questioning if there was strong hostility that was harbored in ethnic lines. This leads to more firm beliefs about the existence of primordial divides that became more manifest during the conflict.

Simmering Ancient Hatreds

Some participants perceived the conflict as deep-rooted in identity divides and groups being against one another solely because of such differences. Khawla, who was part of an organized religious group and a war widow, assesses the cause of the conflict as follows:

> It is obvious that Shi'a people want to destroy the Sunni people. They do not want to let any Sunni [to live] on this earth. Even Shi'a people have a saying that "who kills Sunni enters heaven." (Khawla, Sunni Arab, female, 23, from Aleppo)

Such statements position identities in an essentialist manner where intra-group differences and inter-group similarities are completely erased. People with such a view argue that ascriptive identities carry ancient hatreds, which also explains leaders' policy choices.

Rukan (32, who was a medical doctor in her country and a committed Sunni Muslim) argued that the reason for fighting against the regime was "unequal treatment." She connected this unfair treatment directly to sectarian discrimination as she argued that regardless of education level, "the government differentiated between us and the Alawite." Similarly, Akila focused on the influence of Iran over the regime in discriminatory treatment and connected racism to sectarian differences:

> I think they support only Shi'a or Alawite, so that makes Sunni say, "Why?" Now you see people ask, 'Who are you, Sunni, Alawite, Shi'a, Kurd?' We have sectarian differences a lot in Syria. They are racists. (Akila, an Arab Sunni Muslim, a 24-year-old student, and an NGO worker from Aleppo)

When Farah was talking about memories regarding how she learned about the regime from her parents, she focused on religious differences as the core dividing element:

> My father was in a political party, well, something like a political party. In Syria, you do not have these political parties. They were pro-Gamal Abdel Nasser, [who] was the president of Egypt, and then he was the president of United Egypt in Syria in 1958. I consider [Nasser] a bad person, but my father really admired him. It is a group that worked secretly, and they were against Asad. My mother hates the regime, too. Since childhood, I know that [the Asad] regime was not good. We, the Damascus community, all hate the regime. Damascenes are Sunni,[10] and the regime is Alawite, so [we] hate them.[11] Sunnis say Alawites were servants to our homes, and now they are rulers, controlling us. They hate them. In the beginning, they hated them. And so, we, the children, know that these people are not good, but we don't know why. (Farah, 27, from Damascus, an atheist university graduate, worked in an NGO and removed her hijab after coming to Türkiye)

Farah, when talking from different angles, was one of the interviewees who found connections to colonial legacies and external actors' commercial interests. Still, this particular segment indicates a cross-generational transfer of othering in religious lines. While her family was politically positioned as opposing Asad, her focus on Sunni-Alawite differences and the strong resentment needs to be noted as involving views that connect to ancient hatreds.

A Sunni officer, Tawfik, who defected from the Syrian Army and joined the Free Syrian Army, also felt the discrimination toward the Sunni:

> 85% was Alawite in the military. It was very harsh. There was discrimination; they had all the rights and all the positions, and we were not [given these positions and rights]. We were the poor people there, and they considered us the 3rd or 4th level of people. (Tawfik)

While there is a singular "Alawite" depiction in these narratives, intra-group dynamics are always more complex. This singularity, though, points out the essentialist positioning of Alawites and Sunnis in Syria.

Author eye-camera: The reader should note that I am not translating "third or fourth level" as "second class citizen" into English. Some of the Kurdish participants also mentioned in their narrative that Kurds were treated as "third class/degree." Rather than fitting it to common English language expressions, I urge the

---

[10] For "Islamist movement that are predominantly active in Damascus, the *Kaftariyya* and the *Qubaysiyyat*" see Imady (2018).

[11] While Aleppo and Hama were centers of unrest, Damascus refrained from such rebellion as it was closer to the center of power, which made the Damascene bourgeoisie advantageous far more than the others (Hinnebusch 2005, p. 93).

reader to see the angle of people's camera. This would mean that discrimination and disadvantaged positions are felt in complex layers for different people depending on the identities they carry in the social structure.

Naser lived outside of Syria as a child and had a family with strong connections to an organized religious group. His analysis shows a strong Sunni vs. Alawite depiction not only in terms of the regime but how he perceives "people." When other groups are placed in his explanation, they are also depicted based on religion.

> The regime and Alawite people hate us, the Sunni… People in Syria have been suffering for the last 50 years since Alawite came to power, controlling everything. Even going to the swimming pool was allowed only for Alawite people for a period of time. Can you imagine? Since Bashar came to power in 2000, he tried to make the people love him by letting Sunni and others, like Christians, do everything that Alawites did. But nobody can be president except for him and just Alawite people. They are very privileged; they are the elite!... Sunnis also killed many people; they even killed Sunni. Some of them were fighting in DAESH/ISIS, and you know the majority of the Syrian forces are Sunni, but they are influenced by the Alawites. They just kill us. (Naser, 20, student, Arab-Sunni Muslim)

Naser's explanation of the policies of the regime is taken together with the entire Alawite population, clustering them together with the regime. Further, if Sunni people are doing the killing, he tends to make it the responsibility of the Alawite when he argues they "influenced" them to act violently. Interviewees in this section, like Naser, mostly perceive Alawite as a united group merged with the Asad regime, and their expression was more "us versus them," which is more embedded in the primordial view of identities.

Politically Divided Identities

Not all interviewees held the primordial view of identities; some separated Alawite people from the regime's governing elite and refrained from blaming them, seeing instead that they were structurally cornered into supporting the regime. As there was a focus on ethno-religious identities, a considerable number of people paid attention to regional or local identities. There were statements like "I do not know about Syria in general but in Aleppo…" or "I can only talk about Damascus…" or "The places I have lived in Syria…." The geopolitically divided identities have their roots in how the French colonial administration organized society in different layers to accentuate differences in a competing manner. Not only did the French mandate assume a "*civilizing mission…* 'which was…tied to ideas of assimilation and association'" (Sluglet 2004, p. 111 in Tejel 2009, p. 16), but also divide and rule policy. Rather than the support of unified Sunni Arab nationalists, the French strengthened the ethno-religious minorities. The political organization of Syrian society has led to competition and power asymmetries among identity groups. "Once the conflict was sectarianized, new exclusivist identities were forged that would constrain possibilities for ending what became an intractable conflict" (Imady and Hinnebusch 2018, p. 329). Furthermore, such a structure disregarded the importance of local communities' well-being and focused on colonial/imperial power struggles and interests. Therefore, this section examines how people articulate the identity clashes as politically produced divides.

Some participants find the root cause in political attitude and historical positioning of identities. Suad, one of the oldest participants, was born in the 1940s and raised in a financially well-situated family in Hama. Unlike many other participants, Suad's recollection of her childhood memories indicates the struggles and poverty that were endured by Alawites before Asad assumed power:

> When I was a child, I really did not know the meaning of Alawite or Christian. Everyone was together, and they had no problems with each other in Hama. I did not recognize people as Kurdish or something like that. As a family, we do not like this stuff. My sister and her daughters got married to Kurds. But after Hafez Al-Asad came [to power], he had another problem with Hama. The Alawite people then were really poor, living in the mountains, so people from Hama, and especially people from our street, used to bring women to work in the houses. I used to see them in my neighbors' houses and later learned that they were Alawite. In Hafez Asad's days, when I came to Aleppo, everything started to change. They did not have problems with each other, but they started to point out groups like Armenians and Christians. For me, it was no problem because I used to go out with Armenians and Christians, and even my best friend was a Christian. (Suad, 68, Arab-Sunni Muslim, homemaker)

While Suad argues she did not know the "meaning" of Alawite or Christian, she simultaneously shows an awareness of her in-laws being Kurdish and her closest friends being Armenian and Christian. Therefore, Suad's explanation signals that rather than not having these identities, how these identities are perceived has shifted with the political change. Suad also brings an alternative reading of history, starting with class oppression toward Alawites, and is given as a reason for Hafez Asad's hostility to this particular locality of Hama. Under the rule of the previous governments in Syria, including the French mandate period, Alawites, mostly living in rural areas, experienced poverty and discrimination. Farah's family narrative of perceiving Alawites as "servants" in their past, mentioned above, brings validity to Suad's narrative of the grievances Hafez Asad might have felt in relation to his Alawite identity. Suad grew up in Hama, lived in Damascus and Aleppo, and had a rich, comparative experience of different locations in Syria, while Farah's social context was mostly in Damascus. Suad (68), years older than Farah (27), had more class consciousness. As a result, unlike Farah, Suad's explanation was focused on class perspective rather than the sectarian clash between Sunni and Alawite. Class differences and changing class and power positions are important in understanding shifting hierarchies and enduring resentments, distancing people from seeing identity conflicts as primordial.

Merwan, a Kurdish man a little younger than Suad at age 60, brings a reading closer to Suad's. For him, it was not ethnic differences but the regime that created the problem:

> We were living in Syria all together, can you imagine that? We can go back and live together again. The age of the Syrian Republic is 80-90 years old; we do not have any problems between Arab and Kurdish people. It was only between the regime and Kurds, but [amongst] people, we had no problem. We worked together. We married with them. We gave them our

friendship, we drank, and we had a friendship with Arabs and other people [such as] Armenians. There is a characteristic of Kurds that you cannot find with other people. We use Turkish and Arab names because we are not sectarians. (Merwan, Kurdish, 60, from Raqqa)

Different from Suad, who is Arab, Merwan's narrative shows an ongoing identity awareness as he is Kurdish. However, similar to Suad's assessment, he positions sources of tension to the regime rather than communities from different social identities. Kurdish participants often mention their "third-class citizen" status or how they were not allowed to speak their language. Kurdish is forbidden in state schools in Syria (Tejel 2009, p. 27). "Kurdishness [was] considered…a sign of *fitna* (dividing of society) by the regime" (Tejel 2009, p. 2); hence, the usage of "third class" indicates the positioning of Kurdish identity *vis-à-vis* the dominant power structure.

According to Rashid, the politics of Asad influenced Alawites as they were part of his identity group. His experience is located in Latakia, where Alawites were dominant in numbers.[12] His narrative shows how, more than the group itself, the political decisions are guiding the attitude and perception concerning different groups:

The things that the regime in Syria did were applied twice in Latakia; there was twice more *zulm* (oppression) and injustice. Sunnis were not given rights and freedoms in this city. People who are the elite of this regime and people from his ethnic religion were very comfortable applying such injustice [in Latakia]. (Rashid, 33, married, Arab-Sunni Muslim, Pharmacist)

Rashid's narrative points out that, depending on locality, people's identities play a role in how they feel in positions of power and privilege. The more these identities are given different levels of access, the more people are clustered within the one-dimensionality of these identities.

Husam grew up in Syria as a Palestinian refugee, feeling like a Syrian. He remembers co-existence in Latakia, where Alawites were densely populated. Nevertheless, Sunnis were "distrustful" of expressing any opinion in front of them:

At the time that the conflict started, we discovered that Christian people were Asad supporters. But before, we did not have any difference. Why did they support the Asad regime? The Asad regime told them that "because you, the Christians who are in Syria, are few people, Muslim people will attack you, and they will let you out of Syria." That is why they supported this regime. (Husam, Palestinian-Syrian, 31, single, college-educated)

Husam's assessment of Christians further signals how different identities are politically pitted against one another based on fear of others and cornered to support certain political groups. Malek (male, from Latakia, 41 years old, Arab-Sunni Muslim, holds a postgraduate degree) argued that different religions living side by side could be achieved. Nevertheless, freedom was problematic as "Asad controls these people from the kingdom of fear." Some others, while also focusing on the regime as the main actor of the conflict, also refused to look at it from an ethnic or

[12] Sunni populations held majority status in all Syrian provinces except Latakia and Suwayda (Sorenson 2016, p. 10).

religious divide, perceiving the regime as a group of people who protect their interests:

> Asad's group… I refuse to say that they are Alawite. I do not think that they are Alawite. People like Rami Makhlouf [maternal cousin of Bashar Asad] control the country, thinking the country is their farm. (Reem, 51, Arab-Sunni Muslim, arrested for her Muslim identity when she was 15 and stayed in prison for 9 years, war widow, college-educated, held a professional job in Syria)

For Bilal, religious, ethnic, and sectarian divides were the product of policies that started after the recent Syrian armed conflict[13]:

> In old Syria, you could not see ethnic and religious discrimination anywhere except in the military. They even put an Alawite observer next to a high-ranked general. Things started happening when the external powers came, and outsiders instilled in their brains that 'look, these Alawites are killing you!' My friend, it is not Alawite that wants to kill you! Who wants to kill you is a man who does not want to give up power; there is a man who killed people from his own sect just to stay in power. He does not kill you because you are a Sunni. He kills you because you rebelled against him. The same thing was told to Alawite people: 'Sunnis are going to kill you; they are going to mass murder you.' Why would we do such a thing? People who went for the revolution with good intentions in their heads did not have an idea to kill Alawites. I am going to get this tyrant, this dictator down, they said, even if he would have been my father's son [I would take him down]. But returning to this social fabric is no longer possible. (Bilal, Turkmen-Sunni Muslim, 26-year-old, disabled, college-educated)

Bilal differs in terms of ethno-religious discrimination from the majority of the interviewees but is similar in terms of identities being instrumentalized by the regime for political power. While Bilal argued there was no ethnic discrimination in old Syria, an older Turkmen participant narrated that during the Hafez Asad period, he was singled out at school due to their ethnicity. Unlike people like Khawla, who believed that "Shi'a wants to destroy the Sunni people," and Nasser, who believed Alawites were against the Sunni, Bilal did not equate the regime to the Alawite people. He perceived the use of ethnicity as a cover for a lack of will to share power and resources.

There are several results of the analysis of ascriptive identities. Some people perceive the world from ethno-religious identities. Such reduction makes them see the root cause of the conflict in terms of binary identity differences. Such primordial depiction can lock people in without seeing intra-group differences and inter-group similarities, perpetuating enmity. Some others, even though they experienced meaningful relations in the past after witnessing atrocities of war, tend to believe in the inescapability of ancient hatreds. A third category sees identity divides as sources of political choice, refrains from believing in ancient hatreds, and can avoid the singularization of people based on one identity group. The latter believes it is possible to co-exist and that it is not the difference but the treatment of differences that creates the conflict. However, regardless of seeing identities as primordial or political, most

---

[13] During the uprising, religion was used to rally troops, where rebels relied on the Sunni Muslim majority, and Asad appealed to minorities such as Alawites, Christians, and Shia Muslims (Erlich 2014, p. 12).

believe that after the atrocities, the biggest challenge for the people of Syria is to move beyond the grievances and reach reconciliation.

Author eye-camera: Mainstream writings and journalistic accounts predominantly bring us "ethnic-sectarian" primordial identity differences, and depictions and analysis follow this departure point. My analysis shows that not all people are locked into ethnic-religious-sectarian identity differences and view the world from this angle. What mainstream writings strip away is the awareness of people about how power politics lead communities to insecurity, a sense of threat, and division. Individual experiences and perceptions help us see more diverse views. Social research should capture these diverse views to move beyond one-dimensional depictions.

References

Al-Salhy S (2012) Iraqi Shi'ite Militants to fight for Syria's Assad. 16 October. http://www.reuters.com/article/us-syria-crisis-iraq-militias-idUSBRE89F0PX20121016

Althusser L (2006) Ideology and ideological state apparatuses (notes towards an investigation). In: Sharma A, Gupta A (eds) The anthropology of the state: a reader. Blackwell Publishing, Hoboken, pp 86–98

Bartolomei E (2018) Sectarianism and the battle of narratives in the context of the Syrian uprising. The Syrian Uprising. In: Raymond H, Imady O (eds) The Syrian Uprising: Domestic origins and early trajectory. Routledge, London, pp 223–241

BIANET (2013) Kürt konferansi: Erdoğan'dan Halepçe mesajı [Kurdish conference Erdogan's halepce Message], 15 March. Istanbul BIA Haber Merkezi. https://m.bianet.org/bianet/siyaset/145112-erdogan-dan-halepce-mesaji

Brass PR (1997) Theft of an idol: text and context in the representation of collective violence. Princeton University Press, Princeton

Chilton P, Lakoff G (2005) Foreign policy by metaphor. In: Schäffne C, Wenden AL (eds) Language and peace. Routledge, New York, pp 61–84

Ehteshami A, Hinnebusch RA (2002) Syria and Iran: Middle powers in a penetrated regional system. Routledge, London and New York

Erlich R (2014) Inside Syria. Prometheus Books, New York

Geertz C (1963) The integrative revolution: primordial sentiments and politics in the new states. In: Geertz C (ed) Old societies and new states: the quest for modernity in Asia and Africa. The Free Press, London, pp 105–157

Gettleman J (2018) "These bodies are our assets": Blood and grief in an intimate war. New York Times, Aug. 2, www.nytimes.com/by/jeffrey-gettleman

Goldsmith L (2018) The Alawis: structure, perception and agency in the Syrian security dilemma. In: Hinnebusch R, Imady O (eds) The Syrian uprising: domestic origins and early trajectory. Routledge, London, pp 141–158

Haklai O (2000) A minority rule over a hostile majority: the case of Syria. Nationalism Ethnic Politics 6(3):19–50

Hardin R (1995) One for all: the logic of group conflict. Princeton University Press, Princeton

Hiltermann JR (2007) A poisonous affair: America, Iraq, and the gassing of Halabja. Cambridge University Press, Cambridge

Hinnebusch R (2005) Syria: Revolution from above. Routledge, London

Hobsbawm E (1983) Inventing traditions. In: Hobsbawm E, Ranger T (eds) The invention of tradition. Cambridge University Press, Cambridge, pp 1–14

Hokayem E (2013) Syria's uprising and the fracturing of the Levant. International Institute of Strategic Studies, Adelphi Series, London

Hughes GA (2014) Syria and the perils of proxy warfare. Small Wars & Insurgencies 25(3):522–538

Imady O (2018) Organizationally secular: Damascene Islamist movements and the Syrian Uprising. In: Hinnebusch R, Imady O (eds) The Syrian uprising: Domestic origins and early trajectory. Routledge, London, pp 106–127

Imady O, Hinnebusch R (2018) Conclusion: the early trajectory of the Syrian uprising: from agency to structure. In: Hinnebusch R, Imady O (eds) The Syrian uprising: domestic origins and early trajectory. Routledge, London, pp 329–335

Kaufman SJ (2001) Modern hatreds: the symbolic politics of ethnic war. Cornell University Press, Ithaca

Kaufman S (2023) The roots of ethnopolitical conflict. In: Byrne S, Matyók T, Scott IM, Senehi J (eds) Routledge companion to peace and conflict studies. Routledge, London, pp 17–27

Kelly MJ (2008) Ghosts of Halabja: Saddam Hussein and the Kurdish genocide. Praeger Security International. Greenwood Publishing Group, Westport

Khong YF (1992) Analogies at war: Korea, Munich, Dien Bien Phu, and the Vietnam decisions of 1965. Princeton, Princeton University Press

Khoury GD, Méouchy N (2007) Etats et sociétés en quête d'avenir (1945–2005): Dynamiques et enjeux. Geuthner, Paris

Lefèvre R (2016) Morocco, Algeria and the Maghreb's cold war. J North Afr Stud 21(5):735–740

Lounsbery MO, Pearson FS (2023) Complex effect of external involvements in ethnopolitical violence. In: Byrne S, Matyók T, Scott IM, Senehi J (eds) Routledge companion to peace and conflict studies. Routledge, New York, pp 39–47

Malmvig H (2017) Wars within wars: Regional actors' involvement in the battle for Syria. In: Boserup RA, Hazbun W, Makdisi K, Malmvig H (eds) The Middle East and North Africa between regional autonomy and international intervention. DIIS/AUB, Copenhagen/Beirut, pp 67–78

Najafov Z (2017) Internationalization of ethnic conflicts and impact on regional and international security. J Polit Sci Public Aff 5(4):1–5

Nossiter A (2016) "That ignoramus": Two French scholars of radical Islam turn bitter rivals. New York Times, July 12. www.nytimes.com/2016/07/13/world/europe/france-radical-islam.html

Pearlman WR (2017) We crossed a bridge and it trembled: voices from Syria. Custom House (e-book version)

Pearson FS, Lounsbery MO (2020) Structure-agency, social justice, nonviolence, and relationship building. In: Byrne S, Matyók T, Scott IM, Senehi J (eds) Routledge companion to peace and conflict studies. Routledge, London, pp 81–92

Phillips C (2015) Sectarianism and conflict in Syria. Third World Q 36(2):357–376. https://doi.org/10.1080/01436597.2015.1015788

Phillips C, Valbjørn M (2018) 'What is in a name?': The role of (different) identities in the multiple proxy wars in Syria. Small Wars Insurgencies 29(3):414–433

Reilly JA (2018) Fragile nation, shattered land: the modern history of Syria. I.B. Tauris and Co, London(e-book version)

Rifai O (2018) Sunni/Alawi identity clashes during the Syrian uprising: a continuous reproduction? In: Hinnebusch R, Imady O (eds) The Syrian uprising: domestic origins and early trajectory. Routledge, London, pp 242–259

Savelsberg E (2018) The Kurdish PYD and the Syrian civil war. In: Gunter MM (ed) Routledge handbook on the Kurds. Routledge, pp 357–365

Shils E (1957) Primordial, personal, sacred and civil ties: some particular observations on the relationships of sociological research and theory. Br J Sociol 8(2):130–145

Sluglett P (2004) Les Mandats/the mandates: some reflections on the nature of the British presence in Iraq (1914–32) and the French presence in Syria (1918–46). In: Méouchy N, Sluglett P (eds) Les mandats français et anglais dans une perspective Comparative. Brill, London, pp 103–127

Smith A (1986) The ethnic origins of nations. Basil Blackwell, Oxford
Smith A (1996) Culture, community and territory: the politics of ethnicity and nationalism. Int Aff 72(3):445–458
SOHR (2021) Total death toll | Over 606,000 people killed across Syria since the beginning of the "Syrian Revolution," including 495,000 documented by SOHR. Accessed at: https://www.syriahr.com/en/217360/
Sorenson DS (2016) Syria in ruins: the dynamics of the Syrian civil war. Praeger, Santa Barbara
Tejel J (2009) Syria's Kurds: history, politics and society. Routledge, London
Tschirgi N (2020) Critical and emancipatory peacebuilding. In: Byrne S, Matyók T, Scott IM, Senehi J (eds) Routledge companion to peace and conflict studies. Routledge, London, pp 315–325
United Nations (2012) UN Genocide Adviser warns of increasing risk of sectarian violence in Syria, 21 December. Accessed on 15 July 2022. https://news.un.org/en/story/2012/12/428922-un-genocide-adviser-warns-increasing-risk-sectarian-violence-syria
United Nations (2022) UN Human Rights Office estimates more than 306,000 civilians were killed over 10 years in Syria conflict. Press Release, Office of the High Commissioner of for Human Rights, 28 June. Accessed on 12 July 2022. https://www.ohchr.org/en/press-releases/2022/06/un-human-rights-office-estimates-more-306000-civilians-were-killed-over-10
Volkan VD (2001) Transgenerational transmissions and chosen traumas: an aspect of large-group identity. Group Analysis 34(1):79–97

Chapter 4
Internal Actors of the Conflict

The previous chapter examined the formation of identities by examining the role of international actors and whether participants regarded ethno-religious identities as primordially or politically divided in the Syrian conflict. Building on that, this chapter focuses on one of the central questions in Conflict Studies based on the study participants' perceptions: "Who are the internal actors of the conflict?" The focus is on two internal actors, the Asad Regime and the Free Syrian Army (FSA), and the dynamics in different Syrian localities that led to the conflict.

Perception About the Asad Regime

Some of the ways the government that lasted between 1971 and 2024 in Syria was referred to as "the regime," "the al-Asad regime," "al-Ba'ath party," "Ba'ath regime," "government," "Shi'a regime," "Alawite regime," and "normal government." The most common usage was "*the* regime." Many participants used common adjectives to explain the regime, including *fitna, fasād, zulm,* and *zaalim*. In the literature, "fitna" is translated as factional, civil strife, sedition, or heretical uprising; "fasād" as conspiratorial in nature, causing corruption on earth, transgression, disturbing the peace, and spreading evil on earth; "zulm" means oppression, injustice, and "zaalim" is the oppressor, tyrant, cruel person. For many, the conflict's main actor and source was the Asad or Asad/Ba'ath regime.

Individuals' personal stories and memories are central to understanding how these strong words came to be used and what they mean in their minds. "50-year rule of the Ba'ath Party/Asad Regime" was narrated by merging recent oppressions and historical memory of oppression. Some of the historical memories were narrated by an older generation who witnessed particularly the 1982 Hama uprising and consequent violent repression and sometimes by the young generations who

© The Author(s), under exclusive license to Springer Nature Singapore Pte Ltd. 2025

U. Ozkaleli, *De-essentializing Refugees: Perceptions, Experiences, and Becoming of Syrians in Türkiye*, https://doi.org/10.1007/978-981-96-5519-9_4

heard it from their parents. While their narratives intertwine recent and past events, the first sub-section below will focus on how people's historical memory locates the regime, and the following one will articulate how it is understood today.

Regime Zulm (Oppression): Ba'ath and Hafez Asad

A regime's endurance should not be confused with its internal legitimacy. "Even after great loss of legitimacy has occurred, a state can remain quite stable – and certainly invulnerable to internal mass-based revolts – especially if its coercive organization remains coherent and effective" (Skocpol 1979, p. 32). The below examination of the differently located participants will focus on how they see history and why they question the legitimacy of the institutions and political structure. The state's treatment of individuals positioned in various intersecting identity groups shapes and reshapes how they focus, articulate, and remember stories of past events, which re-present itself in their historical memory. The state has relations with dominant and subordinate classes (Skocpol 1979, p. 31), creating different proximity for different groups and individuals in their relationship with the state. I emphasize here that, depending on whether the state is divisive or inclusive in its treatment of its citizenry, it continuously shapes how past stories are recounted. Identities are "becoming rather than being: not 'who we are' or 'where we came from,' so much as what we might become, how we have been represented, and how that bears on how we might represent ourselves. Identities are therefore constituted within, not outside representation" (Hall 1996, p. 4). In this ongoing process of articulation of identity, how the state positions us and how we connect the past to today's happiness or grievances influence how we look into our past. If we are not "return to roots but a coming-to-terms-with our 'routes'" (Hall 1996, p. 4), how does this shape our current experience of interacting with the state? If, for example, we experience privilege now with a constant reminder of the past history of oppression, how does this shape our narration of history; what does our story of the past look like? How would our past stories be shaped if we faced constant oppression of salient identities we hold?

Interviewees' narratives need to be contextualized with the enduring political system that silenced many. What points of their history are important, and how they narrate this history closely interacts with their experience under the state authority. Interviewees talk about children being arrested and tortured in Dar'aa. In their counterfactual statements, many participants believed and wished that Bashar Asad would detach himself from the violence by taking action against the perpetrator. They believed that the protests would have ended with a compromise point if he had disowned the acts, arrested the responsible, and taken steps to address people's grievances rather than following the hawks in his government. After such a trajectory, some of the young adults in this study might have explained Hama 1982 in a different light than how they narrated it as refugees of war. In other words, the

Dar'aa incident reinforced anti-regime sentiments embedded into collective memory through Hama, linking father and son Asads in *zulm* practices.

Participant narratives varied based on their ethno-religious and political identities, focusing on different aspects of the Ba'ath regime. Some participants emphasized the period of the Ba'ath Party before Hafez Assad's rule. The majority prioritized the fifty years of Assad's reign, while a smaller group began their accounts of zulm/oppression with the 1982 Hama uprising and massacre. Some participants had direct experiences during Hafez Assad's reign, while others, from a younger generation, learned about that period from their family members.

Kurdish Syrian Merwan, born in the mid-1950s, discusses the Ba'ath Party, focusing on well before Asad's rule:

> I am *Agha*, [feudal landowner who has great influence in the region in which they live]. My father had water wells, and there weren't many water sources in those lands. In 1964, he produced one thousand tons of cotton, made all that field a green field, and taught people how to work. After that, the Ba'ath party rose [to power], and they put my uncle and father in prison. They took the land and all the engines, generators, everything. Al-Ba'ath party is worse than Asad because Ba'ath brought Asad to us. Before the Ba'ath party, we did not know the difference between Arabs and Kurds. Of course, it was democracy. After the Al-Ba'ath party rose, they said you are Kurds, and we will move you and erase you from the ground completely. (Merwan, 60)

Merwan's narrative of pre-Ba'ath Syria reflects his privileged socioeconomic position. As a landowner, he was in a position of power, which provided a lot more access to the system, providing a nuanced account between Ba'ath and Asad. In turn, Aykut firmly believes that the regime's strategy for eliminating opposition is fundamentally rooted in Hafez Asad's consolidation of power:

> After being appointed defense minister in the mid-1960s, Hafez Asad gathered all those in the military who opposed him and imprisoned them, including the president. He gathered them all in a prison in Mezzeh. At that time, Israel had an air strike, and they wanted them to hit that prison as well. They wanted to kill the people, but a lot of political prisoners escaped from that prison… Later, after Hafez Asad got the power fully under his hands, he issued political pardons to everyone, but he had already killed all the ones he wanted to be killed. (Aykut)

The construction of historical memory shapes not only narratives surrounding past events but also influences the underlying sources of conflict in individuals' perceptions. Interviewees problematize repressive practices toward any opposition. Indeed, Syria is among countries where peaceful protests "were often countered by widespread repression that fueled more hatred and resistance" (Pearson and Lounsbery 2020, p. 82).

Hama in Historical Memory

A prioritized historical memory within the fifty years of Asads' reign focuses on the 1982 Hama uprising and massacre as a symbol of the repressiveness of the regime that forced people to endure another 30 years until the Dar'aa incident and the uprising. While mostly narrated as a massacre done against Muslim Brotherhood supporters and religious Sunni Muslims, the killings also had strong class dimensions. Hama became a turning point where politics in Syria was perceived to be deadly (Reilly 2018, p. 185).

Though it happened in the 1980s, the massacre in Hama is instilled in the collective memory and has prominence in the narratives of many participants. Suad expressed her faith in Sunni Islam but has strong opposition toward the Muslim Brotherhood (*al-Ikhwan*), blaming them for using children in a mosque during the Hama uprising of 1982. While the Hama is primarily remembered as an attack on the Muslim Brotherhood, Suad also argued that not only were members of the Ikhwan targeted, but also many left-leaning individuals and numerous nonpolitical civilians lost their lives during the massacre. Suad's account was echoed in the literature, as during that period, a "large number of participants were non-observant Muslims, as the Muslim Brotherhood cooperated with left-wing and non-fundamentalist groups…" (Haklai 2000, p. 36).

In order to show the impact of Hama as a historical memory, the narratives below are from the younger generations who learned this historical trauma from their elders. Transgenerational transmission of trauma means that members of a group who experience severe and collective trauma show its effect on all those under the same identity group, which initiates unconscious societal and political processes in later generations (Volkan 2001, p. 87). Chosen traumas create a mental representation of the shared traumatic event, and if it is not dealt with through mourning the loss or reversing the humiliation, the mental representation of the event is passed down to the next generation; the sharing of the chosen trauma functions as a link for the group (Volkan 2001, pp. 87–88).

Ahlaam, as a young generation Syrian, learned history from her mother's experiences, and Hama is one of the events that she narrated:

> My mother was away from Hama, and when she went back in 1980, she saw all the people on the road dead. Her sister-in-law saw her son's deeply cut head wound. It was a disaster. When they went back to Hama, they saw that there were some places that were rubble. Everything was on the ground, and bullets were everywhere. Hafez al-Asad told everyone, "We will let it stay like this so when they want to start a revolution, they will see this, and they won't [attempt]." My mom keeps telling me this story. Hearing about it was very hard for me. (Ahlaam, 23, student)

Younger generations sometimes refer to it as 1980 and sometimes use the 1980s as an approximation. Ahlaam is one of many younger generation Syrians who, after learning about Hama, shifted her view of the Asad rule. Rahman was also inclined to support Bashar Asad when he came to power but shifted his view after his family passed down the Hama massacre memories. Like Ahlaam, he was deeply shattered:

> At first, I knew nothing about Hama; I was like, OK! Bashar is good. Bashar is cool. Then, my mother, from Hama, knew what happened there. She lived in the 80s, and she suffered. I learned from my mom a lot of shocking stuff about my uncle and my family in the 80s. I was shocked, saw what was happening, and turned against Bashar Asad. One of my uncles has a trauma. He was in a mosque for Friday prayer. After the prayer, he left, and his friends stayed in the mosque doing another prayer or reading the Qur'an. The conflict was between

> Hafez and the Islamic group called the Ikhwan, the Brotherhood. So, at that time, everyone who used to go to the mosque, even if they were too religious or to go pray and live, would be suspected. My uncle left the mosque, and then all of his friends were arrested for 10-20 years. My uncle would wake up in the middle of the night screaming, "They are here for me; they are here to take me..." After he finished his senior year, [my uncle] left for overseas. He works and lives abroad because he couldn't handle being in Syria. Sometimes, he would sit normally, then fall to the ground, saying they are here to take me. That was the most shocking story to me because I heard it only 4 years ago. They told me that my uncle had some mental problems, but I did not know it was war-related. That is the main reason why I hated Bashar in the first place. (Rahman, male, 21, student from Aleppo)

Timing of Rahman's family to tell him his uncle's history is indicative of both the level of repression and resentment people felt. High levels of insecurity made parents afraid to talk to their children about the regime to prevent them from expressing their views. However, mistrust and resentment toward the regime resulted in sharing their deep-seated traumas when they observed their children's sympathy and expectation of Bashar Asad as the new head of the state. Bashar Asad is seen as the continuation of the regime rather than a change, which was symbolized through the activation of the Hama massacre trauma.

Unlike Ahlaam and Rahman, who were born much later, Firas was a little boy when the 1982 Hama massacre happened. He connects his family's loss of Kurdish roots to his narrative of Hama:

> We do not speak Kurdish at all, unfortunately. We are originally from Kobanî, but we [ancestors] came to Hama 100 years ago. The family name is Kurdish, but they did not speak the language. "Arabized,"[1] we can say. We also witnessed a civil massacre in Hama if you heard about it in 1982. I was a little boy, they suffered a lot. We moved to Aleppo at that time as many others did from the same city… At the 1982 massacre, you can say 99% hated the regime, and there was a big reaction. They still live the massacre, and every family lost a precious member. That is why they still have this hate inside. My cousins and extended family had terrible stories about the Hama massacre. Many bad stories until now. It was the anniversary of it, 2 February, two days ago. (Firas, 42, from Hama)

Commemoration with an exact date indicates the freshness of the event in the memory of people. Another interpretation that relates to this narrative is the connection of Firas' assimilated Kurdish identity to the Hama massacre. Remembrance of the Hama massacre is directly connected to the mention of the assimilated Kurdish identity. What started as a loss of ethnic identity a century ago continues in his mind with the loss of lives due to the massacre that also led to the suppression of identities and voices that did not fit the expectations of the ruling elite.

Memories about oppression persist in people's consciousness, and many argue that these memories prevented any possibility of opposition until 2011. Reem, for example, narrates her imprisonment from age 15 to 25 starting in the 1980s and witnessing the rape of women in prison (without acknowledging being raped herself). She moves even further down in her historical view of Syria, this time not

---

[1] For an extensive study of Syrian Kurds and the use of the term "Arabized," see Tejel (2009, pp. 1, 63).

from her personal experience but what she read and knows about a time period that is between the end of French colonial rule and the beginning of Ba'ath:

> I read about the history of Syria in the 1950s. There was the Islamist party, the Communist Party, the Left side, and the Right one. They were all living together in harmony. Maybe our dream in Syria can be summarized as: I want Syria in the 1950s to be Syria in this century. (Reem)

Starting from the 1980s personal arrest and moving into the 1950s and believing that different ethno-sectarian groups could form a "national Syria," Reem effectively positions Asad's rule as the root cause of the lack of unity. Strikingly, people like Reem believe in the possibility of a "national unity" within diversity.

Author eye-camera: In Western societies, we commonly see different racial-ethnic-religious groups forming one "nation," particularly in the depiction of the U.S. as being the "melting pot."[2] *Moreover, it is only for Western citizens that we are presented with the idea that they can see themselves coming from "one nation" regardless of diversity in their racial, ethnic, and religious backgrounds. The Global South, particularly the Middle East, is presented with people who are fractured, divisive, and lack the sense of perceiving themselves as a "nation united in diversity." Reem's words, however, echo the desire and vision for such a possibility.*

So far, in this chapter, participant narratives show how they connect the actors and causes of war to historical memory. Hama 1982 (also 1916 Sykes-Picot in the previous chapter) can be considered a myth, which can be defined as "a belief held in common by a large group of people that gives events and actions a particular meaning" (Edelman 1971 in Kaufman 2001, p. 16). The word "myth" does not mean it is "false"; rather, it refers to focusing on how a set of past events are understood by people (Kaufman 2001). In other words, real historical events are framed as morally defining experiences, which most of the time are "chosen traumas" that take a central place in group self-understanding (Kaufman 2023, 18; Volkan 2001). "Hama" is used by the participants as a "symbol" that "evoke…emotions, such as pride or a sense of national grievance, associated with the myth" (Kaufman 2001, p. 16, cf. to Battle of Kosovo in Kaufman's example). The "myth-symbol complex" (Smith 1986, pp. 15–16; Kaufman 2001) can be seen when myths and related symbols collectively define what it means to be from a nation. In the Hama example, people from different identity groups use Hama 1982 to express the meaning of the regime for them and what they commonly endured under its yoke. The role Hama played as a myth was "giving events and actions a particular meaning…by defining enemies and heroes and tying the ideas of right and wrong to people's identity" (Kaufman 2001, p. 28). "Zulm of the regime" has strong ties to this particular history as many people narrated it, identifying the regime as an oppressor and the people as the silenced victims (*maẓlūm*). In 1982, the Hama massacre was transferred to younger generations, and many people talked about Hama. Interestingly though, while Hama "had been one of the nationalist bastions of the colonial era"

[2] Barrington (1997, p. 713) argues that to make a "nation," it is not a prerequisite to have a common ethnicity, such as in the U.S.

(Reilly 2018, p. 176), almost no one among the participants mentioned it in such terms. The colonial era showed its face in the memory via Sykes-Picot. Nevertheless, Hama's position of historic resistance against the colonialists was replaced by the Asad regime's brutality.

Regime Zulm (Oppression) Traveling from Father to Son

The oppressive structure of the regime that was positioned at the beginning of Hafez Asad's rule, particularly the 1982 Hama massacre, traveled through 50 years, which showed its face in the narratives about the current conflict's starting point. Malak's explanation signals the continuation through time in terms of oppressive practices:

> They [people] went to the demonstrations. They had the right because they saw a lot of *zulm* (oppression) from this regime. My family used to sell cigarettes, and the police used to come and tell them [you will hand over] either the cigarettes or money, the bribe. Before the revolution, 8 years ago, my brother came from overseas for a vacation. He was sitting in our store. The police arrested him and put him in prison for a month. They tortured him, hit him, and kept him in a single prison cell. In the end, they told him, "You can go now; it was a mistake. Your name was the same as a criminal's name; even your mother's name matched." They are doing *zulm* to people in the prison, and they are not treating them as humans there... [The reason for all of this conflict] is *zulm* that he [Asad] was applying unto his people [her voice gets high pitched and angry]. (Malak, Sunni Arab, war widow, 34, from Aleppo, studied till 7th grade)

Arbitrary arrests based on "mistaken identity" emerged in other interviews as well. When they mentioned this, participants were not only angry about such "mistakes" happening but also appalled by the fact that there was no negative consequence for the arresters or any recognition of the victimization that the person wrongly accused faced.

The participants often mentioned the power asymmetry in how they explained their perception of the regime. Husam elaborates on the asymmetry and centers the cause of the conflict as the silencing and oppression of the regime:

> We used to live with and were dominated by a dictator [Hafez Asad]. I needed to talk to you about this issue with whispers even among us. As we used to say, "walls have ears" [meaning even in private, one should not talk as it would get out]. It was very difficult. We were not able to speak on our own; if you spoke, you would be taken to jail. So, this was the main reason [for the conflict]. (Husam)

The perception of the regime crosscut almost all participants. Aisha recalls the start of the conflict:

> The war started because of what happened to the children in Dar'aa. After a while, slowly, demonstrations started in Aleppo as well...I saw on TV that Asad took the children away for writing, "Where is the money of this oil going?" on a wall. When the parents went after their children, he also put these parents in jail. He killed the children. Afterward, the demonstrations got bigger as you heard it, I heard it, everyone heard it. (Aisha, Turkmen villager, Muslim, no sectarian identification, 46, married)

Many young people expressed disappointment about Bashar Asad. As he was young and Western-educated,[3] young people expected that he could be a change agent. Amez summarizes such prevalent perceptions about the expected change after Bashar Asad assumed power and devastation by the violence that sparked the uprising:

> When the children of Dar'aa were arrested, and the whole protest started there, we thought that Asad would do something to fix it. He would have been a national hero if he had done that. If he had just taken over or removed the people like Atif Najib and the other politicians who were responsible for the events, what we call police brutality, he would have been a national hero. I was not building any opinion [about Bashar Asad] earlier. Nevertheless, he started bombing and shelling, people being killed by hundreds a day, and there were massacres conducted inside Syria. I said, "This is wrong; we cannot tolerate this." We were too naive to understand how filthy this regime was. We just hated the *Mukhabarat*. We hated the regime, but Bashar Asad was loved back then. But afterward, we knew what he was like; the head of the regime is the root of all evil. (Amez)

Bashar Asad's shortcomings in achieving the change that young adults hoped for created aspirational deprivation (Gurr 1970, p. 46), meaning that while expectations were increased, what was offered to the public remained similar to the previous period in terms of freedoms. Young people had high hopes and expectations for change, which dramatically crashed with youngsters being targeted violently in Dar'aa. Unmet expectations explain why university students were mobilized and became active participants in the demonstrations.

The name *Mukhabarat,* the intelligence agency that carried out the oppressive policies, appeared in the narratives of different participants, signaling the traveling of oppression from father to son era. Some college students developed views about the oppressive and violent approach of the regime, not with Dar'aa but with what they witnessed during the demonstrations, which was instrumental in forming opinions about the regime being the main actor of conflict. Akila was one such college student:

> I am not good at politics at all, but when protests started, I saw my friends going to the protests and heard the words they were saying. The other side came and captured a guy. I remember him; he wore a white shirt, and he was handcuffed. They were beating him to death in front of all the other students. They were putting us in a role where everyone had to go out and see this guy being kicked by them. From this, I saw that they were not doing something fair. We were not doing anything [wrong], just protesting without being violent. We were students, and students did not have guns. They used tear gas. My parents were telling me they were against the regime, and they told us that the regime was not good. When I saw what they were doing to the students while we were not doing anything, I realized that my parents were telling the truth. I had proof; I saw it with my own eyes, how they were killing and how much we were afraid that they would catch one of us. If one of us got caught, they would kick him in front of everyone, and then they would take him to torture. (Akila, 24, female, from Aleppo, student, and NGO employee)

Joumana also claimed that the main actor was the regime, and the cause was the lack of desire by the regime to respond to the calls for change. In her depiction, the

[3] Bashar al-Asad spent 2 years in London, England.

regime and Asad collapse into the individual "he." This is a common expression among participants:

> It is the regime. Because there are a lot of solutions for the regime, and he did not use them from the beginning of the revolution. People did not ask the regime to go away; no, they asked for change. Change in mentality, change in laws, call for change. No one asked for regime change for the first two or three months. But then the regime started to shoot people, kill people, and arrest them. The regime is responsible. (Joumana, female, 28, from Damascus, considers herself Muslim but neutral)

Participants also had a comparison between themselves and their parents in their responses to regime *zulm.* Reem argues that such a revolution should not have waited for 40 years, and Nala, who is a 46-year-old war widow with an elementary school education, believes that the cause of this conflict was keeping silent for 40 years to oppression. Some younger generation Syrians have the same view. While seeing the major problem historically lying with the regime's oppressive structure and practices toward Syrian society, they were also critical of the silence of the previous generation. Walid (23 years old, college-educated, from Aleppo, entrepreneur) argues that "fathers and grandfathers were afraid, and the younger generations are more courageous." Bilal also reflects on previous generations' choice of being silent[4]:

> In Syria, there has been an oppressive dictator regime for the last 40 years, ever since Hafez Asad got into power. He left the authority to his son, and the dictatorship continued. After 2000, when Bashar Asad came and promised reform, everyone knew it was not going to happen. It could happen to a certain degree, but he cannot do all he promised. I think rebelling against such an oppressive, dictatorial regime is legitimate. It is not a right, but beyond that, it is a responsibility. If you have [lived under] a dictator regime and they are oppressing you in every part of life, you need to rebel against it. This is our fathers' fault. It is a responsibility to rise against such a regime. (Bilal)

The unhappiness of younger ones toward the previous generations indicates two things: the younger generations became pivotal agents for voicing democratic demands, and second, they played an active role in the demand for change. It is still important to put into the analysis that, while the younger ones depict older generations as passive, it is the older generation who broke the silence about the regime atrocities, such as the Hama massacre, and caution their children about the regime regardless of being headed by the father or the son.

Shabiha as a Tool for Violence

When talking about the non-violent protests, almost all participants recounted the role of *Shabiha.* Some define Shabiha as "paramilitary hit men (criminal gangs who acted as plainclothes enforcers) to intimidate and murder, and torturing prisoners to death" (Reilly 2018, p. 223). Shabiha means "ghosts" and comes from the

[4] For an analysis of reasons for obedience and complicity to the regime while the internal beliefs of people were different, see Wedeen (1998).

smugglers in the western seaport of Latakia in the 1970s (Erlich 2014, p. 78). Shabiha was responsible for the regime's worst atrocities (for the 2012 Houla massacre, see Erlich 2014, p. 78). The university students who were part of the demonstrations were traumatized by their experience with them. Amez's experience below is similar to many others:

> We were in these protests, and after university security closed the university doors, the buses started to come in. These buses were filled with ex-prisoners. They were not wearing uniforms. They were wearing civilian clothes and armed with large sticks and tasers... When they caught a student, my proximity to them was like the space between you and me [we are sitting at a small table across from each other in a tea house]. The security guard struck him and started pointing at the guy who was *Shabiha*, so he ran towards the student he tasered him in the neck. The guy started flipping around. Foam started coming out of his mouth, and I was choked up. It was the first person I had seen dead. This guy was dragged on the floor. Since the doors were closed, they literally threw him off the fences and took him. I never saw him again. Afterward, many incidents happened, not to me but to others, so I decided not to go to school and stay at home. When there was a protest, I might or might not go; I went just to participate and be part of this beautiful movement back then. After a while, it started getting bad. We started seeing people leaving their areas from Eastern Aleppo, becoming IDPs, and moving from their homes into schools. (Amez)

Shabiha can be an example of "selective incentives" (Hardin 1995 in Kaufman 2001), which means "people may engage in violent conflict because they are promised rewards for killing or threatened with punishment if they do not kill…Aggressive governments may also use criminals, as they can be promised loot or locations for mafia-style operations in exchange for leading their gangs (armed by the state) into battle" (Kaufman 2001, p. 20). People who talk about Shabiha did not focus on these individuals per se but rather the government that utilized them to terrorize people. Hence, rather than the "thugs and criminals," the focus was on the utilizing force which was the state (Kaufman 2001, p. 39).[5]

In Hafez Asad's time, the embodiment of fear was *Mukhabarat.* Bashar Asad time, particularly during demonstrations, had an additional fear called the *Shabiha.* In the narratives, the regime was reduced to first the father and then the son Asad, and they are seen as the main actors of the conflict.

Perception About the Free Syrian Army (FSA)

Many in this study chose to use the "Free Syrian Army," but several who were against the opposition called it the "Free Army." When the duration of a conflict is extended, conflict analysis needs to focus on the time component. Who the parties were at the beginning and how their depiction changed is significant in our understanding of conflicts. Even though the views about the revolution changed, a considerable number of the participants continued to sympathize with the FSA in 2016 when the interviews were done. In the later years of the conflict, "rebels" were

[5] See Kaufman's explanation on use of common criminals and example of Serbia's *Arkan.*

depicted by the media as "Jihadists," but there were supporters of FSA, from leftists to Kurds to moderate Muslims to Islamic groups at the early formation. Regardless of their ethno-religious or political identities, other than the few people mentioned below, the majority of the participants strongly supported FSA and saw it as key to bringing down the regime at the time. Tawfik, who in the previous section mentioned the Alawite majoritarianism in the military, explained his involvement and perception of FSA:

> I was a volunteer in the regime, or Syrian Army, from 1982 until 2012. Then, I ran out of there, joined the revolution, and joined the Free Syrian Army. When I was a volunteer in the military, I knew that I was there to protect and defend my country and my people, not to kill them. And when the regime decided to kill their people, it was very normal that I would choose the people. It was a very hard decision, of course, because my family and all my relatives were in danger. The regime was very bad, and he wanted to take his revenge.

Here is how Zeinab (50), who believes in human rights, left politics and has a firm standing against oppression, positioned FSA in her narrative:

> There was a mother whose two or three sons were in the revolutionary armed forces, the FSA. Once, my sister asked how she permitted her last son to join her brothers. He was only 17 years old. The mother answered if I was afraid for my sons and the other person was afraid of their son, and the other as well, who will liberate Syria?... I think women were the ones carrying the revolution, they were the strongest supporters. Many of them were not only supported, but they also contributed. Some of them helped the FSA by nursing and cooking for them.

Narratives of Amez and Avdel, who ethnically identified as Kurdish, demonstrate intragroup differences and complexity of views about the FSA. Avdel, who places ISIS and FSA in the same negative category, argues that both parties tortured him and states that he left Raqqa and first came to Kobanî because of ISIS and FSA:

> We loved the revolution. At the beginning of the revolution, we loved the youth who were participating and protesting. They were beautiful youth protesting against the regime and wanted to bring down the regime. But after that, the army came and made us hate the revolution. We hoped we would have something better, but something worse arrived. (Avdel, 35)

While Avdel was firmly against the opposition army, Amez identified with none of the fighting groups. His narration of his relative shows the complexities of the formation of oppositional armed groups:

> My relative is a military defect, and that affected my life a lot. He used to be a colonel in the Sy… Asad's Army [he changes his mind and does not say Syria]. He defected and started forming the Kurdish Military Council, which was a part of the FSA-Free Syrian Army's main structure. They were known as the first brigade formed. Along with many other generals who defected from the regime, they created a front.[6] Experienced senior military people formed this front. The Syrian revolution would never dream of people like this. They were kidnapped afterward, and we never heard from them.

[6] See Tejel (2021, p. 436) for complexities and divisions within Kurdish parties on their strategy in regards to the Syrian regime.

At the time, Amez had conflicting feelings about the armed groups, but he did not feel as opposed to FSA as Avdel did.

The way conflict parties are perceived may shift after people become refugees. Some of these individuals directly participated in demonstrations or had family members fighting against the Asad rule. For example, while Tamara's husband was on the side of the FSA, her reflection on both sides shifted after losing him. Tamara lived in housing that was provided by an organized religious group. The majority of the women who lived there saw the regime as the aggressor and the only guilty party to the conflict, yet Tamara brings an alternative voice:

> Because of both sides [this conflict happened]. I think the president, the army, and the free army share the fault. About the president, he did not do what he could, and about the Free Syrian Army, if they did not rise like this, my husband and my brothers may be alive now. (Tamara, 21, war widow, Sunni Muslim)

Author eye-camera: When niqab-wearing women have a strong religious approach to life, the tendency is to position them as embracing the martyr position of their sons and husbands. Such a depiction is not farfetched; it comes from women who hold this position. Yet, they are not as singular as they are depicted. We need to move away from singular depictions of people from the same group. Their experiences, social location, and other intersecting identities may position them differently in terms of their understanding of a conflict. Social research would reach a more accurate depiction of society if such diversity were captured.

Only a few participants in this study were against the FSA and more sympathetic to the Syrian government. They call the Syrian government's army either the "Syrian Army" or "Legal Army." Mariam, who came from a mixed heritage of Muslim and Christian parents, argued that she did not love or like the president (Bashar Asad). Still, she did not believe that if he were removed from power, there would be an alternative person who could be a good president. Mariam argued that the opposition did not have a plan of what to do after they overthrew him. She was critical of the Free Army for other reasons:

> Even before ISIS, some of the Free Army was from outside of the country. There were Muslims, but not the real Muslims. They were killing Russians and Christians, Syrian Christians. They were killing them because they were not supporting them [FA]. Syrian Christians were with the president; hence, they were the enemy. The regime likes the Russians because Russia is with the regime. Who was killing [the Christians]? At that time, there was no ISIS. They had not entered Syria yet, so I cannot say it was ISIS [who was doing the killing]. Free Army was saying, "We are not doing this." Who was doing it, then? (Mariam, student, 23, does not identify with any religion).

Strongly identifying herself as a "Syrian," Mariam's choice of detaching the opposition from the "Syrian" name and stripping connection to anything Syrian is important to notice. Similarly, Fadi, while generally angry at all sides of the conflict, was critical of the Free Army, arguing, "Free Army is just that, a Free Army," implying there was no Syrian aspect to it. He maintains:

> Saudi Arabia, Türkiye, and Gulf countries are giving money to the Free Army so they can buy guns and stuff to kill. I am not judging the Free Army. There are people in the Free Army who are very good, but there are people in the Legal Army who are also good. As in

> every army, there are also bad people. (Fadi, 21, unemployed, some college education, did not graduate due to war, born in Idlib, raised in Aleppo)

When elaborating on the sides of the conflict, Fadi further argues:

> It is actually complicated. Some people say it is because of Bashar Asad, and others say it is because of the Free Army. I really do not know. I just want to be left alone and be happy. I do not want to live in this war…I think we were living well before the Free Army entered Syria. In my opinion, Bashar Asad does not know what is happening on the battlefield. He does not know. Because if he knows, he will stop all of this…The Free Army, the people who started this revolution thing, was good, but now they are all bad. Because they are stealing, they are killing, not in the name of Islam; I cannot consider this Islam. The legal army is, too, stealing and killing. Both of them are bad. It is equal. (Fadi)

While appearing critical of both, Fadi's naming "Free Army" has a similar opposing view when people used "Asad's Army." Fadi also shows his political departure by calling one "Free Army," whereas the other the "Legal Army." His seemingly balanced view, when he said both sides had "good people" in them, needs to be understood within the context that he was currently living in Gaziantep. Most of his circle was against the government and staunch supporters of FSA, believing its role was to stand against oppression. Thus, not only Fadi but others who signaled a critical stand toward the Free Army were mostly subtle about their criticism.

Unlike many others, Lina was openly critical of the FSA, arguing that she could not go back to Syria because of it:

> All of us want to go back. But a few days ago, someone sent me pictures of my home back in Aleppo. They stole everything, even the faucet. If they are not bombing our houses, they are stealing from them, so what do they want from us? They are stealing and bombing everything; the two sides are wrong, and I cannot support any one of them. In the area where the house is located, the group that controls that area is stealing [and that group is] the Free Syrian Army. (Lina, 37, Turkmen, from Aleppo, teacher)

While Lina did not identify herself as a government supporter, similar conditions apply to her as they do to Fadi. People who knew Lina positioned her as a regime supporter due to a close family member's link to the military. It is important to realize that social interactions and political conditions decide how people's narratives are presented. This is where attention to their words and context becomes important to interpret people's life-world meaningfully. No matter the social expectations, people find ways of showing their agency by choice of words or examples, as presented in the cases of Mariam, Fadi, and Lina. Given the context that refugees were mostly against the Asad regime, they considered the FSA as an actor that was standing up to it. Some interviewees distanced themselves from all fighting groups as they did not believe in armed struggle. However, unlike the media depiction of rebel groups as Jihadists, in 2016, participants of this study did not reduce FSA to Islamist groups.

Perception About Different Localities

The majority of the participants were against the regime and wanted and supported the uprising. Nevertheless, turning to guns along with actors like al-Nusra Front and ISIS owning the process led them to express opposition to resistance with guns. Aykut disagreed with the use of guns yet elaborated on the process in different localities that led to a civil war. His narrative starts by telling how, even before the events at Dar'aa, people within Syria started to get excited about Tunisia, Egypt, and Morsi being overthrown. He says that rather than Bashar Asad, Syrians focused on freedom and change. Where the uprising started and when their locality joined were elaborated by many interviewees:

> The civilians never carried guns. From February 2011 until a time span of 8 months, no weapons were used. When has using guns started? Hama. In Hama, there was a demonstration. Regime security forces were in that demonstration. People agreed with the governor. They said, 'We are not going to do anything; we are just going to do the protest. We are only going to demand freedom. We are not going to denounce anyone; we are not going to ask anyone to step down.' The security forces started to position themselves on the roof with guns in their hand, sat on the roof, and started to shoot people. This was a turning point as some officers in the military left the military with their guns and started an armed struggle. I wish it did not become armed. Would we reach a better success [without guns]? No, but unfortunately, this armed way started having different faces. Why did we have an uprising? It was not a political uprising. It was a social uprising. (Aykut)

Author eye-camera: The separation of "freedom and demand for civil rights" as a social uprising and not a political one needs to be deeply thought through. This appears in other narratives as well. I believe the oppressive domination and control of "politics" for decades created the separation of "social" and "political" rights in the views of the participants. A contextualization of agency that actors use in different ways may explain the creation of an alternative language as a way to seek change. Additionally, many who participated in the demonstrations were against arms, as this chapter indicates. Receiving countries, particularly when they are hostile to an increased number of refugees, depict them as people who "ran away from fighting." Some participants in this research reflected a strong "anti-war" sentiment. Non-violence and anti-war views are strong political positions that need to be addressed more and recognized as a conscious choice.

Aykut, at the time, was located in Aleppo and remembers how, after Dar'aa, demonstrations started at Homs, Hama, and Damascus, and at last in Aleppo. His explanation of why the Aleppo demonstrations started later than the others is indicative of the complexity of actors and their positionality in the conflict:

> Because Aleppo is closer to Türkiye, it has a strong economic structure and a particular group of Aleppo merchants work closely with the regime. Through this, the economic power was under the hand of the regime. Another reason is that [many people] who worked in different sectors were taken to prisons even before demonstrations started. 10-20 people gathered, but the regime had a very powerful 50 years of intelligence structure. They saw 20 people working together, and they gradually took two or three people into custody. Merchants did not want this to explode in Aleppo. The regime threatened their family and

> their relatives. In this way, the regime controlled this group. As far as I know, over 800 groups in Aleppo were dealt with this way, and they vanished. (Aykut)

In the literature, Aykut's account of Aleppo is depicted in regard to Damascus. Asad created a business network that limited the traditional urban support to the opposition, particularly to the Muslim Brotherhood. The opposition in Damascus favored Islamization without directly confronting the regime. The opposition leadership in Aleppo was more assertive than the Damascus group, while Hama's *Fighting Vanguard* was more militant (Reilly 2018, pp. 178–179). The strongest mercantile alliances focused mainly on Damascus, and the opposition tended to be in the northern cities (Homs, Hama, and Aleppo) (Reilly 2018). Aykut's account here reveals the Aleppo dimension of these complex relations. Economic interests cross the ethno-sectarian lines, which can postpone, erase, or intensify violent conflicts.[7]

Majed (30) was from Ariha, Idlib, and explains how localities faced different actors that led to turning to weapons because there was no other avenue left available to express political opposition.

> I got arrested and saw that my brother was also arrested when they put us in the military car. We stayed in prison for 58 days. They tortured us and broke my bones. The movement was very civilian and very peaceful at first. It was all about students from universities. In Ariha in Idlib, after I got out of jail, the regime asked to meet with us. They told us that we should calm down. We did not reach an agreement as they kept arresting people. After many people were killed in the demonstrations, people, without wanting, started to take weapons with them... In 2011, my brother, who was a student, was killed. He was armed, but no one from our family knew that. He was seeing everything [that was done] in the military, and he was right. Another brother of mine was killed in 2012 while he was helping wounded people... There were more than five hundred dead people from the beginning of the revolution in the city. Then, Ariha just ended. They burned my and my brothers' houses. We had a library in Ariha, and they burned that down too. I know a guy who was working in the media, and they burned his sister. I have some pictures and videos to prove all of this… The regime encouraged all the Salafies and all the extremist people starting in 2007. No one in the international community thought anything about that. They spread the Salafi ideas and thoughts and the Jihadist thoughts. They created Islamic movements. The regime was very happy because he saw a strong power in that.

Aisha (46), a villager, became internally displaced before coming to Türkiye, was not a part of any side yet lived in insecurity based on two different sides fighting over her village, which victimized the population:

> It was the third day of Ramadan. We got all the food and set the table. They said the opposition entered here so Asad would bomb it and shoot the mosque. We heard the guns and bombs, we got scared and took all our kids and ran…Our children were hungry. We went to other villages, but they did not give us bread because we were not opposition. This side belonged to the opposition in the villages, and Aleppo belonged to the regime. My son said I am going to Türkiye. We have no money left. How are we going to live here hungry? We did not have passports. We came from under the wire, where there were no soldiers to see us, illegally. Now everyone says that Erdogan [Turkish President] brought us here; there

[7] How the regime reduced the intervention to economic life and opened some space for the private sector and included some Sunni segments, see Hinnebusch (1993, 1995, 1997) and Haklai (2000).

> was no Erdogan. We came from under the wire. The next day, we saw that Asad shot the school in the village... All the Turks crossed over to this side of the border, and a lot of Turks became part of the opposition forces. Don't you hear from the news Turkmens are like this and Turkmens in the mountains? (Turkmen villager, 3-year elementary school education, homemaker)

Aisha's words mark that some localities became part of the conflict unwillingly. Aisha's lower-class position allows her to see that parties of the conflict are divided in class lines which is as important as the locality they are from. Elites are in conflict, but fighters come from the lower classes:

> My child is at the age of going into the military. I did not let him, why would I? Brother is shooting brother. Both the opposition and Asad's men are mine. Does Asad fight the war himself? Your kid and my kid are shooting each other. Why are they shooting each other? I am not obliged to send my child to get shot... Is Asad's son fighting? Go there and look. Is his son there? He is in his hotel and home eating and drinking. We are not finding food and salt—no bread. (Aisha)

Author eye-camera: Aisha's narrative draws attention to suffering during the clashes based on people's class position and capabilities, particularly if they did not want to be part of any fighting group. In such instances, fighting sides from all angles become the agents of insecurity. From Aisha's position, the attainment of food and shelter is the main concern, and any side that created food insecurity was equally responsible. Her view about financially more capable people not fighting and her lack of will to send her children to fight are important aspects that need to be explored further. Rich may take sides without fighting, and the poor, without taking any side, may be asked to fight without any benefit. Once lower classes have the opportunity to express their views, it comes to the surface that they have not become refugees because they were mobilized to fight, but they may have consciously resisted fighting as part of any warring side. Lower classes take no part in the war's decision-making process, and some are strongly aware of this fact. Hence, for some, leaving home is an act of defiance to fighting. Various views of lower-class people who refuse to be a party to any conflict side need to be examined more in conflict studies. The depiction of lower-class urban refugees needs to center their awareness in terms of the politics of war rather than depicting them as voiceless, inarticulate victims.

This chapter shows that the regime is perceived to be the main internal actor in the conflict under the leadership of father and son Asads. Bashar Asad's violent response to youngsters at Dar'aa broke the hope the young generations felt for the change that he promised. Youth became actors of non-violent change via demonstrations. The regime's response to non-violent protests was severe use of violence, with the addition of the Shabiha. Such violence by the regime justified arming the opposition. Different localities like Hama and Idlib played significant roles in sparking the armed struggle. FSA, while becoming a long-awaited resistance, also became an actor that created insecurity for people who refused to be part of the armed struggle.

References

Barrington LW (1997) "Nation" and "nationalism": The misuse of key concepts in political science. PS. Polit Sci Polit 30(4):712–716

Edelman M (1971) Politics as symbolic action: mass arousal and quiescence. Academic Press, New York

Erlich R (2014) Inside Syria. Prometheus Books, New York

Gurr TR (1970) Why men rebel. Princeton University Press, New Jersey

Haklai O (2000) A minority rule over a hostile majority: the case of Syria. Nationalism Ethnic Polit 6(3):19–50

Hall S (1996) Introduction: who needs identity? In: Hall S, Du Gay P (eds) Questions of cultural identity. Sage Publications, London, pp 1–17

Hardin R (1995) One for all: the logic of group conflict. Princeton University Press, Princeton

Hinnebusch R (1993) Asad's Syria and the new world order: The struggle for regime survival. Middle East Policy 2(l):1–14

Hinnebusch R (1995) Syria: The politics of peace and regime survival. Middle East Policy 3(4):74–77

Hinnebusch R (1997) Syria: The politics of economic liberalization. Third World Q 18(2):249–265

Kaufman SJ (2001) Modern hatreds: the symbolic politics of ethnic war. Cornell University Press, Ithaca

Kaufman S (2023) The roots of ethnopolitical conflict. In: Byrne S, Matyók T, Scott IM, Senehi J (eds) Routledge companion to peace and conflict studies. Routledge, New York, pp 17–27

Pearson FS, Lounsbery MO (2020) Structure-agency, social justice, nonviolence, and relationship building. In: Byrne S, Matyók T, Scott IM, Senehi J (eds) Routledge companion to peace and conflict studies. Routledge, New York, pp 81–92

Reilly JA (2018) Fragile nation, shattered land: the modern history of Syria. I.B. Tauris and Co, London

Skocpol T (1979) States and social revolutions: a comparative analysis of France, Russia and China. Cambridge University Press, Cambridge

Smith A (1986) The ethnic origins of nations. Basil Blackwell, Oxford

Tejel J (2009) Syria's Kurds: history, politics and society. Routledge, New York and London

Tejel J (2021) The Kurdish Question in Syria. In: Bozarslan H, Gunes C, Yadirgi V (eds) The Cambridge history of the Kurds. Cambridge University Press, Cambridge, pp 436–457

Volkan VD (2001) Transgenerational transmissions and chosen traumas: an aspect of large-group identity. Group Analysis 34(1):79–97

Wedeen L (1998) Acting "as if": symbolic politics and social control in Syria. Comp Stud Soc History 40(3):503–523

Chapter 5
Politics and Politics of Turmoil

Causes of the Conflict: Dominating and Coercive State Politics

The prevailing understanding of the Weberian state denotes the state as the monopoly of legitimate violence, giving the state a central actor role in conflicts. People experience themselves *vis-à-vis* the state. The state is a macro-structure coordinated by an executive authority with administrative, policing, and military organizations (Skocpol 1979, p. 29). "…[T]hese basic state organizations are built up and must operate within the context of class divided socioeconomic relations, as well as within the context of national and international economic dynamics" (Skocpol 1979, p. 29) and social interests of nonstate actors are represented through their involvement in policymaking and policy implementations (Skocpol 1979). Syrian state, with its colonized history, was controlled by a group that had asymmetric power over other identity groups and individuals. Therefore, "when political avenues are blocked by an authoritarian regime, the probability of a group's entrance by violent means into a phase of 'visibility' is much greater" (Tejel 2009, p. 118).

People and communities facing material and symbolic domination in unequal power relationships may turn to violence to defend and legitimize their national, sectarian, or political symbols (Bozarslan 2004 in Tejel 2009, p. 118). The field results indicate that interviewees view the Asad regime as the main actor in the conflict, attributing the root cause of this conflict to its dominating and coercive state politics. Symbolic domination (Migdal 1994, p. 15) could include denial of social, political, ethnic, and sectarian recognition, and lack of recognition may be experienced as an attack on people's dignity as "loss of dignity" was prominent in the narratives.

Before moving into structurally encouraged stereotypes and prejudices, I will briefly include findings about spaces and possibilities for positive interaction and a

© The Author(s), under exclusive license to Springer Nature Singapore Pte Ltd. 2025
U. Ozkaleli, *De-essentializing Refugees: Perceptions, Experiences, and Becoming of Syrians in Türkiye*, https://doi.org/10.1007/978-981-96-5519-9_5

sense of closeness among different identities. Juxtaposing positive interactions with stereotypes and prejudices will highlight that there was a possibility of creating peaceful and meaningful relations if the structurally enforced divisions were not enforced.

Some participants remembered friends, teachers, business colleagues, and neighbors with whom they had good relations from other sects and religions. Khawla, for instance, argues that "the Sunni and Shi'a were just like brothers." Joumana, though rare, witnessed inter-religious marriages, and Aya and Waseem saw that even at first families were against these marriages, they later accepted the union. Nala's husband worked for a Christian-owned firm, and Salah had Christian customers. Relations were explained as "beautiful, loving, and tolerant." Haya's mother had a Druze milk mother/wet nurse, and she remembers her grandparents having Christian and Druze friends. She also remembers her mother telling stories of how "they were eating from the same plates, and there was more tolerance in the Damascus suburbs." Reem, who was imprisoned for reading religious books, misses the diversity she grew up with at home in terms of political views, as her communist father was highly tolerant of differences and never stopped her from praying or fasting. She was raised respecting diversity as she read books in the family library, from religion to communism to culture, including Naguib Mahfouz to Chekhov to the book of Gogol. Zeinan, in her native Raqqa and in Homs, where she studied, never heard people asking about each other's religion or ethnicity, including close friends, when staying in each other's homes because they all considered religion "a special thing for every person." Even after the war, some refused to singularize Alawite. Like Reem, Rouaa says Alawites are good; it is "just Bashar and his group that is not good." The few interviewees lived in either mixed neighborhoods or where the majority differed from the interviewee's religion, sect, or ethnicity. Joumana stresses good relations and friendships, saying: "My mom and dad's house was located between a mosque and a church, and the left of my room was facing the mosque. Many of our neighbors were Christian, and I liked them a lot. We had a very good relationship with them. Now, they also left Syria."

Such experiences of diversity not only in communal interaction but also in familial relations show that a fertile political life would have led to a consociational political structure (Lijphart 1977), which means "a grand coalition of communal leaders, group autonomy, and mutual vetoes to protect vital interests" (Bogaards 2019, p. 519) if the political system were not oppressive to different identities and political ideas. Analysis of the data shows that depending on their identities and expectations, participants, on different levels, experienced being stereotyped and prejudiced and faced repression, persecution, oppression, and domination under the Asad regime. Consociationalism did not work in Syria due to symbolic domination imposed by the Asad regime through reproducing layers of stereotypes and prejudice at the societal level. The chapter, therefore, examines in detail the experiences and perceptions of people from different identity groups that are shaped by these dominating and coercive state policies.

Stereotyping and Prejudice

If various identity groups lack recognition, they will challenge the legitimacy of the political institutions and the legitimacy of the groups holding the state power (Migdal 1994). In such a setting, different identity groups will likely form coalitions to ask for more transparent and equal governance. A state weak in legitimacy may continue to hold on to power (Skocpol 1979) and use the state apparatuses to prevent such a coalition. Through norms and values, stereotypes are carried with the state's institutional mechanisms (Taylor 2016). In other words, controlling the main apparatus (Althusser 2006), a state's camera projects images that influence people's vision of one another, directly affecting their perceptions. The Syrian state under Asad suffered from legitimacy problems, yet it still organized socioeconomic relations. The field data shows that the political structure that Asads operated fueled divisions and pitted groups against one another by using stereotypes and prejudices to create friction among them.

People from different identity groups had positive experiences and sentiments on a micro level; nevertheless, they could not prevent a social conflict that has reached destructive levels in Syria. Stories and memories that indicate fractures and divisions are important to examine as they show how the structure has enforced stereotypes, prejudices, and enduring othering. Nazem's perspective is that the regime widened the gap among groups:

> Looking at society in depth, there were many problems because they treated some areas more special than others. At the beginning of the demonstrations, all people went for the revolution. However, the regime reacted towards various groups in different ways. For example, in Kobanî, which is majority Kurdish, and As-Suwayda, majority Druze, the regime dealt with Kurds and Druze more mildly [than in other places] when they went out and started the demonstrations. The regime did not act with them as they acted with the other people [Sunni demonstrators]. The regime let them demonstrate until the situation got bigger, and even then, the regime dealt with them not in a very heavy way but in a milder way. The regime behaved [differently] in 2004 during the attack on the Qamishli area. There were a lot of Kurds inside of it, but no one said anything about that. [Different treatment of the regime is] to make the gap just bigger and bigger inside one society and to gain legitimacy as a government through protecting a few or some minorities. (Nazem, 28, from Aleppo, strong Sunni Arab identity, college-educated)

Even though Nazem had a consciousness of divisive politics by the state, by thinking Kurds and Druze received preferential treatment, he distanced himself from these groups, putting a hierarchy on who suffered more. Yet, when the camera is turned to Kurdish historical memory, they have a very different account. Amez, an ethnic Kurd, talks about how, in 2004, the Asad government implemented a siege and used military and intelligence operations against them. While Nazem is unaware, the implications of the approach of the regime to Kurds influenced the daily lives of Kurdish people. Amez narrates his school years:

> I will not say discrimination, but [I was] living differently. [My] school was in Aleppo city. Aleppo is a Sunni city… and the location [of the school] was a conservative Ikhwan, Muslim Brotherhood, sympathizing area. Most of the students were of Islamic background,

> and I was not a conservative student. I was pointed out as the Kurdish guy at school… They knew [I was Kurdish], and they treated me differently. I was not part of the group most of the time… They would look at you differently… The discrimination was connected to Asad's regime against the Kurdish ethnicity or Kurdish minority, especially after 2004. (Amez)

Amez connects negative attitudes at school toward him to Asad's policies toward Kurds, which created an intelligence structure that infiltrated even the school setting. Nawar and many other young Syrians stated that they learned a lot about different identity groups in Syria after becoming refugees together in Gaziantep.[1] Unlike Nazem, Nawar's interaction with Kurds made him realize that even the name "Syrian Arab Republic" excludes Kurdish people and adds:

> Calling it the Syrian Arab Republic was a propaganda strategy under Hafez al-Asad to divide the lands and divide Kurds between the Syrian and Turkish sides. Otherwise, they are not Arabs. I was unaware and had no deep knowledge about the Kurdish case. I knew they tried to earn their freedom in the early 2000s but could not. It was reported in the official news all over the country that it is just like a conflict about a football game and has been extended to the neighborhoods. But basically, it was just like the revolution of the Syrian people against the dictatorship and also to get dignity. (Nawar, 29, from Damascus, Deist, college graduate, NGO employee)

Nazem's view of Kurds being treated better is constructed inside Syria under the Asad regime, while Nawar's, who similarly grew up in a strongly Sunni family, is developed more emphatically through meaningful contact and interaction with Kurds in Antep.

Similarly, Haya, while being critical of some Kurdish politics at the time of the interview in 2016, pointed out the lack of recognition of Kurdish identity, including the refusal of schools or TV channels in their language, and argues that Kurds have a right to their own country. She adds:

> You cannot have people in your country and then force them to be Arab or Muslim. Even if they did that, even if they learned our language, they did not have the right to go to university. That is what Bashar Asad finally did when the revolution first started. We said that people wanted their rights, and the first rights were given to the Kurds for their identity. Before, they did not have one [identity rights].

While at first glance, Haya's words sound understanding of the Kurdish experience, if we put her words in a conversation with Afran's experience and observations of how Kurdish people were perceived, it shows the fragments and lack of interaction between people. In her narrative, Afran said that Kurdish people are asked whether they are Kurds or Muslims as if being a Kurd automatically made them non-Muslims. Afran argued that this was regime teaching.

Different identity groups were unaware of each other's self-perceptions, which emerged as a common theme in my fieldwork. Many younger Syrians learned about other groups, localities, and grievances after interacting with other Syrians in Türkiye. Farah self-reflects:

---

[1] This finding is consistent with Pearlman's (2017, p. 7 in Reilly 2018, p. 242) account.

> When I came here [Gaziantep], I did not know anyone from any other city different than Damascus. I met people from Homs and occasionally from Aleppo, but that was it. I had no idea about other areas of Syria. The ideas I had were stereotypes. [I thought people from other cities/regions] were ignorant; they knew nothing. [Some others] were very mean and very greedy. These were all Syrian stereotypes we had. When I came here, I met people from around Syria for the first time. I got to talk to them and learn about their ideas and stereotypes about Damascene people. I now know more about the geographical areas of Syria and the names of the towns. I was ignorant about Syria when I came here, I learned a lot. People, geography, and history. (Farah)

Naser argues that certain aspects deepen stereotypes and prejudices. One is the different accents and the inability to comprehend them within Syria.[2] Another deep-rooted tension between rich merchant Aleppo and Damascus, the political capital, led to negative stereotypes. Fatima met a Druze for the first time in Antep and argued that "When you do not know someone in your own country, it is so easy to judge, to make this decision to discriminate or kill because you do not know the person." Mariam gives a picture of Syrian neighborhoods as being separated by ethnic and religious groups, arguing that this was positive and that no one interfered with the other. Schools, she said, were separated as well, but she had seen a lot of Muslim girls attending Christian girls' schools where religious classes were different for Christians and Muslims. There were some schools that were strict about limiting diversity:

> We have so many Armenian schools in the Armenian neighborhood. [Their attitude was,] "This is my area. I do not want people going to my schools. I am teaching the Christian way. I do not want Muslims in my school." They were not doing it in a bad way. It was not a problem that they did not accept Muslims. Not many people wanted to go to their schools [anyway]. They [non-Christians] had other schools. I know this because my mom's friend is Russian, and her husband is Syrian. She wanted her son and daughter to go to that school, but they did not accept them. They told her, 'Fine, you are Christian, but your son and daughter are not, so they cannot come here.' You can say that Armenian people were more complex than the everyday Christian Syrians. They have [this attitude] I am Christian. Do not touch me. (Mariam, mix heritage of Muslim and Christian, student)

Mariam argued that it was not based on ethnicity but religion, as they were accepting people who were Christians from other ethnic backgrounds. Mariam further states, "But before the conflict, living there was normal. No one was mad at each other." She claims that nobody questioned the policies of school acceptance. They did not take it personally. However, deeply segregated neighborhoods inevitably bring the language of othering, as Mariam's own usage is an example. Miriam singularized all Armenians as having the same approach. Further, someone's husband being "Syrian" automatically meant "Muslim" in her explanation. The husband is not located as "Muslim" but rather "Syrian," indicating that "Syrian" is not an umbrella term for all living in the territory. Non-Armenian Christians were defined as "normal" Christians, making Armenian Syrians an oddity. Such usage suggests that there are dominant identities within groups as well as between groups. The presence of linguistic othering reflects fractures as to who is positioned as the

[2] For the complexity of Arabic vernaculars in Iraqi context, see Collin (2009).

"owner" of certain identities. Normalization of rejection of students into schools based on their parental lineage is a division created by the macro-level (state) to allow meso-level organizations (schools) to influence micro-level relationships (children, parents, teachers).

Ahlaam argued that most of the religious tension was not between Muslims and Christians or from one religion to another, but rather it was within the same religion, particularly within Sunni groups, focusing on dress code intolerance within the sectarian lines. She argues that pious Muslims are "okay with" Christians not being covered and accept this in terms of their religious belief. Yet, when it comes to the dress code of Muslim women, different segments have judgments and opinions of how people should be dressed. While the way hijab is worn in Aleppo is different than in Homs, and Homs one is different from the one in Damascus due to the following of different mosques, the hijab can also be differentiated in terms of class standing. On the one hand, a participant mentioned that niqab-wearing women were referred to as "ninjas" by some in some localities in Syria. Some explained that women who covered their heads with a hijab but wore very tight dresses or jeans were judged negatively and harshly. On the other hand, a niqab-wearing participant argued that secular dress is not "the Syrian way" and that there were no "real Syrian women" with secular dress. Ahlaam, as a Muslim-identifying woman who preferred secular dress, also faced judgments:

> All my life, some just thought I was Christian. Some of my friends' parents did not allow them to walk with me because, as a Muslim, I was not wearing a hijab. Some of them, however, were really open-minded. (Ahlaam)

Haya, as a hijab-wearing, strongly religious young woman, confirms Ahlaam's experiences and says secular-dressed Sunni women were always perceived negatively. Haya's following perceptions, which are similar to Farah's description of negative views and prejudices, indicate deeply entrenched inter-communal distrust:

> In my view, people in Damascus used to be afraid of Alawites. [They tell you] 'Be afraid to talk too much about yourself in front of them, not have a close friendship with them, and be afraid of what they tell you and what they are trying to learn from you. When you are asked a question, you have to be aware all the time when there is an Alawite around.' We say, 'They have nice hand script,' it means they write reports [about others] a lot… I have friends from Alawite and Ismaili and some Êzîdî, and our relationship was the best. Still, Dad did not appreciate it. He knows I have a long tongue [outspoken, bold in expressing views]. He feared I would create a problem with what I said. (Haya)

Believing all Alawites are informants of the regime is prejudiced. How this prejudice is formed is not individually created but constructed via the state behavior. The idea that members of one group spy on others comes from strategies that involve a government using a certain number of people for this end, creating a perpetual mistrust of the entire group. Above, Amez assessed that Asad's intelligence structure infiltrated even the school setting, reflecting the policies toward Kurds. Haya also explains that deep fear from different identities and views dominated even the school settings for young people, causing distrust toward one another. These narratives indicate how government policies set the tone among the population and lead people to develop prejudice toward one another. Farah offers a perspective on how the political tone was set:

> When the focus was on the minorities, like Christians and Druze, [the regime told them] 'Look, guys, I am your protector, and Sunni are the majority and dangerous.' When you [the regime] impose this image or this way of thinking on people, I don't think it creates respect... The hatred among religions was growing, slowly and silently... Slowly, the hatred started between the Christians and Muslims, between the Shi'a and Sunni, and, of course, between Sunni and Alawite. It was very slow. It was silent, but it was growing. At school, for example, we knew this girl was Christian; this boy was Shi'a. And we knew Christians did not like us. I think the regime wanted this to happen. They wanted to look like the protector of the minority to get their support. (Farah)

Intergroup relations had a level of segregated tolerance, living parallel lives without encouraging inclusive relationships. On the contrary, insecurities were nurtured to pit groups against one another, mostly playing majority-minority dynamics and instilling fear of the majority gaining power. While at the start, religious minorities supported the democratization demands, threats and fear from radical Muslim groups dissolved the unity, and fractures grew, which led to a civil war. All of these indicate that cross-cutting ties, while existing for some, were not the experience of considerable others. Deep and continuing interaction through cross-cutting memberships could build community and break social barriers (Brewer and Pierce 2005 in Pearson and Lounsbery 2020, p. 89). Cross-cutting ties would have helped form alliances for democratization rather than fearful polarization, where people who desired more democratic governance would have continued to form stronger cooperation. This would have made them stronger in the long run, both against the authoritarian regime and the radical religious groups overpowering the uprising. State silencing and identity oppression happen with the groundwork of stereotypes and prejudice.

The above section presented perceptions of differently located people about existing stereotypes and prejudices in various ways. Fear was the driving emotion that the regime used for all groups. This was probably the main reason for the immediate disintegration of society. "Syrian" was never made an identity with political cohesion, except for the refugees who were called Syrian out of Syria. Many people learned a lot about other regions when they left Syria and met in Gaziantep as "Syrians" who did not have deep connections as people from different regions in pre-war Syria. As I argued in the theory section, refugees are depicted not even as an aggregate but as a group that singularizes them. Such singularity makes it easier for host/global governance to deal with the "refugee issue." However, Syrians are diverse, coming from different regions and identity groups. Refugee Syrians had an opportunity in host communities to have contact and learn about one another that their political structure did not allow in their home country. This finding is relevant to the ongoing state-building of Syria. Such an opportunity could be turned into a collaborative interaction. Hence, refugees need to be seen as active agents rather than invisible and voiceless beings. The chapter continues by examining repression as a cause of conflict.

Repression

State repression is "any realized or threatened limit or coercive action taken by state authorities to control or prevent challenges that could alter the status quo policy or distribution of power" (Ritter and Conrad 2016, p. 86 in Chenoweth et al. 2017, p. 1953). The fundamental objective is that governments wish to remain in power (deMeritt 2016, p. 1). Rather than focusing on categorizations and typologies of state repression or why states repress, I positioned the camera to analyze how people experience state repression. This section connects the reader to the experience of people who narrate what parts of their minds, bodies, and lives state repression lived.

Repression was applied in different aspects of people's lives. The first aspect of life they felt repressed was political leadership choice. Seventy-eight-year-old Lamia, a member of a financially comfortable merchant family whose ancestors assimilated to Arab Syrian society and detached from her Kurdish roots, explains coercive silencing by the Asad regime:

> I started to hate the father [Hafez] Asad from the old time. The Asad family really destroyed Syria in all aspects, education system and freedom of speech. Nobody is allowed to do anything. It is a very close country. Only people related to them [the family] are allowed to do anything in Syria. They kidnap and torture people. That is why I hated the corruption. People wanted freedom. They could not handle a 50-year-old dictatorship. [Asad] is a person who has done nothing for his people. (Lamia, from Hama and Aleppo, homemaker)

Many participants felt they were silenced and prevented from expressing political ideas or oppositional thoughts. Politically, people were also frustrated that there was no chance of change and opportunity for oppositional politics:

> We are not opposition, we are revolutionaries. This opposition word is problematic…In a democracy, there are parties, and you look at their programs, and you choose whichever is better. We have the voting as well. For the last 40 years, there has been no one who can go against Asad. If I want to say I will be president, there is no such thing. You go, there is a secret room, and there are cameras. There is Asad's name, and there is a "yes," and there is a "no." If you marked the "no," the person sitting next to the room opened the door and said, 'Did you say no? This is wrong! Give me another paper [ticket]!' He put a mark under the yes. We had a play depicting this. Asad always gets 99.99%. You live in a country like this, and you will endure this kind of tension. There is no other party, so you cannot do [anything]. Only there is Ba'ath party, and they can do anything. So, there is no chance. [But] it is over, the world has changed. You [regime/Asad] cannot do what you did in the 1980s [referring to Hama]. (Ziad)

Ziad's point about the difference between opposition vs. revolutionaries is connected to the political system. He finds "opposition" more suitable for systems with at least a minimum procedural democracy. Opposition occurs when "non-state actors within the state collectively threaten to or actually impose costs on the ruling entity to incentivize the government to change a status quo policy, treatment, power allocation, resource distribution, etc." (Ritter and Conrad, 2016, p. 5 in deMeritt 2016, p. 7). Many narratives like Ziad's show that the decades-long repression in Syria in terms of political access was the source of conflict:

> The Asad regime was not equal to the Syrian people, there was so much oppression. We did not feel comfortable. We wanted the right to say we do not want you as the president. We wanted to choose who we wanted [as president], but they did not allow us to do this. (Alaa)

Alaa's experience of being silenced about her rejection of being governed by Assad and Ziad's experience at the ballot box falls outside of accepted standards of judicial and administrative behavior related to the political beliefs of the person involved (Davenport 2007, p. 3).

Interviewees often expressed this profound concern about the repression and limitations imposed on freedom of expression in informal, everyday settings. This repression significantly altered their ability to communicate authentically and engage openly with others.

> You cannot talk about politics in the streets. You cannot gather in 10-15 people groups in the streets, they would immediately break it up. No one did things as a group, even if it was not about politics. If a group of people got together and did something, it would grab attention…There was no legal system. The law was always on the side of the rich and powerful. (Bilal)

Many talked about a deep fear of being reported to the intelligence. This made them very careful of what to say, even in their own homes. Husam talks about this as "walls have ears," and Ahlaam uses a similar expression pulled from her memories: "When my dad wanted to talk about politics, I remember my mom ran over the house and closed everything [doors, windows], and she said, 'the doors have ears.'"

The third aspect of life interviewees felt repressed was a tight grip on social and professional life. Every aspect of life was strictly monitored by the regime. A common theme was the strict censorship of any form of expression. Nour (Sunni Arab, single, 31, traumatized by having her father in prison for long years of her childhood), who volunteered to work with kids, had to send all the written material, including songs, to the *Mukhabarat* for screening.

Fatima (29) removed her hijab after coming to Türkiye. She felt a lack of possibility for different expressions and alternative ideas while she was a student in Syria. As a young woman with leftist political ideas, she was discouraged from expressing herself. She was a volunteer in the *Democratic Youth Union*, an organization recognized by the state, but all the activities of the Union were closely monitored and reported. While some ideas in this Union resembled hers, she found them to be copies of the regime without being open to new ideas. Fatima was bothered by all aspects of life being controlled by the regime, desired to reach alternative expressions and thinking, and needed to experience a becoming that was not dictated by the government. Fahed, who was working in the education field, experienced a similar strict control and stressed that Türkiye was less strict:

> Civil society was covered by the intelligence. We were a Syrian NGO in Syria, but for any work for people to be done, we needed to sign a paper for the intelligence… The center of the conflict is oppression. Everything else runs around it. We will finish the *zulm*, and the rest will not be hard to solve. We should start from the roots, not just from people. Intelligence and military should be built to serve people, not to spy on them. Intelligence [exists] around the world, but it is different when it works only just for one family. (Fahed)

Finally, people experienced repression in terms of organizing against the regime. Haya explains how other students reported and got her into trouble for keeping revolution-related brochures in her dorm. Even though the police searched but could not find the brochures, her friends discouraged her from going to the demonstrations:

> My friend said, 'If you have the brochures, get rid of them and do not go to the demonstrations. Our solution is not in the demonstrations. Once you get arrested, you are raped. Once you are raped, people are going to start talking about you. Just think about it, you are in an Eastern community as a raped girl.' I had an activist friend, who conducted interviews with raped girls. One was kicked out of the house just because some people asked, 'Do you have raped girls in your houses.' So, it is a bad idea to go to demonstrations in the first place.

Haya's words reflect the fear of many others. In addition to rape, parents were afraid of their children being hurt. In turn, younger generations were fearful either to put their families in danger or to have their parents suffer seeing their children in trouble.

Farah explains the fear of talking about the regime by focusing on her parents during the uprising. Before the revolution, Farah's parents shared their negative views of the regime at home, leading her to dislike the regime. However, things changed at the start of the uprising:

> When the revolution started, my family took a step back and became more neutral. They were like, 'ok, we only want peace and security.' They were really afraid. That is when my friends and I started to talk about the regime. But it became a real taboo to talk about it even in front of your family because they got afraid for you. They are like, 'Shut your mouth now and don't talk about it.' (Farah)

Opposite to Farah's, a considerable number of other families were silent throughout the years until the younger generations got older. They broke their silence after seeing their children develop hopes and expectations when Bashar Asad came to power. Political repression infused so deeply into society that people refrained from critically talking about the regime for many years. Miriam, who was against the uprising, argues:

> No one would talk politics before the conflict. I do not know any person who would talk politics out of fear that they would be reported to intelligence. [Once taken] no one knew if the taken person was dead or in prison. [Intelligence would] try to get information from the person in custody, but not in a good way [torture]. You would not know what happened to that person anymore. Fine [meaning I accept], it was bad, but it was, like 100 people [who suffered] may be, but now it is not only 100. [Revolution] didn't change for something good; they made it worse [by doing the uprising]. For example, politics was not good, but other things were good. (Mariam)

Due process transgressions and suffering under criminal and civil penalties (Davenport, 2007) not only relate to individual human rights abuses but also send a message to the masses about what would happen if they showed any opposition. Therefore, Mariam's rationalization of a "small portion" of people suffering does not take into account the amount of fear inflicted on the large segments of society. The above examples indicate that some people were silent for a lifetime raising their children until the uprising, and others stopped even talking at home to prevent their children from joining the demonstrations. Mariam was critical to society in terms of not having the courage to speak up out of fear but, in the end, picking up the guns, which turned into a destructive conflict:

> Before the conflict started, I didn't like the president. I was saying it, and even people I know stopped me [and told me], 'They can take you. They can put you in prison.' Who is going to take me? I am sitting in front of you. If they are going to take me, it is one of you who said something [about my oppositional comments]. They said, 'No, do not say anything.' They were not able to say even a word. When the conflict started, they started to be against the president, going out to the streets. However, before the conflict, they were not brave enough to even say a word, so they couldn't do it [revolution] themselves. (Mariam)

People gave different yet connected reasons for this silence. While some participants were very critical of their parents' generation, "acceptance of repression" is a complex and difficult matter. People's fears were deep and justified because they and their family members were persecuted. While people faced limitations on freedom of speech, government reprisal, and due process transgressions, their personal integrity and rights were repressed. There were constant threats toward their "individual survival and security such as freedom from torture, disappearance, imprisonment, extrajudicial execution, and mass killing" (Davenport 2007, p. 2), which included not only themselves but also their loved ones. The following section focuses on the level of political persecution.

Persecution

Persecution can be defined as "the illegitimate infliction of sufficiently severe harm" (Rempell 2013, p. 292) "especially because of race or political or religious beliefs…" (Oxford Dictionary; Badar and Florijančič 2019, p. 656). Accounts from interviewees show that harm happened in many different ways, from torture and imprisonment to psychological ones. Bilal explained that oppositional thinking was not only punishable for the person but also for their families:

> I was always interested in politics, and my father told me not to talk about these things to anyone at school, including my friends. He told me that they would not only finish me but everyone in my family. And he was right. It was the regime's strategy. If they took a person who did a crime [meaning being an opposition], that person would say I would do it for freedom. However, when it is one's family, some people cannot continue [their opposition]. (Bilal)

Bilal's view about silencing through targeting loved ones surfaced in the narratives of participants who came from different social backgrounds. Rouaa has a college degree and was an engineer in Syria. She was traumatized by how close her husband came to being persecuted because of the oppositional politics of her brother-in-law, who lived overseas. Her experience brings Bilal's assessment to a concrete example of how totalitarian systems persecute family members as a strategy to control and keep people in silence:

> In 2013, when I was at my home, four armed men attacked my home. They were from the Syrian regime. They knocked on the door very strongly. I was pregnant, I opened the door. They asked me, 'Where is your husband?' and I inquired, 'What do you want from him?' They said they want to take him…Thank God he was not home…They asked me 'What is the relationship between… [she gives a name and a surname] and your husband?' I told them he was my brother-in-law [husband's brother]. My brother-in-law lives overseas... He has a page on Facebook about Bashar Asad's crimes and his massacres. They told me that they wanted to take my husband to their branch. I knew that if they caught him, he wouldn't be back. They would kill him because the same thing happened to my friend's husband. They caught and later killed him. One year later she discovered that he was dead. When Bashar Al-Asad's men catch a man, they put him in jail, and without food, he suffers so much. I wanted to rescue my husband. Of course, if they caught my husband, they would have killed him… Bashar Asad's regime, if they saw any ideas or emotions expressed against them, and if one had a relationship with anyone who worked with the opposition or spoke about Asad, they would arrest and kill him. (Rouaa)

In addition to Bilal's and Rouaa's pointing out the structure of the political system and collective punishments toward family members, many other participants explained the reason for the silence, pointing out past traumas and fears particularly mass killings in Hama that included women and children.

The deep fear about political ideas being expressed also has a strong connection to imprisonment stories that people knew about others or experienced themselves. Ayman, who was from Idlib, explains the reasons for growing up being silent toward the regime:

> My father, in the 1990s, was imprisoned. Why? He wrote an article about the president saying how arrogant a man he is without mentioning his name. They took my father for two years. I was young, and if I spoke about the government, my mother pinched me [he shows his arm]. 'Do not even try to say words about the president. It is forbidden,' she said. What if you speak, and someone hears? We grew up like that. All of us… They say that the children wrote on the wall [in Dar'aa], but what was the reason? What happened before that? People did not just say, 'Let's have a revolution and find another president.' No, there is something that Bashar and his regime did that affected people badly, and because of that, they started this revolution… Some people's relatives were in prison for 30 years. 30 years! Some of them died [in prison] …They were raping the girls in the university. They were taking your property, taking anything of yours they wanted. It is something you cannot imagine. Let me tell you just one story so you will understand they are unlike others. If you are driving your car and you pass another car that turns out to be the Prime Minister's car, he will take out his gun and kill you, and it is ok because he is drunk... I can tell you a thousand stories…. My father was in a cell with another person, and he discovered that his cellmate was a big [high-ranked] Alawite officer in the army. Why was he in prison? Because he spoke about the horse of the son of the president and said, 'The horse is eating walnuts more than us.' You are living in a country where you cannot say, 'ok, let me have a try. Maybe I am better than you at leading this country.' NO! Everything has to be for them. (Ayman, 24, student)

As seen in Ayman's account, personal stories of victimization expand to include stories of others being severely punished. People's personal stories become narratives about the reality of the community as they articulate their victimization by connecting it to others. Similar to Ayman's trauma, Nour was also greatly influenced by the imprisonment of her father. Nour's father, a member of the Muslim Brotherhood, was in prison for 9 years, starting when she was a toddler. Her story moves from personal resentment of Hafez Asad for sending her father to prison to being in fear of expressing her views, as it was well known that many people disappeared. Reem, who was arrested at age 15 for 9 years, gave the reason for her arrest:

> During the 1980s, when the Muslim Brotherhood problem existed, I was in the school, and they took me from the exam room. They took me because they said I was praying and giving my friends religious books. After one year, they sent me to court, and the court announced that I should be in prison for four years. After four years were finished, they kept me for five more years for security reasons. I was the youngest prisoner in that space. (Reem)

While Reem's father, who was a communist party member in the past, never changed his approach to his daughter, for Reem, one of the most difficult things was growing up separated from her brothers, who were to this day emotionally distant and very formal with her, referring to her as "Mrs. Reem." Reem was deeply saddened that being persecuted and treated badly in prison had the additional cost of being completely cut off from family, only seeing them four times between 1981 and 1986 and not at all for another 4 years. More than what she went through in prison, she talked about the loss of connection with her family and yearning for a close relationship that seemed unattainable.

Arrest of young women continued from Hafez Asad to Bashar Asad's time. Rashid's narrative signals that an important cause of one of the demonstrations was a protest against political imprisonment:

> People from the beginning did not know what they wanted, but they knew something was wrong. We wanted freedom, and we wanted the arrested people to be freed from the prison. There was a very famous woman, her name is Tal Al-Mallouhi. She is a girl between 20 and 22 years old. We heard from the news that the regime arrested her, and they said her crime was that she was working with Israel. But she was writing [in her blog] about the freedom of speech and aggressive actions the regime was applying to us. We wanted her to be freed. We did not yell that we want the regime to collapse. We put some subjects from the Syrian constitution [to be changed]. Then we understood that the regime would not react to us in a good way, and we wanted him to collapse. (Rashid)

Born in 1991, Tal-Al Mallouhi was a regime-critical poet-blogger at the time of her arrest in 2009, before the demonstrations started. After 15 years, as of December 2024, with the collapse of the regime, she was released (NDTV 2024).

Zeinab talked about her and her husband's arrest by the regime. Her husband was working with a human rights organization, which made him a target of the regime. Even though they were fearful, they joined the demonstrations, never expecting it to become an armed struggle. In 2011, during a meeting in her husband's office, the security members stormed the office, destroyed everything, and arrested them. Zeinab went through psychological torture during her interrogation as they threatened her with the well-being of her children. She was also deeply traumatized and felt severe guilt by the way her children had lasting effects of the deep fear they lived through with the arrest of both parents. Zeinab, moving from her experience, further explains the reaction and resentment that was felt for political persecutions people faced:

> It was forbidden to say anything. When the regime says something, we must say yes. Why did the regime put good people in prisons? Why are the good writers and educated are in

> prison in Syria? Why is everything forbidden in Syria? Why is everything for the regime and nothing for the people? People lost everything. The revolution did not start from nothing. They started from the suffering and sadness. (Zeinab)

For differently located people, joining the demonstrations was also challenging because of the fear of being detained. Firas explains why he wanted to be part of the demonstrations and why he could not continue participating:

> The feeling of freedom was getting very close and [promise of] democracy, it was like a high adrenaline feeling. Those moments were delightful and thrilling. But I could not join more [than a few times] because you do not want to lose your life. [Life is] very, very cheap, and [you] get detained. I had many friends who got detained and I do not know anything about their whereabouts until now. I do not know anything about them or what happened to them. I feel really, really sad about it. Angry, sad, mixture of both. Very difficult for their families. Some got detained for a few months, and they got released, but others, we do not know [what happened to them]. As you may know, many get tortured to death in prisons in Syria. (Firas)

Systemic persecution throughout the years and a lack of accommodating response from the government at the beginning of the demonstrations created a destructive conflict. At the time of the interviews, it was 5 years into the civil war, and the existing government continued to hold power (and was in power until December 2024). What is the consequence of persecuting people for decades once the power shifts hands? This is the question awaiting Syria after the collapse of the Asad regime. Many people who were forced to leave their country experienced increased resentment toward the regime and its supporters. At the time of the interviews, some made predictions that did not project a bright picture. Nawar was surprised at how much people focused and prayed to win the war and observed that "Some are driven, and even if the war is finished, they will follow Alawites and kill them." Nawar argues that while the war is presented as being between the Sunni and the Shi'a, too many Sunnis supported the Asad regime, and many Shi'a or Alawites, including his friends, supported the revolution. Nawar, as a person who saw the complexities and intra-group differences, which made him move away from simplistic and binary formulations, agonized as he argued, "But not even those Alawites who support the revolution will be forgiven. Resentment is so strong in society." Nawar is not alone in his worry that resentment and violence against Alawites can increase in the future. Camil is also worried that Alawites are going to become targets. While not wanting to overgeneralize, Camil argues that the majority of Alawites are perceived to be pro-regime due to the regime's choice of presenting Alawites as the beneficiaries of the system. In terms of population, Camil sees Alawites as the biggest losers compared to all other people in Syria, as "thousands of them were killed and will be killed in the future."

Kaufman (2001), giving former Yugoslavia as an example, shows how simmering and renewed resentments can intensify conflicts. Nawar and Camil's words are warnings for foreseeing new dimensions to the conflict where previous grievances and resentments will set the tone for the future. Works of fiction and academic analysis of these works address the danger of the continuation of a "vicious circle of oppression" in Syria if solutions for solidarity are not formulated (Al Natour 2022, p. 79).

For more than five decades, Syria underwent the tyranny of a secular minority sect. However, within Alawite, a distinct group was the main beneficiary of the system. Syria now has a Sunni government; the rule is seemingly on the majority. However, the extent to which the majority of the Sunni will benefit must be scrutinized. There are different Sunni factions, including the secular Sunnis whose future in Syria is unknown, similar to many Alawites who were against the regime. Syria may find itself in a condition where the names of governments have changed, but the governance ideology remains intact.

Identity Domination and Oppression

At the beginning of the chapter, I argued that stereotypes and prejudices develop under the state-projected light, which prepares the ground for silencing and oppressing different identity groups. Once individuals focus on one dominant salient identity and have a prejudicial attitude toward others, communal solidarity can be easily broken. Authoritarian-structured, centralized single-party rule was consolidated under Hafez Asad's Ba'ath and became a supreme political institution where the army and the police controlled every aspect of the public sphere (Haklai 2000, p. 35) and dominated and oppressed different identity groups. This section focuses on the close interplay between domination (institutional constraints on self-determination) and oppression (institutional constraints of self-development). Lack of autonomy directly weakens the likelihood of self-development. Oppressive practices show their face in different facets of ethnic, linguistic, and citizenship rights.

Aykut, who was economically privileged and educated, experienced hardships in his self-development in terms of ethnic identity. As an ethnic minority, he was told that he had to "endure" problems in government offices because his name was not Arabic. His memories as a schoolboy also reflect oppressive practices:

> We are Syrians, but our blood is Turk... Only because my name is a Turkish name at school and other places, I was insulted, especially by the members of the Ba'ath Party. I have a memory from 10th grade. In the Arabic lesson, my teacher was telling the students the grades. I had the second-highest grade. He called my full name without telling me my grade. Instead, he asked me why I had this name. The Party sent Ba'athist teachers to all the schools. I said because I am a Turkish-origin, Syrian citizen. In front of all the other students, he told me, 'You eat this nation's bread and drink its water. How can you say such a thing? You are a Syrian. How can you add Türkiye?' The regime injected these ideas into all schools. (Aykut)

Turkmen identity in the rural areas had different kinds of barriers to their self-development than what Aykut depicts above as a city dweller. Aisha brings a different experience as a villager who had difficulty having access to Arabic:

> My children could not study much. Only one of my sons studied until the last year of high school, but my daughters did not study at all. They did not know Arabic, which is why they

could not study. Generally, we speak Turkish at home, and we do not go out too much, which is why they could not learn Arabic. Very similar to how you cannot speak Arabic. But at school, there is no Turkish at all. It is all Arabic. (Aisha)

Domination and oppression of ethnic minorities were common. Firas, moving from his family's experience, explained how Kurdish identity was assimilated into Arab culture:

During the 60s and 70s, like Türkiye, they did not allow Kurdish to integrate that much or speak or teach the language in Syria because of Arab nationalism. You can say that there is suppression of identity. In my opinion, even my friends who are Kurdish and know Kurdish are not allowed to speak Kurdish inside the military service. [They can speak] only Arabic. Also, they are not allowed to teach the language. They cannot open schools in Syria. You could say the culture is oppressed. (Firas)

While some people argued that there were no differentiations in terms of ethnic or religious/sectarian lines such as Arabs, Kurds, Sunnis, and Alawites, Afran argued that such identity differences and oppression always existed giving the [Newruz/Nowruz holiday][3] restrictions and prevention of celebrations as an example and she adds:

There was always discrimination and racism against Kurds. Suddenly, in 2011, at the start of the revolution, the government started saying the Kurds are our people, we are brothers. They even said that Nowruz is a celebration and festival that we admit exists and exists for Kurds. Yet, when you open my ID card, it does not say that I am a Kurd. We are not registered with the government as Kurds. We are all [considered] Arab Syrians. (Afran, trans-woman, 27, from Aleppo, college educated, works at an NGO)

Jiwan summarizes the political oppression of Kurdish identity:

We, as Kurds, cannot participate in government, neither to an executive nor to a legislative part. The regime removed 500-thousand Kurds from citizenship; they do not have ID. They do not announce them as Kurds legally in their laws in Syria. There has been no announcement from the Kurdish political parties. There are no Kurdish newspapers or Kurdish schools. I put my name in the 2003 parliamentary elections. One of the intelligence members told me, 'You put your name, but even if the whole of China votes for you, you won't be a parliamentarian in a people council because you are not from the Al-Ba'ath party.' But there were Kurds in the parliament. They were representing the Ba'ath party. They were the members of the Ba'ath party, and they changed the names of the Kurdish villages. The regime never allowed any Kurd to be an employee in any sensitive position. In the time of Ba'ath, Kurdish songs, even the songs were forbidden. (Jiwan, 45, from Raqqa, lawyer)

While Husam felt at home in Syria and mostly considered himself a Syrian, he also experienced being an "outsider within" (Collins 2002) and a certain level of discrimination due to his identity as a Palestinian second-generation refugee in Syria:

We stayed and lived in Syria for almost 64 years without having a nationality. On our daily ID cards, they wrote above our pictures, 'Permit resident for Palestinian refugees.' Almost for 64 years, they did not give us a choice to elect. We did not have election votes. We did

[3] Celebration of the arrival of spring and the new year. For the historical meaning and the Syrian government's suppression of the holiday, see Yildiz (2005, pp. 119–120).

> not have rights as Syrians. Palestinian citizens could get one house, one car, and one shop. But to be honest, they dealt with us almost like Syrians. I am Palestinian, but inside, I feel like I am Syrian because I lived all my life in Aleppo. (Husam)

The above segments show that, in many different ways, ethnic, linguistic, and citizenship rights were denied. When the right to make decisions on one's future is denied, that is domination. Once people's choices are dominated, the practice becomes oppressive as their self-actualization is denied through lack of access to education, jobs, representation, and cultural and linguistic development within their chosen identities.

This chapter explored the underlying causes of the conflict and argued that the state, as the main actor in controlling socioeconomic and political life through its apparatuses, first encourages and constructs negative stereotypes and prejudices among groups, putting them into competition by giving them different levels of access. Once communal solidarity is eliminated, the state uses repression and persecution to dominate and oppress them. Such a coercive approach becomes the cause of the conflict. Multiple layers of oppression and discrimination are factors in the destructiveness of conflicts. The next chapter will continue to explore state behavior as a cause of conflict, this time turning the lens to structural inequalities of poverty, class-based discrimination, and economic oppression.

References

Al Natour M (2022) Home, identity, and place in Syrian literature: Maha Hassan's drums of love and Ghassan Jubbaʿi's Qahwat Al-general. Contemp Levant 7(1):66–80

Althusser L (2006) Ideology and ideological state apparatuses (notes towards an investigation). In: Sharma A, Gupta A (eds) The anthropology of the state: a reader. Blackwell Publishing, Carlton, pp 86–98

Badar M, Florijančič P (2019) Assessing incitement to hatred as a crime against humanity of persecution. Int J Human Rights 24(5):656–687

Bogaards M (2019) Consociationalism and centripetalism: friends or foes? Swiss Polit Sci Rev 25(4):519–537

Bozarslan H (2004) Violence in the Middle East. From political struggle to self-sacrifice. Markus Wiener Publishers, Princeton

Brewer MB, Pierce KP (2005) Social identity complexity and out-group tolerance. Personal Soc Psychol Bull 31:428–437

Chenoweth E, Perkoski E, Kang S (2017) State repression and nonviolent resistance. J Confl Resolut 61(9):1950–1969

Collin RO (2009) Words of war: The Iraqi tower of Babel. Int Stud Perspectives 10(3):245–264

Collins PH (2002) Black feminist thought: knowledge, consciousness, and the politics of empowerment. Routledge, London

Davenport C (2007) State repression and political order. Annu Rev Polit Sci 10:1–23

DeMeritt JHR (2016) The strategic use of state repression and political violence. Oxford research encyclopedia of politics. Oxford University Press, New York

Haklai O (2000) A minority rule over a hostile majority: the case of Syria. Nationalism Ethnic Politics 6(3):19–50

Kaufman SJ (2001) Modern hatreds: the symbolic politics of ethnic war. Cornell University Press, Ithaca

Lijphart A (1977) Democracy in plural societies: a comparative exploration. Yale University Press, New Haven
Migdal JS (1994) The state in society: an approach to struggles for domination. In: Migdal JS, Kohli A, Shue V (eds) State power and social forces: domination and transformation in the third world. Cambridge University Press, Cambridge, pp 7–34
NDTV (2024) Syrian female blogger freed from Assad jails https://www.ndtv.com/world-news/syrian-female-blogger-freed-from-assad-jails-mother-7222961
Pearlman WR (2017) We crossed a bridge and it trembled: Voices from Syria. Custom House (e-book version)
Pearson FS, Lounsbery MO (2020) Structure-agency, social justice, nonviolence, and relationship building. In: Byrne S, Matyók T, Scott IM, Senehi J (eds) Routledge companion to peace and conflict studies. Routledge, London, pp 81–92
Reilly JA (2018) Fragile nation, shattered land: The modern history of Syria. I.B. Tauris and Co, London (e-book version)
Rempell S (2013) Defining persecution. Utah Law Rev 1:283–244
Ritter EH, Conrad C (2016) Preventing and responding to dissent: the observational challenges of explaining strategic repression. Am Polit Sci Rev 110(1):85–99
Skocpol T (1979) States and social revolutions: a comparative analysis of France, Russia and China. Cambridge University Press, Cambridge
Taylor E (2016) Groups and oppression. Hypatia 31(3):520–536
Tejel J (2009) Syria's Kurds: history, politics and society. Routledge, New York
Yildiz K (2005) The Kurds in Syria: the forgotten people. Pluto Press, London

Chapter 6
Economic Instability

Causes of the Conflict: Poverty, Class Discrimination, Economic Oppression

Economic inequalities that disrupt the social fabric are crucial to understanding the Syrian conflict. Unequal distribution of resources and deep income gaps among different groups were particularly important. Poverty was prevalent in Syria, especially in the rural areas, supplemented with deep class discrimination despite the Ba'ath party's alleged socialist equality. In turn, cities had their own problems due to economic oppression that monopolized the financial gains in the hands of the ruling elite through bribing and bureaucratic hurdles. Hafez al-Asad created a complex system in which Sunnis, Kurds, and Christians engaged with small industry, business, and trade while paying their dues to the Asad's ruling class. Also, during his reign, the welfare state, despite its limitations, elevated the working class to certain degrees. Nevertheless, the neoliberal economic reforms after him abandoned the Ba'ath Party's traditional working-class base and concentrated wealth and power in the hands of even a smaller number of government elites. These policies caused increased unemployment, cutbacks in state subsidiaries and services, weakened the infrastructure, and deepened poverty and inequality (Pearlman 2017, p. 27; see also Hinnebusch 2018, p. 396). At the same time, the nature of the new generation rural populations was changing, and they were in need of political and economic empowerment, which they were denied (Imady 2014). Poor supported the uprising for economic and class reasons with the expectation of having a better life, while those segments of society with relatively better-off financial conditions supported the uprising with incentives of dignity and more opportunities. Nevertheless, the war eventually worsened everything, reducing living standards and making people seek basic needs.

© The Author(s), under exclusive license to Springer Nature Singapore Pte Ltd. 2025

U. Ozkaleli, *De-essentializing Refugees: Perceptions, Experiences, and Becoming of Syrians in Türkiye*, https://doi.org/10.1007/978-981-96-5519-9_6

I analyze poverty and class discrimination separately from economic oppression. The reason is that not only lower classes but also middle-class and small business owners suffered from divisive policies of the state, but different classes suffered at various levels and depths. First, experiences of poverty and class discrimination will be examined to show how they are intertwined with the ethnic, religious, and sectarian positioning of individuals. Second, economic oppression within the same economic class will be scrutinized. Proximity to the regime determined who economically benefited from the system and who was othered. Those who benefited were not only decided by ethnic lines. Among the Sunnis "... capitalists who had benefited from political connections to enrich themselves did not generally abandon the regime, indeed, some of them actually financed pro-regime militias" (Imady and Hinnebusch 2018, p. 329). In the end, war made everybody face deeper issues, which led to comparing what has become to what it used to be in Syria.

Poverty and Class Discrimination

Some participants in this study analyzed the conflict from class dimensions and poverty. Born in the late 1940s, Suad spent her childhood years within the early period of Syria's independence. Suad's memories of her childhood in Hama indicate that enduring class discrimination was inherited from colonial times:

> I do not like oppression (*zulm*) or seeing people beneath oneself. We were raised in a neighborhood where very well-known families who owned a lot of land were living. I saw how they acted with peasants or people who worked for them. I did not like the reactions the [affluent] were giving or how they behaved towards peasants and workers. Actually, and honestly, I liked the communist ideas so much because their ideas are the same [egalitarian regarding the treatment of peasants and workers]. (Suad)

Suad's life experience spanned various political eras in Syria, including the early times when Alawites faced discrimination as peasants and lower-income people. As discussed earlier, in another part of the interview, she said the domestic workers at that time were Alawites. Suad witnessed a house owner's violence toward a worker who was building his house, which deeply affected and shaped her views. From an early age, she rejected the undignified and violent way people were treated. Before Hafez Assad came to power, the Ba'ath Party rose during her teenage years. In the early formations of Ba'ath, she developed sympathy for the ideas through her observations of class differences. While never formally joining the communist party, she continued to like the ideas as she saw respect shown to all people:

> Our neighbor was sitting in front of our house. A person brought vegetables and stuff to him with his donkey. I saw him kicking this person and throwing the vegetables onto the ground. Since that moment, I hated these ideas [that repressed the poor]. I also remember another guy in our neighborhood who kicked the peasants who came to his house during Ramadan. He also went out and hit the Ramazan drummer [traditionally, a drummer walks around to wake people up for a meal before the sun rises] and told him, 'Go away, we do not fast.' Then, we did not see the drummer ever again. That is why when I met the communists,

communist principles and ideas [I liked it]. My sister's husband was a real communist, and my brothers were also real communists. I saw that they were acting kindly towards people. They had norms [principles], ideas, and respected people. My sister's husband respected even the little kids like they were adults.

Suad's narrative differentiated communists from the Asad regime, arguing that discrimination and inequalities became central to politics after Asad assumed power.

In pre-war Syria, some participants were not facing financial difficulties themselves but were aware of class differences and the poverty experienced by others. Malak argued that she and her family were comfortable and financially secure, but there were many poor people under the Asad regime. Hasan claimed that Aleppo had two parts regarding opportunities and access: the West and the East. He states, "When we enjoyed the West part of Aleppo, the people in the East suffered. Why should we live a normal life when the others are in a miserable situation?"

Aykut analyzed the roots of conflict from the class perspective by comparing changes in Hafez and Bashar Asad's times:

[Before,] people in Syria could find bread easily, but if they asked for more than bread, it would be very difficult to find. They could just survive. The middle classes, of course, disappeared very fast, right after Hafez al-Asad died and Bashar al-Asad came to power. (Aykut)

Genwa also pointed out how the middle class was getting weaker in pre-war Syria:

You can barely make the ends meet until the end of the month. You cannot think about buying a house for yourself or your children. I am talking about middle-class people. I am not even talking about the poor people. (Genwa, 47, female, from Aleppo, college educated, leading an NGO)

Khalwa's account shows the struggle of the urban working poor, people who worked and still struggled to survive:

They did not allow my husband to work. They did not give him any certificate for driving or any standard certificate. I think he had the right to go to the demonstrations. In the end, although he was educated, he started working, traveling, and carrying things. We were almost living [barely making ends meet]. I remember that just one can of milk [became] 280 liras, and daily, he was earning 300 liras. We were feeding our kids, and we were almost living on the rest of the money. I do not want Syria to be like that in the future. (Khawla)

The income gap and poverty depth were the focus of Nazem, who shares the observations that he acquired through his work with the youth:

I did not have any problems because my financial situation was very good. I studied, and I had a good socio-economic level. Nothing was missing in my life. But when I was dealing with people in schools, teenagers, and young people, there were a lot of social problems and a big gap between societal levels. Every level of the society has its own problems. For example, poor people faced discrimination in receiving any money or social justice. On the children's level, there was a lot of illiteracy. There was also the lateness of the services by the government. There were a lot of bad things coming from the administrative and financial side…after social injustice, illiteracy, and administrative and financial problems, it became just two levels in society, and the gap became bigger. This economic gap caused a lot of problems. (Nazem)

Zeinab's assessment of pre-war Syria, in terms of the income gap and depth of poverty, had similarities to Nazem's observations. Yet, she connects poverty and political oppression one to another:

> Before the revolution, everyone worked very hard and cared for their children. It was a hard life. There was poverty on a large scale. The great number of people hit below the poverty line. They had no political rights, of course. If you speak or have political activity, you would be wanted and arrested and stay in the detention centers for no one knows how long. We experienced a lot under this regime. (Zeinab)

Rashid, who worked in humanitarian aid in Latakia, narrates the profile of the rebels, which points out the class dimension. He mentioned that most of the front-line fighters in the conflict were men in poverty:

> I worked in the humanitarian sector…There were a lot of dead people and a lot of people who got arrested. These were poor people from Syria, so if the men died, there would be no one working in these families. There is no one to help them. (Rashid)

While some, like Rashid, Nazem, and Zeinab, were aware of poverty before leaving Syria, others learned the realities of people from other areas after coming to Türkiye and contacting them through their NGO work. As in a previous section, the findings indicate that living as Syrians in a host community made them learn a lot more about other communities in different cities, regions, or neighborhoods. Akila works at an NGO hotline and feels not only sad about their dire situation but also guilty that she did not know people in such poor conditions existed in Syria. Akila's newly developed awareness shows that, in a certain way, meeting as "Syrians" or working "for Syrians" gave people better access to the home realities of different people with whom they had not interacted when inside Syria. When asked why she was not aware that there were poor people in Syria, Akila explained:

> My friend lived in the next street, and another friend lived in a different neighborhood, so those are the neighborhoods that I was used to visiting. Now, when people call me and tell me from which area of Syria they are from, I have not even heard of these places before. I have no way to go there now. I just know that there were these areas. For me, with my work and seeing these people [made me realize] how they are treated. I feel sad, wondering, even if once I treated someone in a racist way. People are equal, rich or poor; they are all equal from this area or that area. If I see someone speak racist, I really feel sorry, like you have to know that people are equal. I feel guilty that maybe in the past, I treated someone that way. I hope they will forgive me. I do not know if I did it, I did not do it on purpose. I may have done it without noticing. I hope they would forgive me if I treated someone unequally or acted as if I were in a higher place. We are all equal. In Türkiye, I do see a bit of racism among my friends. (Akila)

Perhaps being positioned as a refugee creates a moment of reflection, and she questions her previous behavior in her pre-war life. Akila, in general, was disturbed about the racism Syrians faced in the receiving community, Türkiye. Her awareness about issues of racism increased, which made her look back and recognize class-based discrimination that existed in pre-war Syria. Her guilt is reflected in understanding what it means to be discriminated against and being aware of the conditions of people in poverty. "Becoming a refugee" is a shared experience by all, bonding them to the common Syrian identity.

Amez's narrative explains discrimination at the intersection of ethnic and class identity:

> The first day I knew it was a civil war was when I went to my faculty and was asked to show my ID. They saw my name; it was fine. It is not a Muslim Brother-originated or sectarian name, so it was fine. Meanwhile, all the 'Muhammads' and 'Abdullahs' were left aside to be inspected. It was ok for me to get in. Students who came with cars weren't inspected. Neither were those with money. Only poor people would be inspected. Muslim people who came from the villages would be inspected. When I saw this, well [I knew] it was going to be bad. (Amez)

While Amez witnessed the stopping of students at the university and saw a select people being targeted for questioning, Ziad was focused on soldiers' behavior toward the students:

> What I could not stand was the police would order the university students. I am sorry, but people who could not spell a word would stand in front of our university and sit one leg over the other, eyeing girls. After calling a student near them, the soldier hits the student's hand, which was in his pocket, with a stick. He said to him, 'When you are talking to me, raise your hand.' I saw this with my own eyes. These soldiers, if you look at their faces, are horrible people, and this university student needs to be [respecting him]. Here are the police, who cannot even spell a word, yet are asking a university student about this. They did not know where they were standing [not know their place]. These affected me so much. I have seen it with my own eyes. People who did not have two pennyworth of knowledge treated university kids this way. (Ziad)

Ziad's anger and frustration about the disrespect shown by the police to the student demonstrators came mostly from the status he attached to the police in terms of knowledge and skills rather than the violation of freedom of expression. This could signal a possibility of young police officers being elected from the silenced underprivileged groups who found a level of power through their police status. Such dynamics make it easier to encourage violent treatment of college students. In a reverse way, such class dynamic is reflected in Waseem's narrative. As a regime supporter, he blames the poor for rebelling against the regime. Waseem, who strongly supports Bashar Asad and the Syrian government, refuses to call what was happening a "revolution." He states, "At the beginning of what they called the Syrian revolution, we discovered them; they were 100% wrong." When asked what he calls it, if not revolution, he elaborates, "I call it the revolution of the villages against the cities." Waseem says he came from a "very rich family" whose factory got destroyed by the rebels, and as their house was located in a "hot point," they could not access their house anymore. Waseem was remorseful that the rich segment, like his family, was slowly losing their wealth. He felt deprived as he argued that his family had big plans in business, but because of the war, they found themselves at the bottom:

> The rebellion started with the demonstrations in Syria, but it was not all of Syria. It was just some areas. We saw that the poor, not the good poor, but the bad poor in Syria, started all of this. It went to the suburbs, the villages, and the cities. They tried to transform all of this to the city, but the people who lived in the city did not respond very fast with them. They tried many things like cutting the roads, kidnapping the businessmen and destroying everything, and sometimes even burning things in the city. (Waseem)

When I asked him who are the "good poor" and the "bad poor," he replied:

> The good poor [are] those who work and want to feed their family with *halal* [lawful, honest] money and do not want to destroy anything. They do not want to get money in many ways, like killing, stealing, or kidnapping. The bad poor like to destroy, kidnap, and kill just for the money. 50% of them [who started the demonstrations] are criminals, and those criminals are 100% criminals. (Waseem)

He did not include any explanation about what the good poor were suffering from. Neither did he mention if the poor had any demands or grievances or what the issues of the remaining 50%, whom he did not refer to as criminal, were. His narrative indicates that as long as the poor worked without a complaint and did not rebel, they were "good poor." Also, in his narrative, there is no room for people who left Syria and became urban refugees who suffered severe poverty:

> I would like to say a couple of things. I want to tell you something about the poor, not the good poor, but the dirty poor. The good poor stayed in Syria. He is alive in Syria, defending his country, but the dirty poor became rich, and he became dirtier than before. The rich people, the people in good situations, became poor people, and all the balance is now upside down. Something else I would like to add. In the revolution, *in their revolution*, they started wrong, and they stayed on the wrong road. This revolution is about kidnapping, and it is not a revolution. We faced, in our family, kidnapping. They stole our cars, they stole our factories, so it is not a revolution. (Waseem)

For his family's loss of status in Syria, Waseem blames the villagers:

> Not all the villagers are against us. But who started to destroy all the cities in Syria, not just in Aleppo, at first were the villages, unfortunately. A couple of villages were the main cause of this [uprising]. I think it is because they used to come to the cities to work. The people who have firms and factories used to refuse them just because they are from the villages, so I think they took their revenge this way. Even in the last time before the revolution, there were a lot of powerful projects in the villages, like shopping malls and many other things, and land prices increased very fast. If one sq meter was [worth] 100 dollars, it became 1000 dollars. If someone had a small, cheap land, it became very expensive after a while. Because many malls, firms, and factories were built in the villages, it became powerful, not just for agriculture. (Waseem)

While his own explanation signals a prejudice and discrimination toward the villagers, Waseem's narrative is silent about the causes of their "resentment." It is true that the Da'raa incident was "fueled partly by local grievances. For many rural Syrians, both Damascus and Aleppo were distant both in mileage and in connection to their lives, and the anger of their protests partly reflected their disdain for the urban areas and the political system that had for centuries favored the city" (Sorenson 2016, p. 4). Waseem's narrative depicts the poor who migrated to cities in search of jobs but faced rejection solely due to their rural origins, as perceived by the city's affluent businesspeople. Deep income gaps and discrimination for employment based on their origins need to be problematized and seen as a cause of conflict. With the flowed liberalization of the economy, there was an appearance of growing wealth in major cities, yet this did not reflect in widespread segments of society as inequalities deepened and corruption increased (Hokayem 2013, p. 15).

Mariam, who argued that she did not idealize Bashar Asad, still gave some recognition to the legitimacy of the Syrian government. She was against the Free Army. While some other participants talked about the poverty level in Syria, even though they were not experiencing poverty, Mariam defined Syria as being without poverty. Similar to Waseem, she did not talk about the conditions of either the countryside or the urban poor when she evaluated demands that came from the villages:

> Everything was cheap [in pre-war Syria]. Food, cafes and restaurants, gas, and everything was so affordable. It was not like now; prices go up now. They wanted freedom, and who was asking for freedom? The countryside people. On the one hand, they demanded freedom; on the other, they did not even like their daughters attending school. Yet they are asking for freedom. They want freedom of what? They don't know what freedom is; they do not know what this word means. Their daughters go to just one or two classes to learn how to read in case they need to buy something like medicine. They sent [daughters] to school for their own interest, not because she wanted to study. People like teachers and students did not only demand freedom, they were also saying what they wanted. However, a big percentage was from the countryside, which then became the Free Army. They started to steal from homes, like money and electronic stuff. They were still asking for freedom. (Mariam)

In Mariam's world, where the goods were "cheap," it was presented as a general reality for all while it was relative to the class condition. Neither the above account that Nazem, Genwa, and Zeinab observed about the severe poverty of others nor the personal stories of Khalwa about the shrinking buying power of the working poor was included in Mariam's definition of conditions in pre-war Syria. Studies about the uprising, similar to Waseem and Miriam's depictions, also indicate that the rural and periphery of the urban were the first to join the uprising, and Aleppo and Damascus, as the largest two cities, were the last (Hokayem 2013). Nevertheless, the analysis needs to involve the shifting relationship of the government with rural and urban. Both Mariam and Waseem's view of the rural dismisses different experiences due to the vast economic gap between the rural and urban. The government neglected rural areas and favored urban-centered development,[1] even though they previously were the regime's backbone (Hokayem 2013). Some of the causes of rural discontent include "overall deterioration of the agricultural industry, the lack of public policies to help rural workers adapt to new market conditions, and the devastating effects and public mismanagement of a drought that affected millions of farming families from 2006-2011" (Hokayem, 2013, p. 19) along with "visible withdrawal of the state and the degradation of social services, infrastructure, and employment opportunities" (Hokayem, 2013, p. 28).

The class dimension of "demanding" is striking in both Waseem's and Mariam's perceptions. The group of students and teachers had a degree of justification for Mariam, just like Waseem gave a 50% estimate of some people who were demonstrating that they were not "bad."

---

[1] The Syrian government missed opportunities for creating microfinance networks and dismantling such networks increased the political and economic marginalization of Syrian rural populations (Imady 2014).

For Mariam, the countryside people, as a collectivity, did not know what freedom was, and they all did not want their female children to study beyond a level of survival for their father's benefit. "How can people [men] who especially have no gender equality perspective be truly located in projects of freedom?" A strong class-based judgment here needs to be evaluated along with a gender lens. Mariam did not have direct interaction or experience with people who were located in the countryside, but she had firm opinions about what they knew and did not know and their aspirations for their children. While patriarchy continuously feeds the hegemonic masculinity (Connell and Messerschmidt 2005) by attributing characteristics such as power, capability, and control, structurally, in the rural and urban periphery, men are weaker, particularly in terms of economic access. If, for example, there is not enough money to afford education or send children to distant school locations due to a lack of schools in villages, more than anything else, the underlying reason for girls being held back from schooling is a lack of economic resources. Putting this reason forward, however, means that men must tell their families and outsiders that they do not have the means to send their daughters to school. Oftentimes, excuses like "tradition," "religion," and "mentality" become shields, giving a man a sense of control and power over the education decision.

Author Eye-Camera: Focusing on "illiteracy, ignorance, lack of knowledge" is not particular to Mariam only. Similar to Mariam's statement, an important generalization about traditional and conservative cultures and fathers has been central to mainstream feminist inquiry. This widespread view is used as an approach even in social policy circles that provides funding for increasing "awareness" for shifting cultures more toward liberalism or making women move beyond these "archaic cultural practices." Economic capabilities often become invisible in how the rural or urban periphery is treated.

Mariam also had a low opinion regarding the "lower classes" in the city, arguing that lower-class men created insecurity for women, particularly at night, making it unsafe for them to be able to walk alone. She argues, "They can be Christians, Muslims, Armenians, they were from *low class*, you do not know what you can expect from them, what they can do." Studies show that her class-based views were widespread and common, influencing perceptions about the uprising. "As the perception among many members of the urban middle and upper classes that the revolution was led by the rural working classes or Islamists, bent on taking Syria backwards, contributed to relative apathy in certain areas" (Hokayem 2013, p. 19).

Mariam's explanation subtly does two things: first, blame is placed on the people victimized by prejudice instead of the dominant group who carried the prejudice, legitimizing it by shifting the blame. The second, it generalizes that "bad behavior" comes only from a particular group of people, in this case, the rural people, effectively detaching oneself or one's social class or circle from any negativity or seeing structural inequalities and injustices.

Ayman positioned himself to the "villages" that Waseem and Mariam talk in disdain. In his view, the rebelling villages were not so few:

> In Idlib, there is a mountain called Jabal al-Zawiya. It is famous, because [these were the] 33 villages that started the revolution. There was a massacre there, and we are from this region. We started to send the Free Army medication when they were fighting against Asad's army. Asad's army attacked the Jabal al-Zawiya because, in their eyes, they were rebels, but they were just working in this direction to get rid of the regime. (Ayman)

Ayman's overall narrative indicates that rising against injustice was necessary. His last sentence can be interpreted as "rebel" did not give the true nature of the uprising. When poverty and class discrimination surface in the participants' narrative, this does not mean that the causes of the conflict are the villages or lower classes. It means poverty and class discrimination lead to the dismissal of people's needs and aspirations, which makes them call for change. How demand for change is received and treated usually falls in the domain of the state and its control over economic resources.

Economic Oppression

Poverty and class discrimination point out why rural areas and urban periphery were an important part of the uprising in Syria. Nevertheless, economic oppression was not restricted to the lower classes. Without the urban economic oppression and dissatisfaction, rural mobilization would not be enough to lead to an uprising. Regardless of their economically advantaged position, people compared different accesses given to the capital, Damascus. Suad goes back to the first decades of Hafez Asad's time, comparing Aleppo to Damascus:

> The government did not do anything for Aleppo. When I used to visit Damascus, I saw a very shiny Damascus, and when I went back to Aleppo, I saw it in the dark. Gradually, the Aleppo people started to build their own city. Living in Aleppo was really better than [living in] Damascus. There were no people from the government and no walls on the streets. There were just people who worked in the trades, and they were trying to improve Aleppo. (Suad)

As revealed in the many accounts of the field data, security services such as *Mukhabarat* and secret police played key roles in the daily lives of Syrians. However, their influence goes much deeper than political oppression, as "buying land, building a house or a factory, or obtaining a business license" (Droz-Vincent 2014, p. 38) was also under their control. The accounts in this section show that urban people and small business owners had grievances and reasons for being unhappy with the regime. Aykut summarized the change from Hafez to Bashar Assad:

> Hafez Asad was a very powerful person. Both internationally and regionally, he was very powerful. Also, he had control over the internal organizations. Bashar Asad was not a person like that. He came to power weaker. A little bit distant from these issues. Hafez Asad's men were always more powerful than Bashar. Because of this, by using Bashar Asad, in my opinion, they had more gain, both politically, militarily, and economically. (Aykut)

Mayar (40, architect from Damascus) gives an account that resonated with many others' explanations of the causes of the conflict: "Social, economic, and even religious freedoms [were restricted]. From the economic perspective, Bashar Asad was not allowing anyone to do projects or investments that did not benefit him." As examples were given in the previous section, many people in Syria were left in survival mode. Certain groups within the middle class in urban settings were unhappy as they felt they could not fully actualize themselves. The economic oppression people faced was on different levels. Some experienced economic oppression in terms of possibilities and opportunities to become what they aspired to, while others could not expand their business. Aykut compares Syria's economic development with its neighboring countries with disappointment:

> Syria has ancient cities like Damascus, nine thousand years old, and Aleppo, thirteen thousand years old, the world's oldest city. But when you look at Lebanon, the press is much more advanced. In Jordan, different categories of people are much more advanced. I saw Istanbul in the 1980s. In some neighborhoods of Istanbul, there was no water, and the electricity was often cut. In the 80s, Syria was not like that. But then, we saw that in the 90s, the situation was changing anymore. The industry and economy have greatly improved in Türkiye. The potential in Syria, however, was going toward a downfall.

Aykut argues that the regress in the economy was explained by the regime as expenditure going to defense against Israel while there was no victory on that front. Aykut explains his disappointment about the lack of economic openings in different facets of his life:

> When I was studying at university, we could not do anything as young people. I wanted to work, but there was no opportunity. I wanted to develop an idea. But, immediately, we faced a certain rigid way of thinking. We just wanted to create ideas and wanted to gather freely, as the people in neighboring countries did. So, I went abroad to work. Later, Türkiye-Syria relations were getting closer, economic openings were starting, and freedoms were improving. At least, that is how we felt. We [young, educated people] came back [from abroad] with hope. But unfortunately, the same difficulties persisted. Bashar Asad was much weaker [as a leader]. (Aykut)

Aykut further shares his observations of the situation when he came back, and the difficulties of advancing in the society without limitations put forward by the regime ranks:

> In the Organized Industrial Zone, everyday security personnel were easily coming in the offices, sitting without doing anything. This was a highly normal thing to do. Sometimes, he came in and drank coffee with me, and he could question a job; this is how it was. We were living like this… In Aleppo, there are industrial people and merchants. When a security person [high-ranked officer], military officer, or political authority goes there, they earn a considerable income from industrial people and merchants. It was like the mafia, and they were taking money. (Aykut)

Ziad also talks about how economic decisions were made not based on the benefit of the Syrian community but for the benefit of politically supported businesspeople. Such a choice also triggered the rising reactions toward the Asad regime from small business owners:

> The regime made a trading agreement with Türkiye in 2003. When Turkish goods entered our economy, our industries finished off, and even then, a lot of voices were raised. The people in these industries had trouble. Imagine a big country sending products to a small

> country. Turkish and Chinese [goods came]. Turkish products were expensive, so some people still bought the Syrian ones, but the Chinese were the cheapest. China [goods] came, and I saw with my eyes that killed people's businesses. The cost of a product in Syria is thirty liras, and if it comes from China for ten, the [internal] market is destroyed. In Syria, everything is made in China or, if higher quality, made in Türkiye. There is nothing to protect the local products. Why? The government wanted it this way. Because Asad's cousin, Rami Makhlouf, wanted to do trading, [he said] 'Stop this, I will bring it in,' 'Stop that, I will bring that.' There was a famous incident with cement; someone was bringing cement from Türkiye. Makhlouf also started bringing cement, and he stopped this other person's cement in customs, not letting it get into Syria, which devastated him. People felt exploited economically and politically. (Ziad)

Some participants in this study stated that when Bashar Assad came to power, they expected him to take a stand against corruption, which did not happen. On 15 July 2020, high-ranking military officials were arrested for being "Makhlouf's men." Asad started a corruption charge against Makhlouf. A considerable group would have been satisfied if he had taken such a step prior to and during 2011 (Al-Ghazal 2020).

Avdel (Kurdish, 35), in comparison to ISIS, preferred the regime and wished he lived in the pre-war conditions of Raqqa rather than outside of Syria. Still, he mentioned the economic aspects of oppression experienced by Kurds:

> We had oppression [before the war], but we were living in peace. In the time of Asad, it was forbidden to speak Kurdish and to own real estate. We were just working in the names of our Arab brothers. Asad is better than ISIS and the revolution; this is what I believe. We were paying money for the intelligence, and intelligence was protecting us and giving us a salute.

While Bagir also missed pre-war Syria, his narrative includes the pre-war economic dimensions of oppression, bringing the nuances of injustice toward Arabs and Kurds:

> [When] there was no war, life was better than now. [The focus group discussed this statement, some disagreeing]. We were working and paying as Kurds for the intelligence. Every single day, an officer or his assistant from the security/intelligence would come to my office to take money from me. I was paying bribes while I had a construction business. I paid 100 thousand Syrian pounds as a bribe, and nobody would ask me what I was doing. Not only Kurds but also Arabs [paid]. The difference between us and Arabs is that we could not own anything. We could not have a deed [for the property]. We do not want to do any injustice to the regime. The regime had a good justice in its injustice... For example, I have an auto gallery, and I needed to register this gallery, but they did not let me do this registration. They said for you to register it, you need to own it. I brought an Arabic person who was my friend. I put everything under his name, but after they learned that originally this place was mine, they did not even accept the registration for this Arab person because I am a Kurd. (Bagir, 61, from Kobanî, lived in Aleppo)

Merwan (Kurdish, 60) also brings another example of economic oppression based on ethnicity:

> I created a factory in that area (Raqqa province). The Ba'ath party took the land and gave it as a gift to a lot of Arab people. In Idlib province, I had a factory. It was shot by an air attack, and we left everything and came here. This is a small summary. I studied in the best schools in Aleppo, which are Christian schools. Even though the school was private, the Ba'ath

> party made it a general [public] school. Al-Ba'ath took over education, territories, and everything else. They said differences between people are forbidden. They said everyone was the same, and in the end, they took everything.

Merwan's angle indicates that Ba'ath supported "identity blindness" by singularizing all identities. In reality, certain segments of society benefited economically while others were disadvantaged.

Between the social, economic, and political oppression of the regime and ISIS, many people were left to make a choice within these oppressions and violence. While Avdel, Bagir, and Merwan talk about the corruption and economic gain by the regime before the uprising, Alaz (37), who was from Raqqa, talks about the financial gains of ISIS after the war started. This account is important to show that while the front face of the conflict parties are ethno-religious and political identities, there is a strong economic dimension to becoming an actor in a conflict. Alaz first went to Kobanî from Raqqa before coming to Türkiye and was deeply missing home. He actively worked in a civil society initiation of Kurdish, Turkmen, and Arab people from Raqqa to find a way back home. Alaz explains the economic dynamics behind ISIS aggression:

> After the radicals got control over the Raqqa city, I mean ISIS, they displaced all the Kurds. Something like a *fatwa* [Islamic law-based ruling], they said, 'You are non-believers, and you should leave the Muslim land, territories.' Not less than a hundred thousand Kurds were displaced from Raqqa. [Before the displacement], the trade and real estate markets were controlled by Kurdish businessmen. ISIS started to control all of the Kurds' things [assets], which were worth millions of dollars. For example, my office, my house, my cousins' cars, galleries, doctors' clinics, other offices, and the cars of other people were taken over by ISIS under the name called *ghanimah* [spoils of war]. They took all of what we owned, and there are no Kurdish people in Raqqa city anymore. All of them have been displaced to Türkiye and Europe and are dispersed everywhere in the world. After ISIS attacked Kobanî, we also were displaced as Kurds of Raqqa and Kurds of Kobanî to Türkiye. (Alaz, 37)

Economic access, or lack thereof, has an important influence on how identities surface as economic demands can translate into ethnopolitical demands. "Peripheral groups or groups separated from economic development would be more likely to use ethnic or religious identity as a 'political resource'" (Breuilly 1993, p. 260; Bozarslan 1997, pp. 174–180 in Tejel 2009, p. 119).

Different people reported that either their family business lost income or their factories were confiscated by the regime. Some narrated stories about how some of the businesspeople who supported the regime faced the collapse of production because they were replaced by importing products or the frequency and amount of bribery increased. Some of the wealthy people who were part of the uprising and some who were against it could be connected to the realities that they faced. If their businesses suffered greatly, being part of the uprising would be easier. When the material motives of the majority group were recognized in the past and given a degree of economic progress, there was less incentive for them to revolt (Haklai 2000, p. 27). In other words, "an economic elite that has too much to lose in case the rebellion is unsuccessful might hesitate to take the risk, particularly if it is aware of the regime's military capabilities" (Haklai 2000, p. 27).

From Dignity to Basic Needs

The concluding part of this chapter positions the camera to people's view about what they demanded and desired when they joined in the demonstrations in pre-war Syria and where they located themselves and Syria in the lived moment of 2016. This exploration will help analyze the distance of today's Syria from the visions of people who were situated as refugees some 8 years earlier.

Mayar, who experienced prison and torture under the regime, believes that Syrians hoped for justice. He desires to have "the simplest life" with political and social rights and freedoms where people would express their thoughts without any pressure. He argues that what made demonstrations beautiful at the beginning was people believed these ideals: "We knew that the work we were doing is not controlled from any side, from any outside force, not like in the present, as we are seeing from the military groups or from other political groups that are working now. It was happy and joyful work." Many people desired civilian, non-violent resistance, as they believed it would have a stronger chance of reaching a socially just and free society. Fatima, as a young woman with political ideals for her country, believed that the worst aspect of the oppressive political and economic structure was that it led to apathy and disinterest in things other than material ones, where there was no expectation or engagement in the future of the country. Thus, Fatima and many other interviewees were elated to see people coming together to protest and resist, desiring involvement as citizens in their country.

Depending on their social location, people had different experiences of oppression and discrimination. Still, many explained what was missing for them in Syria in broad terms, focusing on reasons why they joined in the demonstrations and the following things they wished to see in the future of Syria: "dignity," "freedom," "justice," and "equality." Kamal and Majed both summarize the demand as "freedom and dignity for all," while Kamal argues that "the government took everything; they just served for themselves." Rashid also says that at the beginning, the demands were "freedom, justice, and social justice." He adds that the dream is a "United Syria, a regime that represents justice and freedom." Rashid believes in "living in dignity," which he sees as taken away by the Syrian regime. The youngest participant in this research, Anas, who was 18 at the time of the interview, explains going to demonstrations as a symbol:

> [In the demonstrations] you see your friend next to you, your relative in front of you, and you know some people around. This was a very good feeling. You especially know that your goal is very good. Your goal is to live in dignity, peace, security, and equal rules, and there is no place for *zulm*. (Anas)

Camil, who believed in non-armed civilian resistance, explains:

> I joined the civil side of the revolution, believing that justice and dignity for all people should be respected. Differences should be respected. Most of the people I have worked with, myself included, had no financial problems in our lives, which was not the reason we joined the revolution. We were financially in good positions, and we did it for our dignity. Imagine yourself as a Ph.D. holder, taken to prison by security. They want you to be taken,

and they can do anything to you. I think this is a most undignified thing, and I could not bear that idea… I hate liars, and the Syrian government was a liar. I believe that Syria could be a great country. Syria has the people, the resources, history, and tourism. It had the most ancient cities in the world, and this country could have made a great success of itself, but the regime used to plunder everything from people and did not give anything to its own people. I am realistic. I know that no government in the world gives 100%, which is honest and works for the people, but at least they can give people part of their interests, respect, and dignity. This is what I wanted, and this is why I joined the revolution. (Camil)

Yet, after their sense of coming together as a community and belief in resisting for a better future, in the fifth year of the conflict, interviewees made striking comparisons between pre-war Syria and after-war Syria conditions and the situation of people. Rukan, with sorrow, focused on "dignity," which was one of the most central needs:

Now, the Syrians just want some food aid and food baskets. However, the Syrians did not leave their country for that. They want dignity, and all these countries in the world do not understand this. Syrians had everything before. Honestly, they were living better than the Turkish people here. Aleppo was much better than here. We had everything except the dignity. Because you can see someone from Syrian intelligence come and remove all your dignity in one second. The tragedy in Syria is like a trade now. You can see now a Syrian starving and dying because he is very hungry or because of the cold weather. We could not imagine that.

These sentiments, of course, belong to a woman who is well educated and has more access than many, as the previous section of this chapter analyzed. Therefore, it does not reflect everyone's position in the needs base. While class dynamics and accessibility are much more complex than presented in Rukan's words, her views hold true for many who had access to basic needs. The people in poverty were also asking for better life standards, and compared to this, larger segments of society started to experience a lack of basic needs after the war. Ziad also sorrowfully sees that people's needs are reduced to basics such as water and electricity. He mostly focuses on people inside Syria and analyzes their wants and needs by locating them in their pre- and post-war situations. The discrepancy between what they wanted before and what they need now is startling:

A person's honor is shattered to get water or a bit of food. Syrians, I know this. They are honorable people. In Ramadan, you give charity to people. If you go to a poor person, they would be ashamed; even if they knew you, they would say, 'How could I accept this?' But now people are in a situation where they have to accept this charity. They are waiting for the olive that is going to be sent. There is no work, no chance for them to leave. So, for them, Jewish or Christian or whoever is going to come, and whatever happens, [they would say] we want to live like we used to, we want electricity and water. (Ziad)

Even in remembering the pre-war poverty, Ziad argues that with complete loss of basic needs of water and electricity, people would be less likely to care who is in power and who makes decisions as long as they get back some of these basic needs back.

The interviewee accounts indicate that in pre-war Syria, a considerable number of Syrians reached a point where they demanded not only basic needs (survival needs such as safety) but also higher needs in the hierarchy of needs, such as respect and self-actualization (Maslow 1951; Barsky 2020). War conditions dramatically changed the needs hierarchies. Nawar brings an interesting economic perspective on wartime conditions and assesses the consequences of a civil war:

> If you were standing in 2011 and asking for freedom from the Asad family, now you would be standing in the same square asking for something to get better; the prices of the items you need to survive every day [are so high]. In the past, the minimum wage, the salary you needed to survive in a month, would be around 600$ a month. I am from Damascus. I live in Damascus. My salary scale as a normal worker in any sector, especially in the private sector, used to be 400$. This is my maximum; with my best performance, my earnings would be 400$. But I would need 600$ to survive there. The same number for minimum survival right now is around 800$, but at the moment, they are earning 300$, not even 400$, not even half of the money that they need to survive. So, this is a huge damage happened to the lifestyle... When the Syrian people started the revolution, they were at a particular level, looking to get a better thing in terms of dignity, equality, and even culture and education. But now we are way below the level we started the revolution. Also, recovering and getting to that level will take ages. (Nawar)

Nawar and Farah also talked about the importance Syrians gave to educating their children in pre-war times and the worrying levels of illiteracy and lack of schooling for children, both who became refugees and who live within Syria. "Life deteriorates to a struggle for the most basic needs" (Khalaf 2015, p. 41) in conflict zones. Ziad, Nawar, and Rukan depict a regression in the needs hierarchy of Syrians. "A person's attention, motivation, and actions tend to focus on satisfying basic needs first, making it difficult or impossible for a person to focus on higher needs unless and until the more basic needs have been satisfied" (Barsky 2020, p. 217).

In Syria, the rural and urban lower classes wanted social security and better access to goods and services. In contrast, middle classes and small business owners wanted regulations so that the government and government-supported cliques could not swallow their share. Many segments wanted more representation and voice in politics in order to reach their needs and demands. Syria experienced a steep decline from demanding economic and political rights to basic survival needs such as water, electricity, food, and security from violent death. From demands for equal gains, power sharing, and issues of haves and have-nots, the war changed the conversation to survival and reaching basic needs such as food, shelter, education, and physical security.

Author eye-camera: One of the important aspects of wars in today's world that we need to think about and analyze deeply is the gap between the needs of people at the starting point of conflicts and the progress of the conflict. While people in different class positions demand better lives, different segments have different access to resources. Some who have access to basic needs such as health care, education, meaningful and gainful employment, demand for political expression, representation, and access to decision-making structures. Some others start by asking fulfillment of basic needs and demand a better share of resources to pull them out of poverty. The endpoint, however, for many becomes the lack of most basic needs, such as shelter, food, electricity, and security, along with daily engagement with bombs and bullets. Schooling, health care, and gainful employment become luxuries in the wake of displacement, homelessness, and insecurity based on threats to life because of military attacks. People are pushed to believe that "even without dignity and rights, their lives are better." Wars are used as tools against the masses, not to ask for their fair share from the states that they live under. The major task of war, it seems, is to reduce the mass demand for higher-order needs. When the departure point is the individual's experience, it becomes apparent that colonized states turn the struggle between haves and have-nots in the forms of civil wars. Colonizing structures through wars prevent countries and regions from transforming into democracies. Syria today, instead of fulfilling its human potential, is facing political and economic setbacks and growing generations that are cut off from formal education. The last thing anybody talks about is "dignity, freedom, representation, and a system that articulates everyone's rights."

References

Al-Ghazal ZK (2020) Is Putin behind the split in Syria's Assad family? MEMO-Middle East Monitor, 11 May. Accessed on 27 September 2022. https://www.middleeastmonitor.com/20200511-is-putin-behind-the-split-in-syrias-assad-family/

Barsky AE (2020) A capacity-building approach to conflict resolution. In: Byrne S, Matyók T, Scott IM, Senehi J (eds) Routledge companion to peace and conflict studies. Routledge, London, pp 215–225

Bozarslan H (1997) La question kurde. Etats et minorités au Moyen-Orient. Presses de Sciences Po, Paris

Breuilly J (1993) Nationalism and the state, 2nd edn. Manchester University Press, Manchester

Connell RW, Messerschmidt JW (2005) Hegemonic masculinity: rethinking the concept. Gend Soc 19(6):829–859

Droz-Vincent P (2014) "State of Barbary" (take two): from the Arab spring to the return of violence in Syria. Middle East J 68(1):33–58

Haklai O (2000) A minority rule over a hostile majority: the case of Syria. Nationalism Ethnic Politics 6(3):19–50

Hinnebusch R (2018) From Westphalian failure to heterarchic governance in MENA: the case of Syria. Small Wars Insurgencies 29(3):391–413

Hokayem E (2013) Syria's uprising and the fracturing of the Levant. International Institute of Strategic Studies, Adelphi Series, London

Imady O (2014) How a microfinance network could have preempted the Syrian uprising. Syria Stud 6(1):81–122

Imady O, Hinnebusch R (2018) Conclusion: the early trajectory of the Syrian uprising: from agency to structure. In: Hinnebusch R, Imady O (eds) The Syrian uprising: domestic origins and early trajectory. Routledge, London, pp 329–335

Khalaf R (2015) Governance without government in Syria: civil society and state building during conflict. Syria Stud 7(3):37–72

Maslow AH (1951) Higher needs and personality. Dialectica 5(3–4):257–265

Pearlman WR (2017) We crossed a bridge and it trembled: voices from Syria. Custom House (e-book version)

Sorenson DS (2016) Syria in ruins: the dynamics of the Syrian civil war. Praeger, Santa Barbara

Tejel J (2009) Syria's Kurds: history, politics and society. Routledge, New York

Part II
Experiences of Syrian Refugees: Self in Dual Spatiality and Multiple Temporality

Chapter 7
Spatial and Temporal Identity and Belonging

Self in Time and Space

The previous chapters examined the perceptions of Syrians in Gaziantep about the actors and causes of the Syrian conflict. The remaining chapters will locate Syrian interviewees as refugees in Gaziantep-Türkiye. Chapters 7 and 8 investigate identity, belonging, and ways of seeing the future by showing how these concepts are intertwined with the dual spatiality of "here" and "there" and multiple temporalities by showing complexities of the past-present-future in their articulations and agency.

In emplaced lives, we live in constant calculation of the future. The future is something we bring into the present as we plan, act, and aim here and now. Our agency and becoming are usually investigated within emplaced experiences of spatial and temporal understanding of past, future, and present. For refugees, such spatial and temporal experience is much more complex. The spatial experience is multiple due to displacement, and temporalities are multi-layered as the linear expectation of life-course changes forcefully and abruptly. For people who are positioned as refugees, the most dreaded questions include inquiries about the future and going back home. Contrary to how they are structurally perceived as rigidly one-dimensional (the refugee in the singular form), past, future, and present are multi-faceted. These spatio-temporalities need to be analyzed without a sedentary view of space and a linear view of time. In the following sections, space and time are approached through proximity, security, and memory by analyzing refugee-positioned experiences.

© The Author(s), under exclusive license to Springer Nature Singapore Pte Ltd. 2025

U. Ozkaleli, *De-essentializing Refugees: Perceptions, Experiences, and Becoming of Syrians in Türkiye*, https://doi.org/10.1007/978-981-96-5519-9_7

Spatial and Temporal Proximity and Accessibility

For refugees, the spatial experience is dual. They are forced to live outside of the home while constantly feeling a sense of loss and longing for home. The multiplicity of time and space intertwines for refugees, particularly when they live in cities on the border of their home country, contributing to a dual spatial experience. Before the war started in Syria, there was a lot of interaction and cross-border travel, particularly between Aleppo and Antep. Mariam, with misty, sad, and melancholic eyes, remembers:

> [Before the war, people] were coming and going [between the cities of Aleppo and Gaziantep]. My friends *came here* before the war started. On the weekends, we *went there [Gaziantep] and returned* [to Aleppo] on Monday. It was nearer to come to Antep than to go to Damascus, the capital. People were finishing school on Friday and *coming back* [to Aleppo] on Sunday or Monday. It was so easy to go. (emphasis mine)

Mariam was in Antep during the interview, which makes it striking how she is talking about "here" and "there" in duality, sometimes locating herself in Gaziantep, "my friends came *here*" (meaning Gaziantep), and sometimes as if she is currently located in Aleppo rather than Gaziantep, "going *there*" (meaning Gaziantep). She mentally locates herself in Aleppo despite physically being in Gaziantep at the moment.

In all the roads that lead to major highways in Gaziantep, road signs indicate "*Halep*" (Aleppo). As a border city, merely a two-hour drive from Aleppo, Gaziantep was always a reminder of a left-behind home:

> [The last time I was in Syria was] August 2012. Almost 4 years… The thing that breaks my heart is that Syria is 120 km from here, and I cannot go. That breaks my heart the most. My foreign friends say I am going to my country; I am going to Nigeria, to home, and Nigeria is so far from here, but he can go. But me? My country is almost there, but I cannot go there. (Naser)

The physical distance between Syria and Türkiye becomes complex as the reachability of the place is much more distant than its actual geographic proximity. At different times in people's memories, both the meaning and accessibility of the place change:

> Syria is more precious now. The distance between us made it so. Now, for example, I want to go just to visit my family, and I cannot. Seven years ago, I just came here with my ID and stayed for a week. I have no problem with this place [Gaziantep], but I feel Syria is so far away from here now yet so close. (Lina)

Even though the physical distance between the two cities has never changed, circumstances of war changed the proximity along with the emotional distance felt toward Gaziantep. According to relational pragmatics (Emirbayer and Mische 1998), the "conception of agency is intrinsically social and relational" (973), which means the agency is "always agency toward something, by means of which actors enter into relationship with surrounding persons, places, meanings, and events." Also, "viewed externally, agency entails actual interactions with its contexts, in something like an ongoing conversation" (973). Syria, in this regard, not only signifies "home" but also provides the social coordinates for the refugees' anchor in the mental mapping that measures the distance between the self's current location and "home."

Ramez, while living in Gaziantep, accepted a job to cross the Syrian border to carry aid because:

> They were sending these aids near to my village. I suggested they let me take this aid inside because I know the area better. I decided to help them because it is a good thing for my area, and I would go to Syria every week. Because I cannot live without it. (Ramez)

Ramez sought ways to be in close proximity to Syria and to stay connected to home. Ramez was densely emotional and resentful of being out of Syria. Ramez's father and siblings were re-settled in a European country. He was devastated that he could not see his newborn nephew, believing that a new life was to be celebrated with family who were together to share it. While he had the chance to go to Europe, he argued that he "could not leave" Gaziantep because of its proximity to Syria, and his ability to go there even for short periods of time gave him a level of comfort. He felt guilty of sending his father to Europe:

> My father is not happy in Europe! Every day, he talks with me and tells me he wants to come back… He just wants one thing, and it is Syria [long silence; we wait for him to be able to talk again for long moments]. And I can feel him [empathize with him] …I stayed here [Gaziantep] for two and a half years so I could go and come back to Syria. (Ramez)

Ramez is not alone in his fondness for Gaziantep, as it is closer to Syria, offering a dual spatial experience for some, including Ramez, who travel back and forth to Syria. Nazem's dual spatial experience went so far as to argue that "[he] never left Syria." He regularly crossed the border to help people in Syria. Others lived the dual spatial experience by staying connected to Syria through proximity. Rashid left Türkiye but came back to stay close and work for Syria. Other participants said they preferred to stay in Gaziantep as it was close to the Syrian border, and they would be the first people to go back once the war was over. Tasneem was among them, even though many told her it would take ten more years to go back to Syria. Haya also did not want to leave Türkiye and opted not to go to the U.S., where she could be closer to family members. She considered Istanbul too far away compared to Gaziantep. She wanted to stay close to Syria, work with Syrians, and be the first to go to Syria once it was accessible. Zeinan, for example, sees her time in Gaziantep as a waiting period. While she lives in the Gaziantep space currently, her plans are all about Raqqa, her hometown:

> I will not go to Europe. Never! I will return to Syria. I am here because this place [Gaziantep] is nearer to Syria. I see people who come from Syria. I ask everything; I listen to news from every place in Syria, from Damascus to Raqqa. When the war stops, when ISIS leaves Raqqa, I will go back… I will return and start teaching children and open a school. (Zeinan)

For Zeinan, like many other Syrian refugees, Gaziantep offers a liminal space (Turner 2017; Şahin-Mencütek et al. 2023), as she is located between her past and the future while holding Raqqa both in past memory and future aspirations.

Reem's words summarize how some refugees perceived re-settlement:

> I want to stay a bit [In Gaziantep] and go back to Aleppo... I want to stay here not for the sake of staying but to be able to go back to Aleppo. Gaziantep is near Aleppo, and if I go somewhere else, I will be just a number in re-settlement cases. They will give me an ID and a salary. I do not want that. I want to be close [to Syria]. (Reem)

The more distant re-settlement geographies are seen as becoming "just a number," which indicates a loss of identity. People who valued proximity to home connected the space to their identities. Space has an intricate relationship with meaning in one's life. Mariam brings views of people who are forced out of the war-torn structure of Syria to show the complexities of positionality and proximity:

> People who are out of Syria want to go back to Syria. They start getting jealous, [they are] like, 'if my friend is in Syria, I am getting jealous of him.' But they are not understanding! You can't be jealous of someone who is living at war. He does not have anything you have. They [Syrian refugees in Gaziantep] say, 'I am working 12 hours a day; what I am earning is paying for my home, my food.' In Syria, there are people who cannot buy food; there is no food to buy. You should not be jealous because he is living in his homeland. [They say,] 'I prefer to be that.' But this is not realistic. People who live in Syria do not even have money. They do not have what you have to buy food. They do not have the safety to go to work and come back. (Mariam)

What Mariam describes can be read as the insecurity experienced within a war zone and the loss felt by the "thrown out, thrown in" experience of displacement. The sense of emplacement is shaken for people who are outside due to war and insecurity, which brings a sense of search that appears as a dual spatial positioning, here and there, outside and inside. While inside, physical security is under threat, and once outside, the loss of home and identity creates an enormous insecurity and restlessness.

Being "inside" or "outside" factors how Syrians in Gaziantep experience their subjectivity: how they imagine themselves and act. Both Ayman and Ziad focused on the basic needs, such as food and water, that became scarce for the insiders. This shifts their perception in comparison to Syrians living outside. While their desires and visions change from outside, from different spatial experiences, refugees see an inside evolving differently than their outside selves. Ayman is acutely aware of his outside position *vis-à-vis* people who continue to live in Syria. Believing that Syrians, who are inside and outside, have different experiences and expectations, Ayman distances himself from thinking and doing anything about Syria and even refuses to talk to other Syrians. He distinguished "then and now," arguing that even though he actively participated in the revolution when inside, he should not do anything once he left as it would impact the people inside. Spatial positioning makes an active participant in an uprising, refraining from any more action as he believes that the basic needs of the insiders are much different than what his concerns would be for Syria. Ziad also has a split between the "inside" and "outside" gap. He is aware that he wants the revolution to continue from the outside while the person inside wants water and food for their children. The dual spatial analysis that refugees bring startlingly shows how wants and needs are different as experience decides what people need. The duality for the refugees is complex as they both desire something different based on their experiences, but at the same time, they continue to know and feel for people, loved ones, and Syrians who continue to live inside Syria. Refugees who are located on the "outside" also live in the cracks of the spatial duality and have multiple and conflicting desires: on the one hand, they want safety and basic conditions for the insiders, and on the other hand, they want change in the conditions in Syria that made them displaced. Akila's words also demonstrate how, in dual temporality, looking back can make a person feel conflicting emotions about being inside Syria:

> People are asking when you will go back to Syria. In ten years [I think]. It will never be the same for me. Everyone [in my family is] in a different place [in the world]. I do not know what I will do next. After I finish university, I do not know where I am going. I love Syria too much, and really, *if time goes back*, I do not want to go outside of Syria, but at the moment, I do not prefer to stay in Syria as it is now. (empahsis mine)

Akila's words indicate that if war had not happened at home, "past, present, and future" would have been in harmony, and she would always aspire to a future within Syria.

Two different types of refugees surface in this analysis. The refugees, who experience Gaziantep as a liminal space for waiting to return to Syria, focus on the closeness of the proximity of Gaziantep and Syria to stay connected to home. They live in dual spatial experiences, which simultaneously means they connect past and future, shaping their present judgments about what to do. In such cases, refugees are involved with other Syrians through NGO work or local associations and stay connected to their Syrian identity. Others, like Ayman, Ziyad, and Akila, while longing for the pre-war past, feel disconnected from the future trajectory of post-war Syria in their present lives as refugees who have different experiences than insiders. For them, as insiders and outsiders, differently located Syrians exist in a present that is disconnected from the common past. These experiences indicate the disconnection of the future from the past as well. They have complex temporalities that decide what they will iterate and what will change. Their present judgments, in other words, are decided with possible future trajectories (Emirbayer and Mische 1998) that are detached from the past.

How does time within the past, present, and future forms have a direct effect on people's spatial experience? What kind of meaning is associated with the place? Can one keep the meanings associated with the place intact? Does the relationship between time and space influence decisions of return? The following sections will explore these questions for the refugees.

Security as a Focal Point of Return

Return for refugees is always a topic that comes with complex responses. While Western media depicts refugees as desiring to re-settle in Western countries for a "better life," the story of the refugees with multiple and intersectional identities is quite different from the simplistic versions that are attached to such media depiction. How people feel about return is complex, both emotionally and materially, and is interwoven with different issues and feelings.

Badia asserts that if she were afforded the opportunity, she would return to Damascus, as she believes that "the human has nowhere else but her homeland." Nevertheless, for her, as well as for many others, security constitutes the essential prerequisite for repatriation. The definition and understanding of security are intrinsically linked to the experiences of refugees, their social positioning, and the recollection of the past and anticipations about the future. The experience of war causes deep insecurity in people, and during my conversations with interviewees, the Syrian war was still ongoing in its fifth year. Many participants expressed concerns about the safety and security of their children and loved ones. They stated that the primary condition for returning home was the cessation of bombing and gunfire. Tamara is widowed and lost two brothers during the war. Her words echo many refugees' views about the need for security:

> [If there will be peace], I will be the first one to go back, but there is no hope. My family is in Syria, and every day, the bombs are raining, and it is getting more difficult to live there. It is impossible to go back. Then, if I go back, with whom am I going back? Our houses are destroyed, and the people we love are gone, so there is nothing. (Tamara)

Tamara approaches insecurity from different layers. The first and immediate concern is the ongoing violence. The second layer of insecurity encompasses both material and non-material needs. Physical conditions such as shelter and a social network with loved ones are core needs that are forever lost for some people. Similarly, Rouba is doubtful about returning even in post-war times, as she believes Syria would not be as safe as it was in the old days. Camil articulates:

> People cannot be creative, build, or restore their country if they do not feel secure. You must feel secure. I do not care about cutting-edge technology; even basic necessities like water and electricity matter little if you do not feel safe enough to go home. (Camil)

While basic needs such as water and electricity are not counted within safety by Camil, participants understand the concept of safety differently. For Joumana, in the post-war era, the decision to go back will be about job opportunities. Fahed summarizes the importance of economic conditions alongside being free of violence:

> Even now, when we go to the free side of Syria, we see the destroyed houses and buildings… When it is secure, we will go back. In 2013, there were 1.8 million people living in free areas. People were there, alive, and wanted to continue. But then people were shot/killed by the barrel bombs, and everything was ruined. When people go back there, we should be secured from these things, from the regime. Second, help rebuild the economy. The nature of the Syrian people is such that they can build their economy very fast, but security is very important. (Fahed)

In 2016, participants still held hope for victory, but they began to realize that the prolonging of the war meant a regime change would not happen immediately. Their past experiences with the regime, coupled with their uprising, shaped a vision and expectation for Syria's future, which informs their current perspective on their desire to return. Some did not wish to return because they were blacklisted. Others refused to live under Asad's rule as they saw him responsible for all the violence, loss of loved ones, and the destruction of Syria. Along with the regime, ISIS was viewed as the greatest threat to security, as many, like Fatima, believe that a normal life cannot be lived under ISIS. Rashid also claims that returning to Syria is a dream and adds why he cannot go back at the moment:

> Before everything else, I want the regime to be finished. We want a regime that is moderate. On the other side, we have many extremist groups that, if they are controlling the country, we won't return. (Rashid)

Akila's condition of going back is related to one thing, and that is family: "If my parents, all my family is there, for sure I would go back for my parents, my sisters, and my brother and stay there." With the same sentiment, no return is also based on the proximity of the family. In Akila's and many others' expressions, Syria as a space is meaningful, with a past history of the place that includes loved ones. A future where the family is not located clashes with the past experience of having family there, influencing the thought process in the present about return. In this sense, being surrounded by loved ones is more important for people than moving back to certain territories, which Ayman's words also highlight:

> Nothing is over there [in Syria]. Why would I go? Who will I be missing? All of my friends are outside. The ones who died, they died. The ones that are outside, they are outside, so why would I go back? (Ayman)

Walid similarly maintains that "Home is where your family is. If I was with my family anywhere in the world, I do not care [where I am]." Fadi's words also indicate how the space is seen through the concept of family. He explains that some of his family is in Türkiye, some in Sweden, and many of his friends are also outside, in countries like Germany, the Netherlands, and Norway. He adds, "Why should I go back and see the destruction? It is over for me. I cannot go back, and I do not want to go back." Here, the spatial positioning is made to be secondary, and the only persistent thing, through past, present, and future, is tied to the family for defining "home." Home becomes not a space but a concept that embraces the togetherness of family.

Evaluating attention to safety and security in relation to returning to Syria requires considering temporality. Refugees' perspectives on the future are deeply connected to their past experiences and the information they receive about the current situations of family and friends still in Syria. Furthermore, individuals arrived in Türkiye as refugees during different time periods, contributing varied insights about growing insecurity. Newcomers brought fresh information, while those who had been in Türkiye for several years were a bit distanced from the immediate threats of bombings even though the traumas they experienced still shaped how they expressed their future aspirations. Their desire to live in Gaziantep, which is closer to Syria, represents hope and a desire to return. However, their views about the future also influence their current assessment of security as a crucial condition for any return, though the meaning of security beyond basic safety significantly varies among refugees.

Memory as a Focal Point of Return

What makes a place a place is the history, the neighborhood, the memories, and the people that are part of it. The development of local life and neighborhoods constructs "their own self-reproduction… [Meaning is created through] the memories and attachments that local subjects have of and to their shop signs and street names, their favorite walkways and streetscapes, their times and places for congregating and escaping" (Appadurai 1996, p. 191). The past and future can meet in an undisturbed manner in the present if the tangible aspects of places and neighborhoods can match with the expected. Any part that is missing or destroyed creates complexity about the desire to be there and not be there. Aykut's complex views about the place and his fears about going back emphasize the meanings that are created through neighborhoods and memories:

> I am scared because Syria is not my Syria anymore. I am afraid of what I will see. 40% of Aleppo vanished/destroyed. Aleppo is a five million population city. 80% of rural areas of Damascus have vanished. Hama has not been destroyed too much, but there have been enormous tragedies. Homs' 60% has been destroyed. How will I return there? How will I look? What will I see in my street? What will I remember? What will they tell me about my neighbor? About my doctor, what will they say? What happened to them? Every day, am I going to hear a new story? People will tell me stories every day. Because I am outside, I am not inside.

The fear of not finding what was known in the past decides how Aykut associates with home. The outsider position is also related to how what he knew as Syria became something different when he was distant from it. Naser's desire to be in Syria and being afraid to be in contact with the actual place is also similar to Aykut's sense of loss and trauma about not finding the place as he knows it:

> I want to go back to my country and do the things I like, but I lost a lot of people there, so I won't be happy going back to Syria. I have lost the hope of returning to Syria. Even if I go back to Syria, even if everything ends, the country is destroyed. What can you do there? Nothing. Just nothing. You will be crying for the country. (Naser)

The inability to reiterate the parts of the past that make sense changes future projections for Naser. Having no hope of return is not about the ability to be in the place physically but the perception that what has already been lost. Destruction of places has a direct effect on people's sense of identity and belonging. Ahlaam explains this feeling:

> I miss saying that I am from Syria because Aleppo and Damascus are two of the oldest cities in the world [her voice is shaking]. It is like I have very deep roots in the ground, but now I… sometimes I cry very hard when I know they bombed Aleppo city. (Ahlaam)

From the past to the future, the destruction of these ancient cities is in itself painful and directly connected to people's sense of identity and belonging to the space. Aykut, Naser, and Ahlaam, coming from different genders, ages, and life experiences, all feel belonging to Syria and have a deep longing for it, yet at the same time, how they remember the place in the past with its people and neighborhoods intact create a contradictory image of its today after the war and destruction. Spatial duality here appears within the mind connected and intertwined with temporality, seeing it in the past, pre-war situation, and in the future, seeing it in fragments or very different than how it was in the past. The idea of not finding what it used to be influences the decision to return.

Displaced Here and Displaced There

The above sections examined the conditions and meaning of the return to Syria by focusing on different meanings of security and the destruction of memories. This section will examine the sense of loss, displacement, and destruction in relation to people's articulation of their future. A considerable number of interviewees had a permanent feeling of displacement regardless of where they were, which influenced their experiences, feelings, and actions. A capturing narrative below signals the intricate relationship of time, space, sense of loss, and displacement:

> I am now 40 years old, and I feel like I have not lived all the things I have lived. It is that kind of a loss. I was born and grew up on certain streets; I have certain memories of certain people. In the beginning, after I left, it was as if I was living an unreal thing as if it was a dream. It felt like I was going to wake up from this dream and realize I had not lost anything yet. But when the time gets longer, do you know what happens? It feels as if all the things I lived in the first 40 years of my life were a dream, and I was just born. Nevertheless, I was born as a 40-year-old person. What a difficult thing for a person to be born at 40 and lose the first 40 years. As if all the things were unreal. And I was born here, in this environment, but I was born as a 40-year-old. (Aykut)

The time here is connected to space, and the erasure of the spatial connection brings the erasure of time. The place cannot be captured without time, and time cannot be articulated without the place. After the destruction, Aykut did not see going back to Syria as a solution. When time is strongly connected to a place for people like Aykut, once the place is no longer there, the past disappears.

Ayan, speaking as a war widow, first depicts the destruction of Syria and concludes:

> We gave our husbands, our happiness, our children's happiness. They stole our sense of security; they stole the happiness and the childhood of many children. We gave everything to Syria. It is not just Syria destroyed now. We are destroyed as human beings and as persons.

The destruction of Syria is both a reality and a metaphor to explain how, as human beings, they are also destroyed. "Destruction," as a choice of word, indicates harm that involves today and the future. There is no return from the loss of a childhood or the loss of a part of a self. Salwa explains the loss of a husband and home as "memories being gone." While some were holding on to memories, others believed that death and destruction wiped away the memories, in other words, the past. Similar to Aykut, Salwa positions herself as a being standing in the "now" without a "past" and a "future." Malek, a 41-year-old man who worked in an NGO to help Syrians, also had a holistic view of the destruction suffered, arguing that along with stones and buildings, "the minds are destroyed." "Destruction of the mind" leaves the person with a lack of connection to both space and time in terms of past, future, and present. Not only memories and family unity, but Malek's view of how Syrians are positioned as refugees or as people in poverty who struggle to find food is also part of the enormous feeling of destruction. Malek combined loss of memories with loss of life in Syria, the death of friends, and the conditions of Syrians in Türkiye to arrive at a bleak nothingness of future:

> Imagine a tree taken away from its roots. People are a mode of memories, not a body, but memories. You cannot imagine losing all the memories. You lost the road you walked before, you lost the home you lived in before, you lost your friends and neighbors, and everything. It is very difficult. Every day, I cry. Every day, I have to delete a friend from my contact list because they are dead. I lost all my friends. Yes, I have colleagues, but it is not the same. I lost everything [Long minutes of silence after this]. The biggest problem is no future! No future...

For Malek, the past being destroyed and today not promising a desirable outcome led to an understanding that the future does not exist. Similar to Malek, Malak, a 34-year-old widowed woman, is among people who had seen her house being destroyed before leaving Syria:

> We left our house in Aleppo and went to stay in our village. After a month, we came back [to Aleppo], and we saw that the whole building was destroyed. I saw that my kid was happy running into our street. [He searched the rubble] and I saw him holding our pillow. He found the pillow, and he was very happy to be holding our pillow in his arms [silent for a long moment].

Malak's sister, who was still in Syria, sent her videos from Aleppo, and she argues that she recognized the remains of her house from the video of the pink walls. Even though the house was destroyed, Malak wanted to go back if the air raids would stop and there was a sense of safety. Nala, another widow, was the same way, and even though her house was destroyed, she said, "I cannot see my husband, but I dream that one day I will go back to my home." Unlike Ayan, Malek, and Aykut, the destruction of their houses did not stop the hope of tomorrow for Malak and Nala. They hoped to be able to re-capture whatever they could from their past life.

Rashid finds living in Gaziantep beautiful, but that beauty for him is diminished because it increases his sense of loss. He argues, "It is very hard for us [Syrians] because you are forgetting your country." Therefore, the beauties in the host country may come with a sense of being terrified of losing the tie to the home country. Rashid is here but not fully, and he is not there but not entirely.

What Ayla misses the most is her house, which is surrounded by houses belonging to her family members. She feels the displacement tangibly in terms of how spatially she and her loved ones are dispersed:

> I have not seen my mother for four years. I have sisters, and everyone is in a different place, in Sweden, in Germany. When my son was accepted to the school of medicine, no one was here to celebrate.

The feeling of emplacement is directly related to sharing, and the place becomes meaningful, not only with material surroundings but with people. Many people mentioned that in the future, even if the war ends, not all their family members are going to be in Syria like in the past. This reality made them feel that the sense of belongingness that they had in the past was lost.

Najlaa, Hasan, and Malak all missed the smell of their land. Hasan was even specific about missing the smell of his district, while Malak missed even the smell of garbage. Najlaa, a war widow, constantly compared here and there, now and then. She wishes to "smell" her country, which also indicates that smell is a constant reminder of being displaced from the known. She connects this to other aspects of living:

> [I miss] everything; walking, eating something, even the taste of things was different [in Syria]. Now, when I eat something here, it does not taste like the things my husband used to bring. Friday was like a celebration for me because we used to go to our families. Going out on Eid [a Muslim holiday] was happiness. Now, when *Eid* comes, I do not feel it has anything good because our people are dying in our country. When we watch the TV, we see people losing their eyes, legs, and arms.

Najlaa feels displacement through her senses, such as smell and taste. Lack of joy on Friday, which was supposed to be family meeting day and religious celebrations, was expressed through loss of taste and connected to the pain and suffering of Syrians with loss of body parts. Losing family time is like losing limbs. Smell, and perhaps taste, symbolizes the "unobtainable," which "requires looking beyond [lost home's] material form to consider its multifaceted sensory qualities" (Petridou 2001, cited in Brickell 2012, p. 230).

The sense of loss of her life, her social position, and her home makes Alaa feel a continuous displacement in the receiving country, neither completely "here" nor "there":

> I miss everything [a strong, awkward, short laughter]. We have been here for 2 years, but I always tell my husband I do not feel like this is my home. I clean it, I try to put some things in it, but I do not feel it is my home. Something is missing inside. I do not feel happiness, really. I also do not dream; I forget how to dream about the future. Everything is unclear. Yes, I miss Syria and everything. I miss my family and my life. We built our life step by step in Syria [she is silent, she cannot say anything for a while].

Alaa's narrative starts from the "home" she is trying to build in the receiving community, which directly links to the "future." The rupture of their past life, even though she has a job and sustains a middle-class life in Türkiye, makes her unable to envision a future. Dreaming of the future in the now is connected to the past. When the past is forcefully interrupted without spatial connection, people may lose their sense of tomorrow, which stunts their actions. For Suad, the memory of the past is also central to feeling displaced and hesitant about the future. Her family was planning to relocate, and her uncertainty about a new departure connects to the past losses, making her think about what was left behind in Syria. Every move, every departure becomes a moment of remembering what has been left in Syria and the difficulty of feeling emplaced "here."

People sometimes manage to go back and see Syria. Aya explained that during their brief visit, her children could not handle staying at home. Similarly, Lamia felt displaced and alienated in her home country:

> I spent fourteen hours to reach Aleppo. I felt very bad and very tired. When I got home, I just remembered all the memories and the home and felt terrible for one week. I kept crying in the house. I saw that Aleppo had changed a lot. People are sitting in the destroyed houses. There are no walls, no doors or windows inside of it. So, it has completely changed. There is no electricity or water. (Lamia)

Lamia and Aya have multiple spatial and temporal experiences. Because of the ability to travel back to see Syria, they face a complex mix of contradictory spatial experiences. Their spatial experience blends with their temporal positioning. Through their memories, they imagine how Syria spatially felt in the past while experiencing its loss when they observe it today. Being in a place for some is no resolution for the experience of displacement because what it was no longer is.

The feeling of displacement is not only related to being inside or outside. When refugees talk about how their loved ones inside Syria explain their feelings, it shows the dual spatial existence for them as well. Nawar transfers the feelings of an insider:

> I am sure you will not find one Syrian household without drama. Either someone died or was kidnapped, bombarded, or lost their life or money, property, lifestyle, everything. At the moment, some of my friends are in Damascus. Sometimes, when I feel homesick and cannot go there, I call my old friends who are lucky to be alive. So, when I talked to my friend, I told him, 'I wish to go there, go to the old city, sit in that restaurant, and get lunch.' Whatever, you know, stupid, homesick random stuff. He said, 'Do not ever think about it, just keep going because even if you came here, you would be more damaged because it is not the same. Like that restaurant, it is bombed, and that place, you cannot sit there because that whole area is besieged.' (Nawar)

Haya's sister, who is located in Damascus, calls herself a "refugee at home" as the home she knows has no one from her family in it. While physically they are in the same space, after the war and destruction and loss of loved ones surrounding them, insiders also feel alienated and shifted in the place, as if they are occupying a different place. Spatial duality happens with the feeling of change in their surroundings.

Belonging Within Multiple Space and Time

There is spatial and social standardization for national citizens (Appadurai 1996) that regulates the ways of being for people who are part of communities and part of different social segments. Some of the interviewees experienced detachment from this standardization under the authoritarian regime. Reem, who spent her youth in Asad prisons, wanted to live in 1950s Syria in the twenty-first century. She was not alone. Lamia, as one of the older participants in the study, also moves in different temporalities in terms of her thinking of returning to Syria in the future:

> Going back to Syria has always been on my mind. But nowadays, it is impossible to go back. But even when this [war] is finished, I will not be satisfied. I used to live in Aleppo but was never satisfied because it was not the Syria I wanted it to be. I want Syria to be more open. I like the 1950s and 1960s era. Because it was a peak of Arabic singers, literature, and poetry. This is the Syria I want to be in. (Lamia)

Long before becoming a refugee, Lamia aspired to go back to an earlier past in the future.

Spatial and social standardization that was a mismatch for the oppressed citizens is experienced even more acutely by the refugee populations as they are in constant disagreement with their dual spatial existence and imaginings in terms of belonging to a place. Concerned that Syrian children were growing up within different education systems, especially the ones that lacked Arabic language access, Zeinab is saddened that a considerable number of the Syrian younger generation would possibly not go back to Syria. Zeinab is concerned with not being inside and what this would mean for identity and belonging when they would be the people looking from outside. Belonging is related to material and linguistic access and behavioral and emotional expectations that connect with how people engage with time.

Reem's following words signal how she simultaneously lives in multiple temporalities even though she tries to leave the past behind. As a 50-year-old hijab-wearing pious woman, she centers her age to explain her experiences and feelings:

> My psychology is young. But when I focus on my pain and when I feel that I am hurt and I live with that pain, I will be older. I live two moments. With you [now] and tomorrow, [this is] what I should do. The past is behind me. That is why I am effective somehow. After a while, when I came here, I started to attend a course with some girls. They are like my daughter's age. First, they used to call me auntie, and after that, when they saw that I was really competitive with them and my grades started to get higher, they began to call me [with my first name]. (Reem)

She positions both Türkiye and Syria as "Eastern traditional societies" where women "are put in a grave with a stone over it." Reem purposefully shifts her focus from her past, which had 9 years of imprisonment, and the loss of her husband in the revolution. Focusing on today and her future, Reem consciously and purposefully divides the time in which she exists. The rejection of standardization of behavior in lines of gender is apparent in Reem's words as she challenges these gendered expectations by being active in social life. Farah and Fatima experienced challenges to standardization they faced in their past in terms of religious expression, creating a dual spatial experience in the self's becoming. Farah and Fatima donned the hijab very early when they were young girls in Syria. Farah got into hijab because she was influenced by friends and went against the will of her family. They were not against the hijab, but the timing, as they thought it was too early of an age, as they claimed once she was in hijab, she could not remove it later. Despite this, Farah claimed she was "into the religion" and influenced by her school friends and surroundings. In contrast, Fatima argued that she was very young, and it was not related to being a believer or religious oriented, but it was her parents' choice. She argues that: "religion and putting the hijab were two separate things. I never connected it together because I was so young when I put the hijab on. It is like people wearing pants and wearing skirts on other occasions. It was a separate thing, so it was only an outfit, and that is why it never created a conflict of questioning the religion." Later in life, Fatima identified and was surrounded by leftist ideas and people, never wearing the hijab in her friend circles, only out in society. Meanwhile, Farah lost faith in religion during her late teen years but continued wearing the hijab due to the expectations of family and society. Both removed their hijab and assumed secular attire in Türkiye, stating that spatial differences contributed to their decision. Farah explains the importance of place in one's identity construction:

> When I decided to come out here [Gaziantep] a year and a half ago, I told them [parents], when I am out, it is easier for you, you will not have to face all the people with your daughter not wearing hijab anymore, and so they said 'yes do whatever you want.' I removed the hijab after I came here [Gaziantep]. (Farah)

Fatima argues that "[Being in] Türkiye helped make this decision to remove the hijab."

The past and present are positioned with spatial awareness. This indicates that people shift their actions and thinking with the influence of spatial differences. A sense of self and becoming are complex and not one-directional for everyone. Some who are positioned as refugees may find alternatives that feel more embracing.

Noury positions himself in the host community and brings a complex perspective about his future in Syria, in Gaziantep, or a possible third place. In his mind, different places have different aspects that challenge his sense of belonging. When he views Syria from a different place, he looks at it as how it was in the past, how it is today, how he is evolving outside of it, and what this means about how he will see himself in the future in terms of Syria:

> We are living in a similar way here [Gaziantep] as it was inside Syria, the *old* Syria. I am still Syrian inside. But they [Syrians in Syria] are living in a very bad situation. Now, Iranians are in my country, alongside Iraqis. Their mentality is not like ours. The army controls the city of Aleppo. They [Syrians in Aleppo] are seeing the things not as the things I raised for, they have changed, all the people. They cannot trust anyone. After one or two years of war, the Aleppian and Syrian people cannot trust anyone. I cannot communicate with them. When I go back to Syria, it will be dark ages for me. I hope everything will be good for my country, but there is nothing I can do. (Noury)

Not only does Noury see his path diverging from Syrians within Syria as time progresses, but in an intriguing way, he perceives his spatial distance to Syria as an advantage of keeping the "old Syria" by reiterating past practices without the intrusion of violence or other groups who control it. The future would be so different than what he knew in Syria, not because he is outside of it, but because the changes and shifts happening within Syria are erasing the past Syria. He complexifies the spatial positioning by arguing that war interrupts reiteration while the Syrian neighborhood in receiving communities may continue to reproduce what they have always known. Noury is also an example of showing the multiplicity of refugee identities by articulating what would make him feel he belonged:

> We cannot own property here in Türkiye. This is the thing that I could not forgive the Turkish government or the Turkish people. If we could own property, you would see Gaziantep as Syrian. Because we have a lot of money, your houses are less expensive than

> ours. To own a house means you own your peace. This is the first thing about stability. You pay extra [for rent], and you are afraid that this guy will come and get you out, so these things [rentals] must be solved for us. So, it is hard for me. The first thing [owning a house] does not exist. Second thing, ok, I have friends, and I have everything, but my family is not here, so I feel bad. Also, I am afraid if I want to create a family [get married and have children], I would be afraid for their future even if I have money. Until I get another citizenship, which is good citizenship, not being in Gaziantep, I will be so cool. I will be good.

In the eyes of Noury, belonging to any place requires citizenship or the right to own property and the possibility of bringing one's family to close proximity. Noury had a strong sense of local Aleppian identity and was surrounded by a strong network from his community in Gaziantep. His sense of belonging would have been complete if he could have his own home, as he considered peace starting in ownership of a house. His future aspirations were closely connected to experiencing community along with a sense of security where he would have a house that would guarantee his safety. When people experience forcefully being removed from their country without a return in the foreseeable future, in a world that promotes property ownership, it becomes both a real and symbolic safety along with a sense of belonging.

Not all felt similarly to Noury. Amina, who is from Baniyas, has seen her loved ones immolated, including her husband. She lived in an apartment complex that housed Syrian refugee women with their families like herself. She desires a future for her children, and her only wish is to see them get an education. She has expectations in terms of the future of her children, but she argues that she does "not want anything else." She argues that even though her children are at school, "[Türkiye is] still a foreign country, and we are still foreigners here." Her sense of belonging is not complete as she argues, "I feel strange here because I am from Baniyas, so I cannot see someone like me from the same area. A family from Baniyas came here, but they went to Europe, and I did not know them anyway. There is no one else from my area." For Amina, the past holds an important element for her sense of belonging, which is the essence of locality. In her present condition, particularly for her, there are no people from Baniyas, which is more challenging as she cannot find any connection. The present has no resemblance to the past as she knew it, which reflects her "not wanting anything else" than the future for her children. In this case, routine and iteration of the past are lost, causing a vague purpose of "a future for children" without any possible future trajectories, causing the present to lose its deliberation capacity for evolving situations. Najlaa, from a different approach, chose to skip a part of the near past when her husband was killed. She introduces herself not as a widow but as married, arguing that "when I look at my daughters, I feel that [my husband] is with me." Najlaa's positioning as still a married woman encourages her to adapt to life in Gaziantep. Ayan and Najlaa depart from different ways of positioning their past life and present moment. The feelings within the multiplicity of the time perception and envisioning of existence in multiple and complex ways of past, future, and present change the experiences of these two women. Najlaa has family members who were also in Gaziantep, while Ayan had only her children. Ayan states, "Maybe because I lost my husband and I do not have any relatives here,

I am living a standard life, and I cannot feel anything." Ayan goes through the motions with what she identifies as "not feeling" when she considers herself only in the present moment with the painful realization of the non-presence of people she loved in her life. Laila sees people like herself as a "sacrifice to the oppressors" and calls herself a "victim." Her reason is that "As a person, I think I am in this situation because I neither support the revolution nor the regime. Asad's soldiers destroyed my house and my life. That is why I see myself as a victim." Laila sees herself in "the now" without any hope for the future because her life, house, and past are destroyed. Her "now" is painful because the destruction of the past brings her no future expectations:

> My husband always says to me that I am such a negative person. I think my life is over. I think my son will be able to see Syria again, but I do not think I will.

When refugees position themselves within one dimension, their alienation, and expression of "numbness" were more often the direction of their feelings. In sum, there are at least four ways that temporality plays a role in refugee experiences. The first adapt themselves to life in the host community, the second is mostly focused on their desire to go back, and the third only focuses on the future and impossibility of going back either because of the conditions or because Syria as they knew it no longer existed. The final group was severely cut from past experiences, could not envision a future, and solely focused on the "here" and "now." Their engagement with time set the demarcation among these four groups of refugees. In other words, temporality is experienced differently. Some experienced it singularly by either focusing on the "now," the "past," or the "future" alone, rejecting one or the other, and some experienced multiple temporalities simultaneously. How temporality is positioned in their life showed differences in their experience of holding a refugee position.

How one has relationality with time influences one's present experience. If one experiences a severe cut from the past, such as the loss of a husband or no human connections from their past, they focus on the severity of the now, which may end up making them feel numb as they cannot envision any future for themselves though some still could project it on their children. If they are positioning themselves constantly to the past (nothing but a desire to go back), they appear depressed. If they continuously think about not wanting to ever go back to Syria in the future (the corner store is no longer there, my house is in shambles, my relatives are not there), they appear to be in extreme pain. Some others cannot envision a future due to a material lack of money, residency, citizenship, or clarity for owning a business, permanent job, or a house, which makes them anxious and in the sense of inertia. In other words, some cannot live in the present, while others live nowhere else but the present; some live nowhere else but in the past, which shapes their articulation of self, belonging, and becoming. Refugees show more resilience if the past and future are connected to the present. The following chapter will examine how the interviewees articulated the future of Syria. There was a difference between what they foresaw and what they envisioned.

References

Appadurai A (1996) Modernity at large: cultural dimensions of globalization, vol 1. University of Minnesota Press, Minneapolis

Brickell K (2012) 'Mapping' and 'doing' critical geographies of home. Prog Hum Geogr 36(2):225–244

Emirbayer M, Mische A (1998) What is agency? Am J Sociol 103(4):962–1023

Petridou E (2001) The taste of home. In: Miller D (ed) Home possessions: material culture behind closed doors. Berg, pp 87–106

Şahin-Mencütek Z, Gökalp-Aras NE, Kaya A, Rottmann SB (2023) Syrian refugees in Turkey: between reception and integration. Springer International Publishing, Cham

Turner VW (2017) Liminality and communitas. In: Turner V, Abrahams R, Harris A (eds) The ritual process: structure and anti-structure. Routledge, London, pp 169–187

Chapter 8
Between Foreseen and Envisioned Future of Syria

Past Informing the Future

Depending on people's worldviews, beliefs, and experiences, there was a lag between Syria's foreseen and envisioned future. The chapter discusses how Syrian refugees portray the realities they encounter. Additionally, it offers insights into their expectations and hopes for Syria's future governance structure. What shaped interviewees' view of the future was determined by the kind of past they focused on. There are different layers of the past. There is a "life-course past," meaning their past is concentrated on either their own past or recent past events. There is a "scriptural past," particularly for the pious or "historical past," meaning that they looked at either the prophetic times or the history of the country and the region for reference. The past perceptions are linked to the present articulation of refugees' future expectations and visions, especially in discussions about the post-Asad period. Therefore, the political governance section in this chapter will examine what refugees consider possible political structures after Asad. As a new governing structure emerged after 2024, the findings in this chapter may shed some light on the new era with the elaboration of potential advantages and disadvantages.

Scriptural or Historical Past Informing the Future

For the pious war widows, who were living in Islamic group-funded apartments, the future was blended with their belief, showing again multiple temporalities intertwined with the scriptural past and future. When answering their realistic expectation of the future of Syria, Khawla argues that even though "Bashar Asad took control of Syria… it is written that after the conflict and the problems, we will see the light at the end." She explains the source of her belief:

© The Author(s), under exclusive license to Springer Nature Singapore Pte Ltd. 2025

U. Ozkaleli, *De-essentializing Refugees: Perceptions, Experiences, and Becoming of Syrians in Türkiye*, https://doi.org/10.1007/978-981-96-5519-9_8

> It is written in the Qur'an. That God's victory is really close, and the martyrs who died are written in the Qur'an. The martyrs are alive, and they are in the hands of God. And there is a verse about one who is *maẓlūm* (oppressed) that says, 'I will let you see the victory after a certain time.' (Khawla)

Khawla intertwines multiple temporalities, leading her to believe that power will shift in future Syria, as the *mazlum* will replace the *zalim*. She envisions a future that will deliver justice for the oppressed, connecting this anticipated future to the scriptural past. For her, the scriptural past shapes the near future, prompting her to evaluate expectations based on her connections within this dual temporality. When they focused on the present destructions, some of the pious found explanations in religious script, believing that the war was the punishment for losing the religious path and focusing on material aspects of life, suggesting that good fortune will come as people find the right, i.e., religious, path, though not all are so optimistic. Ayla, another pious widow, focuses both on the religious scriptural past and the life-course past and gives a two-level assessment juxtaposing her hopes nurtured by faith and facts on the ground. She brings her observations from refugee-Syrian schools located in Türkiye to predict the future of Syria. She argues that because all the injustice and corruption (*fasad*) were already embraced by the new setting, building a different kind of Syria on top of the old one was not promising:

> [I see the future] black. There are no positive signs going around. On the small level, for example, they opened a lot of Syrian schools here [in Gaziantep]. The principals, the teachers, everyone is Syrian. We went back to the same behaviors we were doing in Syria, even here in Türkiye when we are foreigners. Now the situation is like this in the school: If someone is the son of the principal or manager of the school, he will get higher marks. If you know someone in the school, your child would be registered there easily. Bashar Asad was really smart. He finished the intellectual people in Syria and let go of the rest of the people. Our hope is in God. I hope that Syria will not be lost. The reality is not saying any good things about what will happen… I have a lot of hope, but this is the reality. We are sleeping, getting up, and just waiting for a miracle that God will do. If God says something, it will happen, as the verse says. (Ayla)

Like other widows who see the losses of war, Ayla's life-course past and present show a conflictual difference from her scriptural past connection that informs her envisioned life-course future. For the pious self, the multiple temporalities work in complex ways in their articulation of future provisions they have about Syria. The fear for the future that will continue to include *fasad* (corruption and malice) does not hinder her envisioned future for Syria, where Syrians will be able to overcome such unjust practices:

> We should repair everything. Why did we go out for this revolution? We wanted to remove *fasad* (corruption). We want everyone to be comfortable. We want justice; we do not want someone to prefer someone else over the other. We want everyone to have their rights. If we want to have good vegetables, we should look after the land well. We should put the appropriate person in the appropriate position. Money and bribes will let *fasad* come back, and we will be really far away from God and his rules. (Ayla)

Ayla's vision was articulated and pointed out wrongs in the system, desiring a future that included meritocracy, equality, and justice. She finds these values in the scriptural past. In the envisioned future, Nala, another pious widow, states, "I want [Syria] to be like [prophet] Mohammad wants us to be. It is all about *Shari'a* [Islamic law that regulates society]. Everything is included inside of it [*Shari'a*]. All the rules are included in Islam." Nala does not give any specific points about what rules are important, claiming they are difficult to explain. Batul, also a pious widow and a religion teacher, believes in patiently raising children for future Syria and states that how she envisioned future Syria is "first not to let our country to be secular. *Shari'a* and religion should be applied in a good way. With tolerance to everyone. Islam is not closed; Islam is open, and we should be open with everyone." For Batul, secular rule in Syria meant keeping The Ministry of Education close to the people who studied Shari'a under The Ministry of Religion, giving them lower salaries. What is central for the state to be secular and religious, in this view, is who and in what way provides education for children. While Batul is adamant about the formation of an Islamic state in the future, she argues the necessity of the co-existence of different religions and religious sects under Shari'a rule. She presents her ideas about how such co-existence is going to be formulated:

> This is a big question [how different religions and sects will co-exist]. We always take examples from Prophet Muhammad, looking if Islam is deleting everything before him. When we look at the lifetime of Prophet Muhammad, we see that he dealt with all religions. He has tolerance for all religions, and he used to love all religions. He has relationships with Christian and Jewish people. There should be tolerance among all religions. Religion is peace (*salām*). Tolerance and love (*mahabba*). It is not about the power and who will control whom. (Batul)

While Batul wanted Shari'a as the base of society away from secularism by solely focusing on the scriptural past without a connection to the life-course past, Reem, as a pious widow, reached a different kind of conclusion after her experiences about the role of religion in the future of Syria:

> I started to feel scared of the extremists that entered the country. They did not exist before. We are a religious people, but from the middle level [moderate], DAESH or El-Nusra Front do not represent us. We should take them out of their roots and kick them out of the country. Unfortunately, we have a lot of young people from our families who joined these groups. Syria has really changed. It is not like before, especially in the religious situation. It should take, or it has to take, a lot of effort to take this thought away from it, and we have to tell our kids about our religion, the middle level of [moderate] this religion. Especially in Aleppo, we have Christians, side by side with Muslims, Armenians, and Jewish people. We should all live together, reconstructing Syria. However, with religion, it is a very difficult thing. I think, as I said, the future is in our children's hands. They should educate other people about it. It will take a long time, and I think a lot of blood will be spilled on the streets. (Reem)

Reem's difference from Batul's Shari'a-based envisioned society comes from the temporality she focuses on. Reem sees the religious base as undesirable, as extremists would change the fabric that would not allow plurality to exist. Reem's reference point is the recent past after seeing how the use of religion as a source created DAESH and the El-Nusra Front, which she did not find any similarity to her own understanding of religion. Both women consider themselves religious and argue that their husbands reached martyrdom, which makes them proud. Yet, Reem's life-course future vision shifted as she focused on the recent life-course past, where she observed the effects of religious governance on her country. In contrast, Batul's words continuously echo prophetic time, connecting her desire for a future in Syria with a religious governing structure. The only temporality Batul is taking is the scriptural past, believing that the long-ago past and religious tolerance could be achieved in the future.

It was not only pious women who formulated views that took different temporalities as a base for their formulation of the future of Syria. Bilal, a young Turkmen man who did not mention religion much up until the question of the future of Syria, explains a mix-and-match system where religion and civil rule are combined in the future. Bilal was worried at first about being judged as a radical Islamist reactionary, arguing that he was not at all radical:

> I would prefer to live in a society in which Shari'a rules. For the societies in this region, it is the most suitable system... That system had governed the people in this region [the Middle East] for a hundred years, maybe a thousand years. I do not mean we should be against democracy. Shari'a does not have a lot of characteristics that are in contradiction with democracy... In the end, in one society, the Shari'a says Allah's word is the valid one, and the Qur'an will be your constitution. But this does not have a contradiction of choosing people you want [for governance] because, in the end, in Western societies, there is a constitution as well. If we put principles from the Qur'an and create a constitution from these principles, and if we say this is the constitution of this country, you can elect the man you want, but that man has to follow the articles/rules. So, it does not have a contradiction with democracy. This does not have to be an imam or Shari'a graduate, but it has to follow the religious rules. In its usage and customs, in the ways of governing, the state has to follow religious rules. (Bilal)

The reasons he gives for finding religious constitution a necessity show that multiple temporalities are at work in Bilal's thinking. He moves beyond Syria and argues that in the region, Shari'a law existed for "hundreds, maybe thousand years." His argument may not necessarily focus on the scriptural past, as the pious women mentioned "prophetic times," but he still takes "religion as history," which he attributes to the whole region. Bilal's way of reading history is not limited to his views on religion. He also believes that having a "dictator" even after Asad is gone is inevitable for Syria. While he says it is possible to have democratic elections, a combination of his view about the inescapability of a dictator, along with his desire to have religious rule, would lead to a theological dictatorship. This omission probably came from his desire for a Sunni majority rule. A considerable number of male participants, regardless of whether they wanted a religious governance or a secular one, argued that Sunnis were the majority, which meant they should hold control of the government.

Similar in age to Bilal, Amez and Amir expressed their views quite differently, holding a secular understanding that shaped their distinct vision for Syria's future. Scriptural past also plays an important role in their articulation, though it marks what they are against. While Amez and Amir are a non-believer and an agnostic, respectively, they also used historical argument, blending today to past temporalities, arguing that "religion was the cause of conflicts for centuries" and must be removed from the political equation. Seculars do not have a scriptural past to take as a reference point, but they do have a "past as history" (Hakli and Kallio 2018) that informs their future projections. Both men and women who were from secular worldviews argued the necessity of moving religion away from the future governance of Syria. Zeinab's views further capture the secular approach:

> I think it is essential to keep politics apart from religion if you want to build a good, constructive country. You need to let the religious people and religion in mosques. That was a key for Europe to enter a very different stage of its time. The Middle Ages were so dark that churches murdered many. Europe got rid of all of this and started to build good, developed countries out of politics. This is your religion, your belief, your opinions. This is how you belong and how you want to live. No one can take these rights, but religion is something spiritual, related to heaven. Live it there in that place. This is the ground we are living on, and we want to put rules in this life in order to build a democratic and open-minded government. This needs to put religion aside. (Zeinab)

It is important to notice that while pious people look at the scriptural past to shape their expectations and their judgments of today according to it, seculars look at the same past to develop arguments about future expectations against it. "The dark period of the Middle Ages" is a past history that is shaping future projections and present judgments for the seculars. While the prophetic time is taken as an ideal point for the pious, the Enlightenment is for the secular. Neither the prophetic time nor European politics is questioned.

The focus on the scriptural/historical past diverges between the secular and the pious. Yet, in terms of the need for co-existence between different communities and religions, there is a potential for commonality. Some pious people believe in civil governance, others believe in tolerance toward different religions by referencing prophetic times, and for seculars, the aspiration of democratic rule is co-existence.

Seeds of Enmity and Children as Embodiment of the Future

Participants, like Ayman, are concerned about the enmity seeds planted in the young generations. In his envisioned Syria, if he could change anything, he aspired to change the mindset of children who were going to be the future of Syria. He argued that "the fathers" hate each other and the only way "sons" were not to follow it was to know that their fathers' way was wrong. If they are smart, raised with education, awareness, ethics, and an open mind, they will have an opportunity to think freely and change. Unlike the older generation, who would always fight, the children would go on a different path and never speak of the past but focus on the now. While Ayman envisioned such a future, he was not hopeful:

> In reality, it is more complicated. His son is raised hating me, and my son is coming asking what has happened, and I will say he fought me, he killed me. Both will be like their father, so there is no solution.

In Ayman's mind, the way people in conflict relate to the past would always be destructive in its influence on the present. His formulation is to shut down the past completely. As this is not possible, detaching children from their fathers' hate appears to need magic. What he aspires to and what he knows from the past do not match. This results in a sense of detachment, making him refrain from involvement even though he started actively supporting the revolution. Ayman's concern about "forgiving and forgetting" was shared by others. Akila, for example, worries about how the future is going to be built after the atrocities:

> I do not have a good image of a future Syria. Everyone has something broken inside. Maybe a Shi'a person killed your son; I will never forgive him, for example. Maybe he is from ISIS, and he took my land, and cut my head. I do not think, and I do not know if people are going to be able to forgive and forget. It is really too hard… (Akila)

For Akila, the future and past were in constant comparison: the future looked bleak as she lost hope of finding or reaching a Syria like in the past that she knew. Akila's, very much like Ayman's, constant imagining of the past and the possibilities of the future paved the path of how she felt in the present, mostly losing hope for the future in comparison to the past of Syria.

Children, in different ways, were the biggest concern for several different participants. Lamia was worried about 3 million children being without school and wished a nationalist and strong leader would come to power to protect these children. One of the most disadvantaged urban refugees in terms of class in this study was Karima. She refused to position herself in many other topics, arguing that "no one would listen or care about people like me." Nevertheless, she expressed that she wanted nothing more than to go back to Syria when it was secure. Her main concern was the safety of children:

> Children should be able to go to their schools without being killed or without a rocket or plane bombing their schools. What is the guilt of children that they are dying? I just want Syria to be secure and to be stable.

In his envisioned future, Nawar argues that it is so far away from the possibility that he cannot even dream of a utopian future. His future desire for Syria is connected to the fact on the ground, he sees Syria's future like children who are deprived of schools:

> The recovery is not going to be easy, that is for sure. It is destroyed, and now we have to go to the level of poverty. The reports show that a huge number of children are out of school. Sure, we were not the most developed country, but somehow, my country used to admire education very much. If you are a taxi driver, still get a university degree, and this is not for the sake of money but for the sake of society [was the understanding]. We have lost even that view. Too many people, particularly children, do not know how to read and write. My number one focus would be on this. (Nawar)

The conditions of children were tangible observations. People who paid attention to the conditions of children both inside Syria and for refugees had difficulty envisioning Syria's future. In such cases, children have become the symbol of people being confined in the severity of the present realities. Haya was also worried about children who were cut out of school due to war. Her narrative compared the education gap between children who were living under regime rule and those outside of it:

> If I were in power, the first thing I would do is to re-build the schools. Because many regime supporters' children still go to school. Five years ago, if a child was five years old, he is now ten. This child did not go to school for five years and received no information or educa-

> tion… So, the first thing I would do is rebuild the schools. The organization that my husband works with built four schools inside Syria, but unfortunately, three of them were bombed. The other was under a basement, so the aircraft could not get it. (Haya)

A future cannot be built without an educated population. Haya is worried because the number of schools is much less than the number of children who need education. Zeinan had to leave Raqqa despite not wanting it because she did not feel safe as she came face to face with ISIS in her home. She is a teacher with seventeen years of experience, loves her job, and aspires to return home and open a school. She is deeply worried about children who are without any school:

> Many children left school, and many children lost their chance to learn. My nephew and others do not go to school. When I phone them, they cry. They tell me, "Auntie, I do not go to school, I want to go to school, I want to…" [her voice rises when she says this, and at this point, she stops. She is crying with anguish]. It is too bad for Syria. (Zeinan)

Her view of the future, due to the knowledge about the lack of schools, was grim. However, as her occupation was teaching, she was sure her skills were needed and envisioned a future where she could be of value. This gave her a contradictory emotional state at the present. On the one hand, she was frustrated and even in anguish that she could not reach all those children who needed her. On the other hand, she saw herself as capable and one of the people who were going to be needed in Syria in the future. This gave her the strength to continue and wait for the day she was going to be reunited with children in Syria who were denied schooling. Unlike some others, her devastation of seeing the conditions of children did not lock her in the now as she connected her past experiences as a teacher to her future possibilities. This gave her the strength to envision herself being active in the future of Syria.

Two men, Nazem and Fahed, worked in NGOs that granted them a chance to work in the education field for children and youth within Syria. While Zeinan was in anguish at the present as she could not work with children, Nazem and Fahed demonstrated energy and strength, positioning themselves today in accordance with their future expectation of reaching as many children as possible to bring them education. Syrian refugees who had access to work, particularly with communities inside Syria, showed a lot more aspirations and hope for the future of Syria. Particularly, working with children brings a strong connection not only for being able to work with valuable groups but also the hope it generates as children are the embodiment of the future of their country.

Political Governance

How participants envision the future governance of Syria is closely linked to their past experiences, current conditions, and future expectations. While many are not overly optimistic, they discussed their visions for Syria's future governance. Some participants mentioned ways of establishing a sustainable governing structure, while others expressed doubts, fearing that Syria may face a future marked by stalemate, conflict, or even dictatorship. Some participants drew specific analogies from Afghanistan or Iraq to illustrate their perspectives on the future. There was also a mention of Bosnia as a "bad scenario" for Syria's future, as Faysal argued that Bosnian people were still under oppression. Others used Lebanon as a negative analogy. Salah argued that the situation might become a stand-still position like Cyprus, a stalemate if the peace talks do not produce any results. Many believed that conflict was going to continue for at least ten more years, while others expected it to last fifteen. Our conversation happened in 2016, which was close, as the end of the Asad regime came in December 2024. Most participants in this study indicated that it would take about twenty years for them to be able to return. While some believed they could return after the war, many felt they would never be able to live there permanently again. Some only hoped to take their children to visit Syria. Suad, who is one of the oldest participants at age 68, believes refugees like herself will not ever go back. She explains the reason as "because I am not finding any person who has ideas or principles for new Syria or good thoughts for Syria unfortunately ... The leadership should be very charismatic, and they cannot find any leader to show this."

Some believed a new direction would come with a parliamentarian democracy with civic rule, while others believed that Islam-based governance was needed. Many of the participants believed that the future of Syria held division. How they named this division and how they felt about it showed differences. Few people who were not against the regime, like Lina, wanted everything to be like it was before and stability that would allow refugees to go back home. Some others also wanted things to be like before, only with the change of power where Bashar Asad would no longer be in power. Some thought certain autonomous governing entities or recognition of different groups, such as the Kurds, were good approaches, while others aspired to have a united Syria. United Syria came with different opinions. Some argued the need for uniting Syria as a multi-ethnic, multi-religious, multi-cultural society where everyone was represented without any religion being in the governing structure. Others believed tolerance and diversity should be under the rule of the Sunni majority in a secular structure or under Shari'a law.

Division

The possibility of division brought the situation of Kurds to the focus for many of the participants. While all of the Kurdish men in the focus group wanted to go back to their homes in Syria, they had different articulations of political endpoints. Jiwan explains how he sees the future of Syria:

> New Syria will be under the control of the regional and external agenda of Americans and Russians. Syrian people are weak. They cannot do anything. All the Syrian elements are the victims of the international community, and they are only fuel to this fire. Future Syria will be for all Syrians, but it will be non-central authorities or a federal government. (Jiwan)

Jiwan looks at ethnic and religious minorities as being victims of the international community and their future being shaped by the superpowers. He desires at least some sort of autonomy. Merwan, in turn, is concerned about the possibility of such an aim:

> We have the Kurdistan dream. We need to implement it, however, having this dream is like having the dream of uniting the Arab people. It is the same dream, but logically, we cannot actualize this dream. We need to live in Syria as a Syrian minority. (Merwan)

Behram takes the word from Merwan and argues that while he does not want to ignore the dream of Kurds, he thinks that his people need to think according to the realities. He qualifies the "minority" position by rejecting a "majoritarian" democracy as he claims it would not work. He argues that Kurds need to be recognized in the political system. Merwan takes the word again and explains:

> Kurdish Street is divided into three groups: the first one is the Kurdish National Movement. The second one is PYD, which is led by Salih Muslim. The [third one is] independent people that we call civil society. [When we look at] these three sides, their programs, their statements, and their goals, do not say they need a Kurdistan or an independent Kurdish country… I read all the programs of Kurdish parties in Syria, and I am part of an independent civil society. I am there with them in the street, and I know. At the same time, there are dreams inside, but we should have a foundation for that dream. We cannot change a map of 5-6 countries in the region. Logically, you cannot. We could do such a thing only if the international community needed it. (Merwan)

Amez's, a young Kurdish man, articulation of what would happen in Syria is not only blended with his community of refugees or his interactions with the host community but with Western academic institutions' discourse that he works for:

> There will be a transitional phase, which will happen very soon. This transitional phase will either be accepted by the local population, or it will fail miserably as it did in Iraq, where Sunni tribes started fighting the jihadists alongside the Shi'a government installed by the Americans. That was a major failure because it was a temporary solution for two or three years managed just to decrease the influence of radical Islam. If the Syrian model does not win the majority, it will collapse. We will enter this dilemma similar to the Afghani or Iraqi models. This is for the general Sunni areas of Syria. No, not Sunni, general Arab areas. In the Kurdish areas, I would see a federalization. I know we are in Türkiye, and I should not talk about this, but I see the current Kurdish-Turkish war that is going on now between PKK and the Turkish government. I would see a solution will come soon. Local governance will take place in the Kurdish areas. Now, the Kurds of Iraq have local governments, and the Kurds of Syria have a local government, and it will turn to a federalization. The Kurds of Türkiye will take their own governance, and now the Syrians have their own governance. The Syrian Kurds and the Iraqi Kurds have their local governance. Those are federations, as they call them, cantons. Those cantons will open up to each other and form a similar state to the state thing. (Amez)

Amez gives this answer as his realistic articulation, as his expectation of what will happen in the future. He also provides his envisioned future for Syria. Similar to some of the above ones, there is a connection between how one sees the real situation and how one adjusts their envisioned future:

> For now, I would prefer the Syrian state to have cantons or local governance for each state: a Sunni federation, a Sunni canton, a Kurdish canton, an Alawite canton, and a canton that

> would connect all of them. A confederation similar to models such as Belgium and Switzerland, but Belgium is the correct one. That is the best scenario to see Syrians live with each other without major problems. (Amez)

In addition to intra-Kurdish differences, others have different views about Kurdish separation. Farah, an Arab female, sees Kurds as being supported by the U.S., while Russians and Iranians are supporting Alawites and Shi'a. She believes there will be division based on these identities. The feelings about the partitioning of Syria are in a clash, which is captured in Farah's expression. She explains that she continuously discusses the possibility of division with her best friend:

> I am not very optimistic; I am pessimistic. I don't think you can solve this… It [division] is sad. My best friend and I have a continuous fight about it. She is okay with the division and sees it as normal. I know it will happen and end the war somehow, but it is *sad*! I mean, I don't want Syria to be divided. I think it is not normal not to be sad, she is not sad at all. Be sad! At least be sad! [she laughs nervously]. I am with the rights of the Kurds. But I am more likely to have them in Syria somehow and have their rights when they are Syrians. But I do not think this will happen. (Farah)

Like Farah, Aykut, a Turkmen man, does not welcome the division but says there is already partition in Syria. He interprets Kurdish independence very differently than Amez did. Aykut sees Syria as a "fire" that burns everyone indiscriminately, from poor to rich, religious to atheist to laicist, from men, women to elderly. Aykut believes that Europe is using Kurds in the region, and he is doubtful about the survivability of a Kurdish state:

> I think there are very good Kurds, but there is also a side of Kurds that do not read the history well. I mean, Turks, Arabs, Turkmen, Armenians, and Circassians are all in these places. They have been living together for 2000 years. We are not leaving this region. We all live here. If Kurds do not live in a good manner with these people, America is now here, Europe is here, and Europe has been using them in very clear ways. I see that, for example. But when you look at it, how will this Kurdish state live? Seriously, how will they exist? If they create a state, even if that state reaches the sea, it is very difficult for it to sustain itself. Inevitably, they have to depend on their Arab and Turkish neighbors. If they were going to live in conflict with these neighbors, how would they continue? (Aykut)

Aykut has a different articulation than Amez. He reads about the establishment of a Kurdish state by engaging multiple temporalities, going all the way back 2000 years, and bringing an argument based on a reading of the past to make a judgment about the future. In this case, forming a state is read as "behaving badly." As Aykut sees partition as a problem for all sides of the conflict, his "brightest dream" for Syria is a united one even though he knows it would never be the old Syria:

> The question is how we are going to re-construct this country again together with all ethnic and religious groups, Alawites, and others. Someone showed cruelty, and a part of society supported him in this, but the opposition also showed cruelty, and they had big faults as well. That is why we need to forget all the wrongs, a point zero, or we need to stop it and re-start everything as a civilized country where human dignity is protected. If we start from this point, there is nothing we cannot do for Syria. (Aykut)

Ahlaam also examines the political situation of division from a spatial and temporal positioning. Unlike Aykut, she believes that it would be necessary to divide and recognize the Kurdish part. While she is firm on her standing and argues this for peace, she also brings in her spatial separation from Syria, acknowledging that she endorses division as a Syrian who is positioned outside of it. While she wants to believe that she would argue the same thing if she were in Syria, she is conscious about being "here" and talking about "there." Still, her spatial "outsider" position does not change the fact that she thinks about her future children and her family's future in Syria. In other words, her views are shaped by these multiple temporalities of today and the future, formed in dual spatiality.

Nawar was against the division and the idea of two flags in Syria and perceived it as an aspect of propaganda to divide the country. Nawar believed that if there was one flag, it would signal Syria's shifting from the old government to new ideas, logic, and philosophies. Two flags, for him, felt like the creation of new stories that artificially divided the people who were from the same history, making it only about eliminating the other and "who controlled" the country without much difference in ideology. The duality comes as "stories" in Nawar's narrative. He approaches the creation of a new flag as an attempt to create new stories, separating the history and, hence, the people from one another. The new formulations, in other words, would change the understanding of the past. Creating a new now would also create new stories for the past, which would not hold the country together. Nawar says the possibility of division is "hurting" him because he believes that division will take its power and weaken Syria and stresses: "We used to say Kuwait is like a neighborhood, and they called it a country, but now we are driving ourselves to many Kuwaits."

Farah desired a united Syria where people loved each other and lived together, but the realities of war made it difficult to believe in such a possibility. She argued that for people to forget the bloodshed, there was a need for a strong government "to impose everyone, whether they like it or not, to live and love each other." "Imposition of love" is not only a contradiction but signals desperation to sustain the lost unity. The strength of the desire for unity may mean that another authoritarian government may be acceptable for some.

Many believed that division was awaiting Syria, some seeing it necessary and even desirable but many others being against it. When people explored the idea of a future government in a united Syria, they articulated what that government should look like. Some argued for an authoritarian government, following Farah's idea about needing a government with "tough love," while others believed in the possibility of democracy. Each will be examined in the following sections.

United Syria Under Democracy

In connection to the realities she sees on the field and her sadness and rejection of the division of Syria, Farah fluctuates with what she deems a reality of needing a strong government and her vision for a Syria that is much more localized:

> Now, we have these Islamic, Islamist forces spreading, and they have power over people. It is really dangerous. I wish I could unify all the civilian actors or civilian organizations, which are Local Councils that are not affiliated with any armed group or any Islamic vision group. This alternative governing body must be civilian. It must not be Islamic. The Local Councils and Provincial Councils represent a good percentage of people, and they are not Islamists. (Farah)

During the uprising, Local Councils[1] became the manifestation of the grassroots challenge to the Asad regime and examples of homegrown democratic governance bodies (Ozkaleli and Byrne 2023). Several other participants also had a high opinion of them as an alternative, and few had experience working in local councils. Nazem firmly believed that Local Councils would play a role in helping people explore the meaning of identity and citizenship, their rights and roles in society, and practice cooperation. While seeing their potential, participants believe that due to the existing power struggles, armed groups' and outside powers' interference, the Local Councils would not be allowed to gain strength to lead the country to a democratic structure. People like Nawar aspire to a future that would bring social justice, freedom, and dignity to society at large. Nawar argues that people in the besieged areas and suburbs of Syria were asked what they thought about the peace talks and conferences that were held in Geneva, and they had no belief in any kind of solution that would come from these talks, and they did not believe that they were represented in these talks. He connects issues of representation to local councils:

> We do not have other alternative solutions. We have nothing to defend on behalf of our names, no one to speak for our case. Democracy is still beyond reality. Now is the time of war. Even, for example, [suppose] there was a huge international program to replace the services that regime used to provide, municipalities or hospital or to fix infrastructures or road systems, whatever it is, and all of the areas, [this would be] implementing through Local Councils. The Local Councils are the elected body in the country. [Currently], each area also has a military group, and military groups always have a powerful influence on the local council and in the area. So simply, the local council is controlled by an army group while it should be the other way around. (Nawar)

This is mostly confirmed by Camil and Mayar's interviews as well. There are few alternatives to this where armed groups spare villages from fighting (Bell and Wise 2022), but mostly, the dominance of the armed groups is observed. This analysis is important to show the conditions for preventing the development of democratic alternatives that people like Nawar, Camil, and Mayar believed possible.

Tawfik's assessment of the existing situation signaled division. Yet, he continues with the aim of the revolution, which was to have one "Syrian" identity regardless of religion or ethnicity. After the collapse of the regime, he envisions a democratic Syria, which he defined as "a government that serves its citizens, not the people who serve the government. The people have always been slaves to the government in Syria. We want a democratic state that respects human rights, that respects justice

---

[1] For an extensive literature about Local Councils and civil society, see Berti (2020), Brownlee (2015), Hajjar et al. (2017), Khalaf (2015), Khoury (2013), Ozkaleli and Byrne (2023), Sosnowski and Hamadeh (2021).

and equality." While the defining characteristic of Syria was its "one Syrian identity" for Tawfik, Mayar, a pious man who was arrested and tortured by the regime, envisioned a future that reflected his expectation that came from his suffering: "political and social rights, and freedom" where "people should [be able to] say their thoughts without any pressure." The concepts of democracy, freedom, and justice meant different things depending on people's intersectional identities and past histories. It is not a coincidence that Mayar, being punished for his views, envisioned freedom of speech while Tawfik, who always was secondary as a Sunni Muslim in the military ranks, wanted to eliminate ethnicity-defined hierarchies.

Zeinab stressed her desire for a democratic country, which included women having their rights and playing an active role in Syria. Her understanding of democracy entails "people rul[ing] themselves by themselves. Freedom of joining parties, participating in the political process, in elections." When it comes to Syria, Zeinab is both realistic and hopeful, thinking that Syria, in time, with different steps, could achieve democratic rule if it engages in institution building. Zeinab sees democracy as possible because "experiencing a lot of conflicts and [intra] religious fight makes Syria understand the matter very well." Here, not only is Zeinab's ideas about the future shaped by the articulation of the past in the present moment, but she also hopes that the same will be done by society, learning from the past to change course for a better future.

Firas also wanted a secular and democratic future Syria with a strong civil society. While seeing the future as complex and hard to predict, for there are many different actors involved in the country's processes, he, like Zeinab, thinks the experiences prepared Syrians for democratic governance:

> I wish that, after five years of revolution, or if we can call it an uprising, it would give people more maturity, freedom of speech, and experience in many issues. We have many civil society organizations. We paid a high price, so I hope this fight will end and the new democratic Syria will come. (Firas)

Zeinan, who is a young college student, defines herself as a liberal like her family, and she argues that she likes to see a liberal party in Syria. Liberal party for her is:

> A very good party where there is a lot of difference and a lot of open-minded people inside of it. A party that separates religion from the state.

Amal, a divorced, pious woman and mother of three, also desires a democracy and explains the benefits of democracy as follows: "Democracy guarantees the freedom of everyone. It develops people to think about politics and the politicians to think about people." Fatima, in her view, sees the problem closely relating to the fragments of society and the lack of interaction among them. Therefore, creating the Syria she envisions entails a democratic, multiparty, and secular system. Fatima argues that there is a need to start from the beginning, having people learn about each other and interact more. She desires and envisions a different governing structure that she calls a "parliamentarian democracy," arguing that she does not believe that the presidential system is suitable for power sharing.

Genwa, who is a pious hijabi woman and women's rights activist, dreams of becoming a minister in the future of Syria. She argues that she would rebuild Syria based on her understanding of diversity. Here is how she defines it:

> As an engineer, I know that there is diversity in the environment of Syria. You can find a temperature in one area, and in another, the temperature is ten degrees different. So, we have diversity at the geographical and environmental levels. In a small area, this diversity makes a lot of plants and a lot of flowers open. [We need to] reflect this diversity of the environment to the people. As an engineer, I look at the environment and tell you that it is unique. When I look at the diversity in Syria, as a Syrian, I should look at the diversity in humans as well. I think it is a treasure, and we should rebuild Syria with that diversity. (Genwa)

When asked about the future of Syria, different interviewees started either from their experiences and observations and blended them with their knowledge to argue for democracy. Participants who believed in the possibility of democracy worked with people at different levels both in pre-war and wartime Syria. Experience of Local Councils inside Syria and working with different sub-groups of Syrians as refugees made them believe that they could build a Syria that appreciated diversity. Not all, however, were as hopeful for the possibility of a democratic governance in Syria.

United Syria Under Another Authoritarian Rule

In the previous section, people shared views and visions that see the possibility of a democratic rule and want a substantial change in the political system. Others focused on "who" should govern rather than a systemic change. Rouaa, a 37-year-old college graduate woman, explains her vision:

> I want a new government. We need a new government and a good man to be the president of Syria. We do not want a president from the Alawite segment, we have seen how they are killing a lot of Sunni. We want [a president] from Sunni. Most people in Syria are Sunni. It was not important if it was from Sunni or Christian, but this Alawite segment made a lot of massacres in Syria. That does not mean that some people who are Alawite are not good. There are some, many people who are good in the Alawite segment, but we need a new government, and we need a good man to be a president in new Syria. You know he [Asad] destroyed a lot of schools, hospitals, mosques, churches. We need support from a lot of countries, and we need a new Syria. (Rouaa)

It is important to note that, in Rouaa's vision, another "man," a "good man," is desired, so in essence, there is no challenge to the existing system per se but to the person who is the president of the country.

Supporting majoritarian rule was common. While some believed in majoritarian (parliamentarian) democracy, they also believed that immediate transitioning to democracy would be an unattainable goal. People gave different reasons for seeing immediate trial for democracy as a challenge. Some argued that people lived under dictatorial rule for long years and needed to transition to democracy gradually, not immediately. Others believed that the effects of war, destruction, and enmity people experienced have not created a conducive environment for democracy yet. Ziad explains that he desires a democracy where the parliament controls the government to stop wrongdoings. Moving from an analogy of a company, Ziad argues that just like a project can be carried out by the best people in business, he wants the governments to be run by the most eligible people. Right after affirming his belief in a parliamentary democracy with strong checks and balances, he takes a dramatic turn in his argument:

> After this situation [war] in Syria, there cannot be a democracy. The person who comes after this will be a bit dictatorial but a just [benevolent] dictator. In Syria, if you have normal democracy, the situation would be like it is in Iraq now. Why? In the last five years, people have not followed any rules. They have forgotten about them. How are you going to make them follow the rules? You cannot... The Middle Eastern people have a head on their own. They are not good at obeying. How you would put them into the right path is [through] violence. The question is, what sort of violence is just violence? We live with violence now, so I do not mean violence in the sense of fighting, but an authoritarian, strong man will come and then slowly will go to democracy. You cannot just have democracy in one day! ... [In] 2011 we could have gone to democracy. How are we going to get people used to democracy now? They need a process... We need something: a man who is full of wisdom, knows what he is doing, and is a little bit of a dictator just to take the country under control. Then, slowly, the process will go to democracy. They need to get used to democracy and what it means to be free. They have not practiced freedom for the last forty years, and now, after these five years, it is even worse. (Ziad)

In his "institutionalization before democratization" argument, Paris (2004) makes a similar claim, not suggesting a benevolent dictatorship but focusing on building institutions without completely denouncing authoritarian rulers. Ziad's depiction of "the Middle Easterner" is a projection of a Western camera that readily generalizes and stereotypes people. An important element in Ziad's statement is that there was a moment in time when he thought Syria was ready for democratic governance. Analyzing his narrative through different temporalities brings us to crucial interpretations that need to be addressed. His argument about Syrians being ready for democracy at the beginning of the revolution in 2011 is a meaningful one, as many participants in this study argued that Syrians, particularly younger generations, demanded change for the betterment of their social, economic, and political rights. The society encouraged its members for education, and people wanted more opportunities to be provided, and they demanded more representation. Connecting this information to how Syrians created Local Councils at the beginning of the uprising shows that home-grown progress toward democratic engagement was flourishing. The step taken back from democratic practice and expectation is the product of the war. In other words, war stole away progress.

Amir's view and belief in creating an "anti-religious" government mirror some of the religious views where they insist that religion needs to regulate all aspects of life. Amir argues that for "the greater good," a future government needed to be anti-religious as religion had the tendency to "get out of hand." Amir argues that peace cannot come democratically as many people are angry at each other for the war atrocities. In Amir's forceful views, a temporal element is at work. For Amir, democracy is not workable because "everyone is angry." Not very different than Ziad, his evaluation of the possibility of democracy in the future is related to the recent past, war, violence, and people's anger toward one another. The conditions created by war are the main reason for him to firmly believe that democratic governance cannot be applied.

Ziad and Amir connected the difficulty of democratic rule in Syria to war experience, the anger of groups toward one another, and distance from normalcy. Unlike them, some other participants are against democratic rule in Syria as a principle. While working in the interim government that was located in Gaziantep at the time of the interviews, Kamal, who is a strongly religious man, argues that:

> Of course, democracy is not a good solution for Syria! Because when we get the authority, I am afraid they will control the way the previous regime controlled the country. Most of the Syrians are religious people. It is in their mind that democracy was applied to us after our independence, and the result was a failure. They should take care of the religion. The Syrian people will decide on this after a free election, and the Syrian people will decide on the type of governance and constitution.

Kamal's temporal evaluation does not consider war as the reason for being against democracy, and there is no gradual shift toward democracy like Ziad is formulating. He looks at the independence of Syria for his reasoning and by generalizing the entire Syrian population, sees democracy as being against what they want and need. Kamal's words were indicative that he firmly believes that the majority wants a Sunni Islamic rule. Through majoritarian decisions, he sees a future in which religious dictates will control society in the future.

Haya, while believing in democracy, also believes that Syria is not ready to practice democracy but brings a different perspective than the above views. She offers a strong gender lens to her assessment:

> Not in the very near future Syria can be a democracy. Because I think people are not ready for it. People are going to Europe, Türkiye, and Syria to experience democracy in Western countries. Actually, that is one of the positive sides of the revolution. They are going to learn something about democracy. Then, democratic control will come to Syria, not now, but one day. For now, I think we are just not ready. Now, we have dictators within the families itself. The father says 'you are forced to stay at home and not go to the university because I said so.' People are not open-minded. We need to reach a point where a considerable number is open-minded. After people accept the idea that only one man controlling them and benefiting from this control is a problem, they will be ready for democracy. Now, everyone wants to be the leader. Everyone needs to be in control, so that is why we are not ready for democracy. (Haya)

"Being ready" was Ziad's approach, but not at all like Haya's. Haya's assessment is accurate for a certain segment. As emphasized in previous quotes, both men and women referred to a possible leader/president as a "man," and their desire for a "strong man." Haya also brings time into her analysis. As more Syrians throughout the years travel to different countries and experience different governing structures, over time, she believes that will reflect on Syrian political life in the future.

Unlike Ziad and Kamal, Nawar did not believe in the need for the authoritarian system but was afraid of the actualization of it in a possible new Syria. While Nawar desires a revolution in the minds of people to shift for freedom and justice, he does not see such a shift occurring. Nawar and several others talked about "continuing regime mentality" even in the host country, Türkiye. They are worried about the authoritarian, corrupt, and unjust system continuing with just a change of people and names who are holding the power. Nawar gave an example of part of the opposition that functioned in Gaziantep-Türkiye as an interim government (until 2017) and argued that they are no better than the regime. He, just like Ayla, who was talking about the Syrian schools in Türkiye, claims that the "Interim government follows the same old concept of the regime. We even call them the new Ba'ath Party because they have the same ideology, and they just changed the brand. They came up with a new name, a new flag, and new characters, and applied the same thing."

There are, then, four streams of ideas regarding the political governance of Syria. First, people who believe in the religious-based rule where Sunni Islam is the base of the society as it represents the majority of the population in a system that is not democracy. Second, people who believe in democracy, but are firm in their conviction that there is a need for a transitional dictatorship to prepare people for many facets of democracy. Third, people who believe in democracy but do not see it possible in the foreseeable future as conflict continues and there is no clear and acceptable leadership to represent society. Fourth, people who believe that Syria needs to start building an institutional structure for a democratic future, and with all the experiences, it is possible for Syria to have free, fair elections and a democratic system where freedom and justice are prominent.

Author eye-camera: Orientalist depiction of Arabs lacking the ability to self-govern is a long-standing colonial construct that is supported by movies like Lawrence of Arabia (Erlich 2014*). In many instances, demands from different Arab communities have been dismissed, and oftentimes, local population demands have not been considered by Western powers. Instead, they supported authoritarian leaders who, in turn, supported their policies (Erlich* 2014*). Orientalist discourse and colonial history need to be a central part of the analysis when people express self-doubt about their communities' potential for democracy. Not only the Westerneyed construction of identities that are internalized through colonial histories but also actual power relations need to be considered. Democracy is a process, a trial and error for all communities. In order to progress in democratic governance, there needs to be an opportunity for "lessons learned." In today's world, post-colonial settings are still mostly not at a "post" moment, meaning that power politics are played on these communities' future. The involvement of regional and global powers in Syria is a clear indication of the interruption of democratic leanings and efforts of these communities. Therefore, the mindset about the necessity of authoritarian rule has traces of the colonial legacy of how power could be acquired vis-à-vis politics of greater powers.*

Chapters 9 and 10 turn the camera to the meanings of becoming a refugee in the eyes of the receiving community, as well as the structural inequalities and challenges that shape their articulation of self.

References

Bell C, Wise L (2022) The spaces of local agreements: towards a new imaginary of the peace process. J Interv Statebuild 16(5):563–583

Berti B (2020) From cooperation to competition: localization, militarization and rebel co-governance arrangements in Syria. Stud Conflict Terrorism. https://doi.org/10.1080/1057610X.2020.1776964

Brownlee BJ (2015) The revolution 'from below' and its misinterpretations 'from above'. The case of Syria's neglected civil society. Syria Stud 7(1):31–59

Erlich R (2014) Inside Syria. Prometheus Books, New York

Hajjar B, von Burg C, Hilal L, Santschi M, Gharibah M, Sharbaji M (2017) Perceptions of governance-the experience of local administrative councils in opposition-held Syria. Swiss Peace January/2017

Hakli J, Kallio KP (2018) On becoming political: the political in subjectivity. Subjectivity 11(1):57–73

Khalaf R (2015) Governance without government in Syria: civil society and state building during conflict. Syria Stud 7(3):37–72

Khoury D (2013) Losing the Syrian grassroots: local governance structures urgently need support. SWP Comments, 9/2013, Stiftung Wissenschaft und Politik (SWP), Berlin

Ozkaleli U, Byrne S (2023) Inside and outside: government and governance experience of Syrian refugees. Syria Stud 15(2) https://ojs.standrews.ac.uk/index.php/syria/article/view/2739

Paris R (2004) At war's end: building peace after civil conflict. Cambridge University Press, Cambridge

Sosnowski M, Hamadeh N (2021) "The right to have rights": legal identity documentation in the Syrian civil war. (GIGA focus Nahost, 4). German Institute for Global and Area Studies (GIGA) - Leibniz-Institut für Globale und Regionale Studien, Institut für Nahost-Studien, Hamburg. https://nbn-resolving.org/urn:nbn:de:0168-ssoar-75531-7

Part III
Becoming a Refugee

Chapter 9
Self in Traveling

Crossing the Border of Clarity

Passing the physical border was an important mental demarcation line for many interviewees in terms of experiencing the self as an individual and as a Syrian refugee. Through the receiving community's gaze and the conditions they faced, they experienced becoming a refugee. By crossing the physical border between Syria and Türkiye, their self-identity is also forced to go through a mental portal between being Syrian and becoming a refugee.

Many of the interviewees reported a traumatic experience of shifting from home to the receiving country. Some narrated the challenges of border crossing, others focused on the decision to leave Syria, yet others remembered what it was like to settle in Türkiye. Some focused on how they were treated in state institutions, while others focused more broadly on the unclarity of rules and regulations applied to their status. For many, language and choice of schooling for the younger generations were intertwined with their identity. On the one hand, they tried to hold on to glimpses of the familiar in the new structure; on the other, they struggled to separate their sense of self from the structurally forced identity of "refugee."

Leaving Home in Insecurity

One of the common feelings was fear and insecurity when deciding to leave home. Tasneem explains her fear for her husband, which led to her decision to leave home. Tasneem's time frame of explaining leaving Syria starts before the war. Her marriage as a starting point symbolizes putting down roots:

© The Author(s), under exclusive license to Springer Nature Singapore Pte Ltd. 2025
U. Ozkaleli, *De-essentializing Refugees: Perceptions, Experiences, and Becoming of Syrians in Türkiye*, https://doi.org/10.1007/978-981-96-5519-9_9

> The first condition I had when I wanted to marry was not to leave Aleppo. Unfortunately, when the war started, we were forced to leave. It was because one of our friends participated in the demonstrations and was arrested. We still do not know where he is. He disappeared. My husband thought maybe if we went out, he could help the people from the outside better than inside. We were thinking that we were going to stay outside of Syria only for one to three months at most. But not this long [she was in Gaziantep for several years]. When we left Aleppo, I could not feel happy or satisfied. I always felt, *alhamdulillah* [praise to be God, an expression of gratitude for the conditions], I have my children, who are good, my husband, my family, but you cannot feel happy. Because you see all that is happening on TV or social media and everything you left in Aleppo. The moment you see all that, you must start again, and it is very hard to start again. (Tasneem)

Tasneem's spatial separation from Syria is something out of her will and due to fear for the safety of her loved ones. Her explanation is striking as it indicates that while spatially in Türkiye, any news or visuals from home made her freeze in time, have a feeling of erasing the present and then re-starting it again. Every time she sees something related to the horrors in Syria, her spatio-temporal experience shifts, destabilizes, and re-focuses on the present, *now*.

The meaning of leaving home and coming to Türkiye was articulated from different angles. Bilal always wanted to study in Türkiye. He felt his disability was presented as an obstacle and an excuse to hold him back. His father promised him to go to graduate school, but he considered it a delaying tactic. Years later, when ISIS took over their village, his disability and medical condition were seen as a way to get him out of Syria. Syrian authorities gave permission, but Bilal explained in detail the physical challenges of crossing the Turkish border. His disability was disregarded, and he had to pass from a spot where soldiers were not present: "It was a deeply dug ditch, two or three meters deep. People were passing from there. It was so very difficult for me. I could get out of it with two people's help. It was too steep. My shoes got ripped from the stones and dirt, and the ground was slippery. Finally, we got out of there, and we were on Turkish soil." Bilal's narrative of his long-dreamt Türkiye and his first memory of stepping foot on Turkish soil is an embodiment of what was left behind, imagined and real experiences.

Genwa, who was a professional woman in Syria, came to Türkiye for a workshop with only one of her four kids. While in Türkiye, the village where her sister and children were staying was bombed. The Syrian government was searching for her. Therefore, she had to stay in Türkiye under very difficult circumstances. Even though she eventually moved to an NGO position, her beginnings in the receiving community were challenging. She adds, "I started to work, and I could bring my children here from under the border fences. One after another, just like the cats, four of them came. They are all here now."

Salwa, a war widow who became the sole parent, remembered her departure from Syria. Her difficult conditions before being placed in Gaziantep show similarity to many other refugees who did not have the means to settle in the host community:

> After they killed my husband, I went to my village and lived in my brothers' houses. I went to my home in Aleppo when my husband's brother got out of prison. When my husband's brother also died, I moved to a camp in the North of Syria. It was just one room without

> anything, no water. It was very difficult, so I left. My brother found a house in Kilis, and I stayed in Kilis with him for two months. I was getting some support from my husband's family. My brother could not find work, so he went back to Afrin to find a house, but there were no houses left by then. In Kilis, they did not let me live with my brother because Turkish people did not allow crowded houses. Then, the northern side of Aleppo was hit by the army, the Syrian Army, so all my family and relatives came to Türkiye. The house was really crowded by then. I lived in a garage alone until a relative told me this place for widows [an apartment complex for martyr men's wives supported by Islamic organizations]. (Salwa)

Salwa's detailed narrative shows the fear and insecurity that started at home due to violence, followed by the level of uncertainty and lack of opportunity to plan or coordinate a new life. Going to the unknown for an unclear duration was one of the trying aspects of many refugees who faced shelter and employment precarity. Moments of experiencing self as a refugee started with leaving home, experiencing passing a border, and experiencing the unknown. What followed these moments of travel was the insecurity of being in Türkiye.

Becoming a Refugee in the Gaze of the Receiving Community and the State

In some places, like Kilis, the demographics shifted to such a degree that the majority of the city became Syrian. Such a population shift frustrated the locals due to the dramatic cultural change and economic impact (Dogramacioglu 2022). In addition, the effects of the Syrian war showed itself when Kilis was hit by ISIS rockets in 2016 (Cantenar and Kozera 2022), turning negative attention to the existence of Syrians. Salwa summarizes this:

> A part [of the host community] hates us because we changed their country, especially after Kilis. Everyone started to point their finger at us. Maybe they are right. It's like, you are in a house, and it gets more and more crowded. You will feel stressed and get mad at that. But not all of them are acting this way. They were living in a calm environment, but we had more children than them and were very noisy. I just pray to God that I will go back to my own country. (Salwa)

Salwa seeing herself through the eyes of the receiving community reflects the complexity of her beginnings as a refugee and the changing perceptions as time progressed. Spatially being who she is challenged in Kilis, making her desire to return to Syria. The presence of an increasing number of Syrian refugees is perceived as "crowding the space," which reflects how Salwa sees herself through the eyes of the receiving community. While not justifying the "hate" and living through its burden, she can see the changing attitude "before" and "after" Kilis being hit by rockets. Her narrative also emphasizes cultural differences as a source of tension. Experience of space, according to Salwa, has changed dramatically, as she mentions the number of children and "noise." Syria was a space of comfort for her, and the norm changes intensified the feeling of dislocation. This duality creates an in-between position of being angry and appreciative, feeling guilt-ridden and accusatory simultaneously for the person holding the refugee position.

Ayan presents the duality of positive and negative treatments as well:

> There are really very kind people among them [people of Türkiye]. They let you take that beautiful image of Turkish people and Türkiye. They feel very empathetic with us, and they say, 'Poor people, they lost their country.' But on the opposite side, there are people who are aggressive somehow. They say, [Syrians] 'deserve what is happening, they destroyed their own country.' (Ayan)

Yasemin expresses her feelings about this duality:

> Dealing with people is hard. There are good people, but also, many people make weird faces toward us or look at us in a different way. We are traumatized, and we keep hearing that they are calling us *Suri* [a pejorative term for Syrian]. In the end, we tell each other we are guests we should shut up and stay inside. (Yasemin)

The data showed a pattern that many Syrians experienced this structurally enforced emotional state of being in-between, and the unacceptability of discrimination on the one hand, and empathy and understanding of the negative attitude of the receiving community on the other (Şahin-Mencütek et al. 2023). They appreciate that while Europe closed its doors to them, Türkiye opened it to millions. The main source of difficulty was seen in numbers that reached millions. They sympathize with the frustrations of the receiving community. Refugees have an additional disadvantage in terms of addressing poverty and social injustice, as they are in a tight position of being "grateful" to be accepted into a country. While they talked about Türkiye opening its borders to them in gratitude and gave examples of "good people" in Türkiye, the structural violence (Galtung 1969) they faced was too sharp not to be mentioned. Nala articulates how negativities affect one's view, "There are a lot of kind and sweet people here [Türkiye], but as a human, when something wrong happens to you, you forget all about the good people."

Author eye-camera: Individual-level analysis carries indoctrination, positioning the issue between the receiving community and refugees. Methodic examination of this data shows the patterns of how refugees, as a vulnerable group, can see the situation from the perspective of the receiving community. The reason for focusing on this finding is to enunciate that even though people are encouraged to think from their identity perspective and focus only on their experiences, they are capable of seeing the world from the perspective of others, i.e., *the receiving community. No matter the overwhelmingness of the negative attitudes and treatments that some of the Syrians faced, they still demonstrated empathy toward the difficulties of the receiving community. Most of the time, we do not hear these voices. Instead, the dominant focus is to look at the communities, either seeing the challenges refugees or the receiving community endure and not so much the power dynamics that position these two segments (local-refugee) against one another. The global structural elements that produce wars, the making of refugees, and the lack of systemic solutions to change the existing structures that position people artificially as refugees and receiving/host communities should be focused more.*

Some refugees consciously distinguish the community's reactions from the state-level treatment and regulations. If negative reactions were coming from the people, some Syrians were not angry at all, thinking the conditions created such tension among people. However, if people in the state institutions were discriminatory in their behavior, they saw this as a significant problem. When talking about the experiences of Syrians in Türkiye, Aykut reluctantly states:

> In a state institution, showing people inhumane treatment [is unacceptable]. When a personal thing happens [from an ordinary person], I can digest that it is very normal. But when they are punished collectively in a state institution… it is different. Unfortunately, they hire people to [state] institutions that work directly with refugees only because they know Arabic, but it is not enough. You have to know how they [professionals] are behaving. (Aykut)

Aykut's words separate individual-level discrimination (micro level) from institutional discrimination. Assigning such jobs to people who are either not equipped to understand refugee positioning or people who are against the opening of the borders to the refugees without proper training (meso level) creates systemic institutional discrimination that has structural and continuous negative effects (macro level) on refugees.

Author eye-camera: During my fieldwork, I met a refugee center manager who was against accepting refugees to Türkiye. He claimed that while he was fulfilling the job requirements of supporting refugees, he stated that personally, *he held the right to oppose their acceptance to Türkiye. States undoubtedly need to be concerned about who they hire and how this leads to tensions, prejudicial treatment, and ineffective policy implementation. The eye-camera of the person who is employed (or appointed) to these jobs as an officer or manager influences the implementation of the policies. The data analysis in this section reveals to the reader the eye-camera of refugees who are left to the mercy of a person who emotionally is against their existence in the receiving country. Continuous dealing with such individuals changes the everyday experiences of refugees. Their sense of belonging and becoming is shaped through these experiences.*

Bilal was very frustrated when he was working with Turkish officials and their treatment of refugees:

> When I see screaming, pushing refugees out [from the offices], I feel it is wrong … not because they are Syrians and these are my people. I would call this wrong if this is done to any human being. The people who come to these centers are from villages. They are not cultured or educated. You cannot expect too much understanding from these kinds of people. These are not the elite segments of society that come and ask for your help. When they do not understand, they ask the same question ten times. It is normal for them to keep asking the same question over and over. These are the most oppressed and most needy. People who are in the worst position need understanding, but there is no such understanding. They are screamed at and are told the meeting is over if they ask the question a second time. (Bilal)

While Bilal directly observes the institutional treatment of Syrians as a person who works in one of these institutions, Naser brings in his experiences as a person who receives the service. His perception that Syrians are treated differently amongst other nationals is strongly connected to how he reads the refugee position of Syrians in the host community:

> It is something really hard to do [getting a residence permit and using state institutions]. You need to speak Turkish to do it. I always bring one of my friends who speaks Turkish fluently so they can help me. The way they deal with Syrians is not good compared to the other foreigners. Just being Syrian, it is different. They would make you wait 6-7 hours to get the residency and then tell you to come back after a week or a month. The other foreigners are taking residency on the same day. (Naser)

Anas's experience in the state institutions was strongly tied to othering based on language:

> They [state employees] act like 'you are in Türkiye, and you should learn the Turkish language. You should learn how to act with us. I have the right to get angry with you if you do not know it. I have the right to kick you out of my office.' Some Turkish people know English, but they do not speak with us because they like to speak in their language. (Anas)

Interviewees mostly compared themselves with other foreigners and perceived that they were treated more negatively in the state institutions than the other foreigners. As people who were othered under the Syrian regime as citizens, they were conscious of separating state institutions from people on the street. The level of maturity for seeing the distinction between people and state institutions made them develop different expectations. The level of awareness of institutional discrimination is reflected in their thinking. While they had no expectation of change at the communal level, they expected improvement in state institutions.

Between the Border of Guest and Refugee

"Self" is a social product. Dual spatial positioning *vis-à-vis* different communities and social structures, along with simultaneous multiple temporalities, have a direct influence on how "self" is experienced. Positioning the self as a refugee in a country is full of contradictions, tensions, and emotional ups and downs. The general findings of this study show that the early days of Syrian populations arriving in Türkiye had a very different tone from the receiving community toward Syrians, and accordingly from Syrians to the receiving community compared to the later years. Syrians who arrived in Türkiye during the early days of the refugee mobilization often mention that the host community was friendly and supportive, and showed solidarity in providing housing and food. Referring to Syrians as "guests" fostered an impression of "temporariness," which in later years developed a negative connotation, leading to perceptions of them as guests who have overstayed their welcome (Akar and Erdoğdu 2019).

The "guest" perception brings problems and contradictions. Are they refugees? Are they guests? Are they foreigners? Are they Syrians? They all mean different things in terms of how they are treated. Application of the 1951 *UN Convention Relating to the Status of Refugees* created a two-tier asylum policy based on geography. In Turkish practice, only European nationals (Convention refugees) are able to attain refugee status, while non-European nationals (non-Convention refugees) would be granted temporary asylum in Türkiye, and Turkish authorities would work in collaboration with the UNHCR to find them a third country for re-settlement (Memisoglu and Ilgit 2017, 319). What emerges from the data analysis is striking in terms of the status of Syrians. On the one hand, Syrians do not want to be positioned as "refugees," which makes them feel like an objectified number. On the other hand, not being legally recognized as refugees makes their status and circumstances unclear. The majority of the participants, whether they wanted to return to Syria, re-settle to another country, or were happy to stay in Gaziantep, had a common issue with the unclarity they faced in terms of rules and regulations due to the complexities of their status.

Fahed is not necessarily bothered that there are a lot of rules but argues:

> While rules are not really negative, they are not stable, and this affects us. The actions of people inside the institutions are not very clear to us. This is the biggest challenge Syrians living here have. (Fahed)

Compared to other countries, Türkiye was seen as more accommodating toward Syrians, but at the same time, the unclarity of their situation made refugees ambivalent about their perceptions of Türkiye. While Salah expresses being grateful to Türkiye, his wife Alaa demands more:

> We want rules and rights, we do not have anything. Yes, we are a lot of people, and it is difficult for Türkiye. But because [Türkiye] allowed Syrian people to come here, you have to have rules to make their lives better and better. We do not want our people to go to Europe. We do not want our children to be there. If they have a chance here, right to work, right to live, right to learn Turkish [they would stay]. Thank God my company gave me a work visa. One of our friends helped me to enter this company, but not all Syrians can do this. Thank God we are safe here, but it is not enough. The Turkish government also recognizes it [the shortcomings]. Rules are not clear here in Türkiye. (Alaa)

Many agreed that the problem was not the "rules and regulations" but the rapid changes in procedures that made it difficult to follow or plan for the future. Additionally, unclarity resulted in a lack of solutions for everyday needs. While Syrians empathize with the challenges brought to the receiving community, the structural inequalities, particularly in terms of economic conditions, housing opportunities, job availability, and lack of clear regulations, make it inevitable to talk about the challenges they face in Türkiye. Ziad argued that, unlike lay people, governments and politicians were more aware that Syrians were going to stay in Türkiye for a long time. Yet, they did not have the foresight to start planning earlier for the millions that needed to be managed. Kamel touches on a myriad of aspects, from citizenship to opportunity for business investments:

> I am happy in Türkiye but still expecting better regulations. As a Syrian, there are no fixed regulations like there are for other foreigners here. Think about citizenship. I have a work permit, and the idea behind this is to have citizenship after five years. I have an ID and medical care but no clear future. For small things, if I am renting a home and if I need to turn on the water, electricity, and gas, I am unable to do so. In Istanbul, it was easy to do with my passport. They reacted to me as a foreigner at that time. Now, it is changing even in Istanbul. We are treated as a Syrian, not as a foreigner. I am trying to work, and Türkiye allows all foreigners to work with regulations except Syrians. I feel discriminated [against]. I have no problem following clear regulations, but if I attempt to invest some money and then they stop me because I am Syrian, that is a problem. (Kamel)

Kamel's words need to be contextualized and understood in terms of the conditions of a person who has a work permit. Many Syrians do not even have that right, and this should be indicative of the level of uncertainty they face. While there are over 1 million Syrians actively in the labor force, at the time of interviews, the number of work permits was around 30,000, while the number of citizenships was 102,000 (Erdoğan 2019). Kamel's words also indicate differences in having a valid Syrian passport issued by the Asad regime. Valid passports gave them more access within Türkiye and to travel outside of Türkiye. Haya gives examples of the status that affects travel, which has a temporality dimension. As time passes, the condition of documentation fluctuates for some:

> We still do not know if we are refugees, guests, or any other foreigner. I have a student permit. I went to apply for my mom to go to Saudi Arabia to visit my sister, who was going to have a baby. They said yes, we will permit you to go for fifteen days. We bought the tickets, and two days before she left, they said she could not go. We needed permission from Ankara, so we had to cancel the ticket, my sister gave birth [without mom]. If we are refugees, we should be given a paper that says we are refugees. If, however, we are foreigners like Italians, Egyptians, or someone from Saudi Arabia or the Emirates, give us similar papers. My husband and I are [treated] as if we are foreigners. I go to school, and he has a job here. My passport will expire in two years, and the [Syrian] Embassy in Istanbul won't renew it because my husband is wanted [by the regime]. After that, what will happen? Will they give us papers that tell us we are okay with leaving the country for a job or travel, for example? (Haya)

Documents, traveling, and access to Türkiye also relate to the ability of people to see their families or the possibility of them being in the same place with their loved ones. Some people get the necessary documents, while others in the same family cannot. This affects the future of families, with people facing many years of not seeing their close family members. Husam, who grew up as a Palestinian refugee in Syria, provides his account:

> Syrian people who have a travel document or passport need to get a visa to travel to Türkiye. I used to get a visa before the conflict. Because the Turkish embassy closed in Syria, I couldn't manage to get a visa to enter Türkiye. I suffered a lot until someone helped me to apply for a visa for residency, and I got it, thank God. But most Palestinian people who come from Syria are staying here illegally because they cannot get a visa from Syria, including my family. My family could not come here even for a visit because they needed to get a visa. I haven't seen them for three years and two months. (Husam)

Many people's visa and passport issues were a challenge. Majed explained a recent experience:

> The Syrian is lost here, he has no rights. He is not a refugee; he is not from this country. A year ago, Rukan [wife] had a Syrian passport, and she traveled a lot including going to Syria. We gave some money to the [Syrian] regime to get this passport. After a while, the regime announced this passport number to Interpol, and Türkiye took it from us because they thought it had been sold to someone. We are afraid here because we do not know our rights or we do not have rights. Now, from Reyhanli [Hatay district] to Gaziantep [two cities in close proximity in Türkiye], we need permission to travel. It is like you are forced to stay here. Türkiye or other states from the international community keep saying that the regime is guilty, but in the end, they always consider the regime letters or regime papers as formal papers. (Majed)

Even after the war and the creation of rebel-controlled areas, marriage, birth, property, and inheritance were recognized if it was issued by the Syrian regime (Sosnowski and Hamadeh 2021). Nazem also articulates the continuous effect of the Syrian regime holding the validity of documentation:

> There are challenges like the documents that they want here [in Türkiye]. When the children are born here, you must attain a lot of papers. The freedom to move from one place to another [is challenging]. I know many things are better than other countries, but they always want documents from us from the regime side. To charities like us [he was leading a charity for Syrians], [Syrian] regime looks at us as criminals or terrorists. Many young people do not have passports and cannot do anything about that. (Nazem)

Rukan was a medical doctor who felt a deep emptiness in her life that she could not practice medicine in Syria to help her people, nor could she do her job in Türkiye as many qualified people, as their diplomas or certificates are not recognized.

Camil clarifies the unclear aspects of the future with the status that Syrians hold in Türkiye, also focusing on the denial of freedom of travel in terms of actualization of self:

> Generally, living in Gaziantep is great, with some exceptions. The future is not clear. Syria needs a decade [for war to be settled], so what will be my legal situation here? The majority of Syrians work here illegally, and the government turns a blind eye, but can I lead my life legally here? I have an AFAD [Directorate of Disaster and Emergency Management] card, and I applied for a tourist visa, but these are all temporary things. What about later on? Most of us have dreams. My dream is to see the world. 90% of countries deny visas to us. Even if you are working for an NGO, you cannot attend a conference or anything. I do not want to be in prison. When I cannot leave a certain country, I am in prison. I love Türkiye. It is a beautiful country. It will take me a few years to travel around Türkiye, but being here in a forced way all my life without travel, tourism, seeing other cultures, and being unable to go are my concerns. It is an unknown. Nothing is clear, and this is really bad. (Camil)

While they are all called "refugees," class differences among Syrians show great variety. Accordingly, their concerns may not be singularized. Some are more related to basic subsistence needs, while others are more about self-actualization. Educated and multi-lingual Syrians who found employment in foreign NGOs face structural problems. Firas, who works without a work permit for a German NGO, explains that some foreign NGOs are not registered. He connects the problem of unregistered NGOs to the unstable rules and regulations that negatively influence Syrians working in these organizations.

Camil, along with freedom of movement, was concerned about building a financially secure life:

> Financially, I want to be free. Can I work legally and start investing, even if it is a small investment? Can I think about it or not? Will it be ok in two years? Settling down is complicated. I have not forgotten about Syria, but I would like to be able to settle with my family where I am living. This is not happening here, which is a really difficult situation. (Camil)

Fatima, an NGO worker, does not see herself as a "foreigner" in Türkiye in many ways. She argues that compared to other countries, "there is no discrimination towards Syrians because lifestyles of Gaziantep and especially Aleppo are similar."

However, when she connects her analysis to legal documentation and the status of Syrians, this is where she signals an insecurity:

> My only problem is that I always feel this is not my country. Sometimes it makes me feel depressed. I do not know if it is only in Gaziantep or, in general, in Türkiye. Still, they have a point of view from the Turkish people that poor refugees are living here in a similar and sometimes better situation than the Turkish people [who are in poverty]. However, there is also another dimension, stability, in this country. There is nothing in this country, as stable rules to make you feel comfortable or better. I know that a refugee document in Türkiye is a political document, not a humanitarian document. The refugee document is putting pressure on the EU and the USA. At any minute, they can use it in any way they want, so it is not for our benefit. We cannot leave here, and this makes me worry. (Fatima)

Author eye-camera: Fatima's transnational analysis and positioning of Syrian people as objects of global politics is rare. Just like people are positioned to look at each other as being part of the host community or the refugee community, many people see the regulations in Türkiye as only related to the country and not as part of global political decisions. Unlike their articulation of global actors in the Syrian conflict being ignited or the way it progresses, many participants did not see policies in Türkiye as part of global interactions and decisions. Türkiye grants refugee status only to European nationals which is guided by the United Nations. Similarly, the status of Syrian refugees has a direct consequence of their right to travel or access other countries, which makes European countries particularly influential over the decisions of Turkish authorities.[1]

Traveling between being guests and refugees brought class-based challenges. For the lower to lower-middle class, concerns were mostly gainful and legal employment to increase the chances of survival on basic needs, which will be examined in the next chapter. For the middle and upper-middle class, concerns were about attaining professional jobs within their area of expertise, right to property, investments, and travel.

Not only rules and regulations but also issues of language and choice of school for children were focal points for their identity in the new space. They will each be examined in the following two sections.

Language Dividing the Spatial Becoming

Regardless of differences in their class and educational background, one of the common challenges study participants faced in Türkiye was the language. Aya's view is representative of many:

> Language is the most difficult thing. I tried many times [to learn]. I know the English alphabet, so I can read some signs. I can go shopping and use the bus, but the problem is communication with other people. (Aya)

[1] For EU involvement in Syrian refugees in Türkiye, see Rygiel et al. (2016).

Husam captures the language challenges and shows how the feelings of people may be very different depending on their access to the local language:

> If you do not have the language, you will be misunderstood. My Syrian friends at work mostly do not know Turkish, and most of them rely on me to translate for them…I am really grateful to be living here in Türkiye, I love it. As soon as I started learning the Turkish language, life became easier. I can understand people, and they can understand me easily. I feel dignity here. (Husam)

Even though Husam was concerned about his work permit issues, he found a level of satisfaction as language and interaction with the host community made life more positive. Reem, unlike Husam, does not speak the language, and she finds this as a big barrier in building bridges with the receiving community:

> The language is a psychological border between Türkiye and us. I really need someone to talk to me because, in the courses, we are just taking grammar and not conversation lessons. Many of us Syrians here come from places close to the borders of Türkiye, so we all know about this culture. There are not many differences between us and them. Even in the language, we can see a lot of similarities between our and their language. (Reem)

Tamara and Bedia, who are from Aleppo and Damascus, respectively, find so many similarities that they did not feel strange or like a foreigner in Türkiye at the beginning. Spatial similarity and cultural elements that are familiar make people feel closer to home. At the same time, language plays, in a way, a Brechtian puncture of coming back to the reality of being positioned as a refugee. Badia wanted to work as a teacher as she was in Syria and expressed that even though there was no such requirement at first, later on, Syrian teachers were asked to learn Turkish. How people interacted with the issue of language showed connections to how they related to the space and the larger community.

Tamara, who is mostly pleased with being in Türkiye and her child having a positive experience at school, points out the essential role of language: "Türkiye is beautiful, its people are beautiful, and they are respectful toward us. Nevertheless, language is difficult. If I needed to go to places such as hospitals, I should have a translator with me." In Tamara's words, language becomes intertwined with basic needs that change one's experience of the host society. In this line, Nour explains how lack of access came with a lack of opportunities even to express frustration:

> When I first came, it was very difficult. I did not want to go out. We first went to Mersin. Until I got used to Mersin, I used to go and look at the sea and hit the waves with my foot because I was very angry. I was very scared to go inside a shop and ask anything because of the language difference. (Nour)

While there are university students who are also resistant to learning Turkish, younger generations are expected to learn Turkish and help the family in their day-to-day dealings. Hasan, a university student, became the breadwinner for the family. He claimed working was not possible for his 60-year-old father because learning Turkish was impossible. Still, regardless of age, language influences the degree of relationality and access refugees have to the host community. Rouba says from flirting to making new friends, the lack of Turkish language becomes a barrier, affecting the quality of her friendships. Many Turkish students expect her to speak Turkish, and once they realize she cannot, they refrain from making an effort to be her friend. Walid also observes that the receiving community's attitude toward Syrians changes based on their language skill:

> People are very loving, but they want you to be in the system. When I speak Turkish, they will try to understand, but if I speak English, they will never try to understand. (Walid)

Some of the participants stated that they consciously refused to learn Turkish. Refusing to learn the language is a resistance of sorts to the permanency of the spatial shift. Zeinan states:

> It is possible that I do not like life here because I want to go back to Syria. I am not trying to learn the language. Never [will I try]. I do not want to. I know some English [she is a beginner in English], and I know my native language, which is enough. Why do I need to learn another language? I will go back to my home. I will not need any English or Turkish! I will go back! [she hits the table to show her assertiveness]. (Zeinan)

Holding on to the native language and refusing to adopt the language of the host community is used as a strong symbol for going back home for a considerable number of people like Zeinan. Zeinan's refusal of language was not reflective of her views of Turkish people as she explained that while she did not speak the language, she had good Turkish neighbors who found furniture for her, and the husband and wife joined her for coffee and dinner without a language to communicate. Her rejection of learning the language was to keep herself oriented to return home. While she liked the good "simple people" in Türkiye and the country, she did not want to live her life in Türkiye. Zeinan holds on to her language and speaks of the days in Raqqa with such affection and yearning that language becomes a source of holding on to the possibility of returning. Naser has a similar approach to language. Both he and his brother are college students, and their experience with the Turkish language is very different:

> It is nice, everything is nice but the language! I do not know how to learn this language. My brother is learning and speaking fluently now. But I believe that it depends on your will. If you want to learn, you learn easily, but I am telling you I do not want to learn it. (Naser)

Naser deeply felt the spatial separation from home, which made him willfully resist learning the language that symbolized a deeper divide from home. Zeinab connects the lack of will to learn the language to several things:

> I find it difficult to learn [Turkish language]. I do not know why. It is difficult to live here in Türkiye. We do not feel we are finding a kind of settlement to live here. The laws are not dealing with us as refugees but as guests. And that makes a difference for us. Restrictions accompany the laws of residence. We feel Türkiye is similar to our home, Aleppo. Everything is intimate and kind: the weather, the mosques, the people, everything is similar. Everything reminds us of Syria, but we wish that the situation in Türkiye as refugees would be better for us so we don't have to leave here.

The familiarity and similarity for Zeinab are disrupted with the legal status, which is reflected in the engagement with language and the host community. She did not want to invest time if she was not to make a permanent home in Türkiye. According to Zeinab, not learning the language is also caused by the lack of communication and interaction with the receiving community members. The social structure is the reason:

> We do not need to mix with Turkish people because we have our community inside the community. All week or a month, we do not feel the need to speak Turkish because there are Syrians all around. Everything we need, we can get from Syrian shops…It prevents us from communicating with people in [the receiving] community. Two years is not a short time [to spend in a country]. And yet, we have no friendships. Only my son has friends because he is fluent in the language. (Zeinab)

Not all are emotionally or psychologically resistant to learning the language. What prevents them is the lack of time. Some interviewees worked for NGOs focusing on the Syrian conflict. They mostly work in Arabic, interact with Syrians regarding aid, or use English professionally. Rashid captures many other NGO workers' situations:

> The biggest problem is the language. I could not learn the language because I did not have enough time. I am still involved with the revolution work, and the remaining time is spent on my work in the humanitarian sector. Unfortunately, I did not learn [Turkish], which caused me many problems. (Rashid)

Zeinab and Rashid both work in NGOs, and their experience is very similar to Joumana and Nawar, who are also NGO workers involved in Arabic and English and no Turkish at work. Joumana, even though she was in Türkiye for two years at the time of the interview, could not speak Turkish, and she gave the reason as a lack of time from her work and taking care of her young child. Nawar also connects work requirements and time to his lack of opportunities to learn Turkish and interact more with the host community. Nawar had to support many family members, which made him work long hours rather than learn the language of the receiving community as he could not invest time to sit with neighborhood people and learn the language over tea. The importance of this structurally enforced language divide creates a sense of detachment from the host community. Nawar reflects on it in terms of belonging:

> When I was in Syria, I would choose Türkiye as a place to travel, visit, and have a vacation. But I have not even heard of Gaziantep before, even though it is very close to my border [Nawar is from Damascus, not Aleppo; Aleppians are familiar with Gaziantep]. In the long term, I cannot see myself in Türkiye because Türkiye is not helping me to see myself in Türkiye. For example, now, after four years, I am not eligible to gain citizenship. This is something I need to resolve. I wake up every day, and I know that I am secure for that day, but I am not sure where I am going to be after a year. I am not sure where I am going to be after five years. I may be in Türkiye in the same situation, surviving day by day, which leads you to a horrible situation if you reach retirement age without a proper retirement plan in such a country. I am also not a very big fan of Europe, to be honest. Although I work for a European agency, my dream is to go to Uruguay. (Nawar)

Nawar wanted to relocate to a place where he could find a future and not be treated as a "number." Lack of access to language, along with lack of a firm status, led him to think of a future elsewhere. Spatially, being in a place for five years with a lack of opportunities and time to learn the language and have a meaningful connection, Nawar dreams of a new, far-away beginning where he can feel like an individual.

Schools and Becoming Identities

The language issue is not only determining adult Syrians' spatial becoming in the receiving community but also their experiences and feelings about the language of their children's education. Selection of children's education language is central to how becoming of these identities will evolve. Spatially, learning Turkish integrates children, but it is not an easy decision. Temporality stands at the core of their view in terms of how close or far the return to Syria is. Ayan draws attention to one of the tension points for many refugees in terms of the language and education of their children:

> The children got used to the Turkish language. My son is 12 years old, and he dreams of having the right to study with the Turkish people in Turkish schools because the hope that we are going back to Syria is really small. (Ayan)

On the one hand, parents and children alike want to be part of the Turkish language and schools as they provide a better chance for survival and advancement. At the time of the interviews, many Turkish schools offered higher quality education compared to the Syrian schools in Gaziantep. In addition, knowing the dominant language is always an advantage. On the other hand, families had a lot of anxiety about the loss of the Arabic language and, hence, the culture. Many people believed that excelling in Arabic was a lengthy endeavor, given the difficulty of the language. Many Syrians believed that learning Arabic as a second language could never reach a native level, and without schooling, writing in Arabic would not be possible for children. Therefore, they believed if children dedicated their time to Turkish education, they would lose competency in their Arabic. Families lived in constant ambiguity. They wanted to keep their children within their cultural milieu and prepare them for returning to Syria. In contrast, they did not know how long this would take and hence faced the risk of making their children less able to integrate to the system they were living in. Decisions about learning Turkish and children's schooling are important to show how identity and spatial and temporal conditioning influence people's choices and dilemmas. Firas captures this:

> The barrier of language and communication is the biggest issue for Syrians. Maybe Syrians do not want to learn [the Turkish language], or they do not have this ability to learn [Turkish] because they always think they will go back. The integration, particularly for their children, is a big issue. I have many friends who have families, and they are always confused about whether to put their children in a Turkish school or a Syrian school. If they enroll them in Turkish schools, they say, they will lose their language and their cultural side. I believe they need to adjust because maybe they will be staying in Türkiye. (Firas)

What is important here is that spatial and temporal positioning makes refugee experiences complex and conflicting emotions. While spatially they are located in Türkiye, people who did not want themselves or their children to learn Turkish continue to position their belonging to a different space. They integrate a temporality that includes not only today but also a future where they do not want to be disconnected from their cultural and linguistic identity. They envision a future for their children that carries a language essential to their self-definition. Refusing to learn the host society's language becomes a symbol of refusing a detached future and, more importantly, holding on to the hope that not only will they return home, but they will ensure that their children will also own the Syrian future.

Some go strategic with schooling, dividing it with consideration of needs. For example, Aya made a necessity-based decision. While sending others to Syrian schools, she sent her son to a Turkish school which makes him the translator in places like hospitals. Conversely, Nala is very happy that her daughter is continuing with Syrian/Arabic higher education. Both are future projections informing decisions of today.

Once the decision is made to send the children to a Turkish school, there is the challenge that they end up being the "only Syrian" at school, which may result in their isolation. Salwa explains the difficulties many iterated:

> Because they are Turkish and he is Syrian, there are a lot of problems happening between them. The Turkish students do not want the Syrians to be with them. Sometimes, they talk and shout at him, and he does not understand. But it is okay. We finished this year, but it was very difficult because I used to take him to school every day by holding his hand. (Salwa)

Nala feels at a loss and in the constant realization of being ripped away from her cultural and familial setting, connecting it to her children's challenges at school and how they were made fun of at Turkish school by other children because they did not speak Turkish. This resulted in her children hating to learn the Turkish language. Children's integration to schools was not prepared where the dominant group could appreciate the differences and challenges.

In many cases, the first contact at school is not a positive experience. If the children stay and learn Turkish, they are more likely to be accepted. Alaa explains her son's initial start at a Turkish school:

> We told him [our youngest son] to stay in the Turkish school only for two months. [We said] if you are comfortable, you continue there, but if not, we will return you to a Syrian school. In the first month, it was very difficult. He refused so much to stay there. Some students fought with him and said, 'You are Syrian.' It is normal. After the initial two months, he felt comfortable and said, 'I will stay here,' and *ma sha'allah*, he is now the first [highest GPA] in all of his school. (Alaa)

When asked why they preferred him to go to a Turkish school, Alaa answered:

> Because we wanted him to learn Turkish, you know it is good [to learn another language]. Even if we go back to Syria, it is good for him to learn a new language. When we were in Syria, he was in a private school, and he learned French and English. Also, we discovered that the level of Syrian schools is very low, very bad here in Türkiye. Even though the government of Türkiye is dealing with this educational plight, the quality of education is very bad. (Alaa)

Alaa's other son, who was in high school, refused to learn Turkish altogether, but she was able to encourage her fourth-grader son to go to a Turkish school easily as he was literate in Arabic and spent his early school years learning his own language. Alaa and her husband faced a challenge for their daughter, who was much younger and not school-aged when she was in Syria:

> Now, the challenge for us is to hold on to the Arabic language. We believe it is our natural language. It is such a rich language that if you do not study it, you will lose it. Now we have to do more and more to try to teach them our language. My daughter is in kindergarten, and we will put her in the Syrian school in the summer to learn the language. Also, at home, we will teach her how to read and write in Arabic so that she not only can talk but also read and write in Arabic. (Alaa)

Amina, who came from Baniyas after witnessing the traumatic loss of lives in her community, talked a lot about her children. Due to traumatic departure from home and all the traveling, she said that her children became "shy." One of her daughters even refused to talk. At the time of the interview, her children attended a Turkish school where afternoons were designated for Syrian children. Amina's children started to get better after starting school:

> One of my daughters did not even talk, but after she came here, she talked with a teacher. My daughter is very polite and very clever. She did not used to talk to me about what was happening to her, but now she is talking about everything with me. My children missed some school years. My son needs to be in the 9th grade, but he is now in grade 6. The daughter is in the 4th grade, and she should be at the 6th. She is 13 years old.

Lina, who worked as a teacher, explained the way schools were designed:

> When Turkish schools are done for the day, it is the Syrian children's turn. All the teachers are Syrians, but the headmaster is Turkish. In primary school, in one class, there are 40 students. My class has 40 students. There are no books in Arabic. We have just one book, copy it and give it to the children. (Lina)

While Lina gives the situation from the perspective of a teacher, Amal talks about the conditions of Syrian schools as a parent:

> Even schools, Syrian schools for my children have many problems. This year [2016,] they started to be controlled by the Turkish government. There is one Turkish manager in every school, but it is not enough because the Turkish manager cannot communicate with the teachers, and there is only one translator, which is not enough. My son has many materials missing for five lessons. Not all the courses are taught, and the number of courses is not enough. Some of the teachers are not educated. Some of them are high school graduates, not university graduates. (Amal)

There are different dynamics when people send their children to Turkish schools, where they have to negotiate cultural expressions and what they are willing to accept. Tasneem talks about the school experience of her children:

> My Syrian friend, who is married to a Turkish man, helped me and advised me to put them [children] into a Turkish school. My kids speak Turkish fluently. They translate for us. They started learning English as well. They are going to a public school, and it is good for them to learn English from the beginning. In the first year, it was very hard for them and for me, but in the second year, it was easy, and it is now good. I like the respect; they told them from the beginning to respect each other [students] and the teacher. For example, I never give my hand to my children to kiss [as a respect to the elderly, children kiss the back of the hand and place it on their head]. We do have this tradition in Syria of kissing hands as well, but I do not like it myself. Last year, my son's teacher extended her hand to be kissed. I was shocked because I did not like my son to kiss hands. But for respect, I let him do it. I am not satisfied, I do not like this idea, but I respect that she taught him to read and let him be better. I know that she has rights over my son, and I respect her. (Tasneem)

The symbolic importance of kissing the hand of an elderly person, in this instance, the teacher in a position of authority, signals a willing submission to that authority. Tasneem's lengthy narrative exposes how she sees a different cultural group and authority figures being influential on her children's lives. Those who have access to one's children's education have a position to influence and shape the becoming of a child. When Tasneem goes back and forth about permitting a cultural practice, it combines the past, the present, and the future in her articulation. She thinks of her past, her own practice of not kissing hands except her father, and how she would have acted in her cultural setting. Then, she sees her child's inclusion in schools and its dependency on teachers in the current position that they are placed as students. All the shift in the behavior (allowing the kiss of the hand), regardless of it being contrary to her desire, has implications for the future, as with the embodiment of this teacher, this new culture and its authorities will have a "right" over her child.

Amal talks about her son's kindergarten and first-year experience, praising the teacher who taught the students to be inclusive, which succeeded in making her son develop friendships. Her articulation of this is, "I put my youngest one in a Turkish school, and now he is a Turkish person." The feeling that a child who goes to a Turkish school is "a Turkish person" is an important indicator for positioning as a refugee in a receiving community where language and culture are different.

The dilemma of being seen as an outsider and as a refugee on the one hand and not given refugee status to have a firmer status is an ongoing situation in Türkiye. The school decision is one of the most clearly identifiable areas in which people perceive their position in the receiving community. As the time of stay extended, some Syrians changed their decisions about where to place their children. Genwa captures this dilemma as time progresses:

> One of my children is in 10th grade, and the other is in 7th grade. They go to a Syrian school, but I will place them in a Turkish school next year. The education system in the Syrian school is not very good. Also, I think that in the end, they will study in a Turkish university, so I wish I had put them in a Turkish school from the beginning. The younger one, at first, I was very afraid for him. He was coming from a war, and I did not want to put him in a very different place, but when the time comes, I will put them in Turkish school. (Genwa)

People who plan to leave Türkiye and those who hope to return home in a few years refrained from sending their children to Turkish schools, which showed that their future projections influenced their present decisions. The ones who focused on the past and home country's culture and native language, regardless of future expectations, wanted their children to stay in Syrian schools. Two groups of participants targeted to send their children to Turkish schools where they could master the Turkish language and learn to be part of the dominant culture. A group who was certain that they were to stay in Türkiye for many years, and another who could not envision what their future would be like. Their reasoning for the decision was different, though. For the former, the motivation was to prepare children for the future and equip them to survive in their new home. For the latter, the focus was on the "now," surviving in the moment regardless of what the unknown, unclear future held.

This chapter examined the crossing of the borders of clarity and the meanings of becoming refugees who were treated as guests. Spatial and temporal dynamics influenced the decision to leave home and become refugees in the gaze of the receiving community and the state. Language and cultural belonging became spheres of staying close to the Syrian past to project it to the future or finding new expressions for a different future that did not include Syria. The next chapter brings social and structural problems of becoming refugees.

References

Akar S, Erdoğdu MM (2019) Syrian refugees in Turkey and integration problem ahead. J Int Migr Integr 20:925–940
Cantenar ÖF, Kozera CA (2022) Fighting ISIS in Syria: operation Euphrates shield and the lessons learned from the al-Bab Battle. Small Wars Insur 33(3):350–381
Dogramacioglu H (2022) The effects of refugees on Kilis culture and economy. Black Sea J Public Soc Sci 5(2):56–61
Erdoğan M (2019) Syrian refugees in Turkey. Konrad-Adenauer-Stiftung Report
Galtung J (1969) Violence, peace, and peace research. J Peace Res 6(3):167–191
Memisoglu F, Ilgit A (2017) Syrian refugees in Turkey: multifaceted challenges, diverse players and ambiguous policies. Mediterr Polit 22(3):317–338
Rygiel K, Baban F, Ilcan S (2016) The Syrian refugee crisis: the EU-Turkey 'deal' and temporary protection. Global Soc Policy 16(3):315–320
Şahin-Mencütek Z, Gökalp-Aras NE, Kaya A, Rottmann SB (2023) Syrian refugees in Turkey: between reception and integration. Springer, Cham
Sosnowski M, Hamadeh N (2021) "The right to have rights": legal identity documentation in the Syrian civil war. (GIGA focus Nahost, 4). German Institute for Global and Area Studies (GIGA) - Leibniz-Institut für Globale und Regionale Studien, Institut für Nahost-Studien, Hamburg. https://nbn-resolving.org/urn:nbn:de:0168-ssoar-75531-7

Chapter 10
Self in the New Social Structure

Social and Structural Problems

Loss of Status

Refugees are generally depicted as poverty-stricken. Such portrayals do not reflect the different socioeconomic layers among them, ignoring their past or their pre-refugee social status. Individuals who once enjoyed material wealth and comfort may become refugees due to their politics or the insecurity of war. Their sense of loss encompasses their previous social standings along with their citizenship rights. Alaa, when demanding more rights and assistance from the Turkish government, felt compelled to justify her demands not only as a matter of human rights but also to frame herself as an "affluent" member of her community in Syria.

> You have to fight to have a comfortable life. I want to talk about Aleppo especially. We came from a good life. Generally, we were not from a low level. We were not poor people. We were rich and cultured. (Alaa)

Stressing that she is "cultured and rich," she grounds herself as a "deserving" (Zadhy and Erman 2023) individual. Such a class-based view inevitably creates hierarchies among people, justifying better treatment for some more than others. Ziad focuses on qualified Syrians not given professional jobs. His views point out deservingness:

> There are 180 universities [in Türkiye], and a lot of them are missing faculty members. Why don't they use them [Syrians]? This is a strength for you [Türkiye]. Now, the Turkish government treats and creates policies for the educated the same way they create them for the illiterate. This is harmful to Türkiye as well. They complain, but let's be honest, rent prices increased, and the more rent money went to whom? To the rich, people with property, the stores benefited because the number of people [who buy goods] increased. But people without properties and stores are harmed. Also, Syrians are oppressed by economic exploitation as well. (Ziad)

© The Author(s), under exclusive license to Springer Nature Singapore Pte Ltd. 2025
U. Ozkaleli, *De-essentializing Refugees: Perceptions, Experiences, and Becoming of Syrians in Türkiye*, https://doi.org/10.1007/978-981-96-5519-9_10

Ziad, in his own explanation, sees the class dimension of which segments are more harmed. Yet, he expects better-educated people to be treated better than uneducated people. While he believes that it is unfair that the rich had better options than educated people like himself, he continues with class stratification to think that the conditions of the undereducated should be less than those of educated ones. He continues this hierarchy in his critical approach to Turkish people when they give priority to "who is considered a Turk *via* citizenship":

> You cannot judge people with ID [citizenship status]. I am Syrian, and three days after I got a [Turkish] ID, am I ok? How does this work? I know a man who is Syrian, but based on his ancestry from his grandfather's father, he got a Turkish ID, and now is he the best? He is not literate. He is an okay man, but I am not good if I have three diplomas but am Syrian. If this is how we evaluate people, it is not right. These types of people are ignorant people, and we know who they are. If you evaluate this way, if it is just an ID, you get a fake one and become a citizen. (Ziad)

The class and education-based hierarchies in the world mostly go unchallenged in terms of unequal opportunities for education and jobs. Yet, when it is about the refugees, what emerges from the narratives is that even the well-set educational hierarchies are turned upside down when one is positioned as a "refugee."

Ahlaam narrates her feelings about a job setting focusing on refugee rights in Türkiye. Ahlaam is unhappy that all Syrians are depicted in one way, for example, women are stereotyped to be all wearing hijab. Also, disregarding their education and work experience, Syrians are considered to be all poor and undereducated:

> In Gaziantep, they do not see people who are studying, have businesses, or are in the interim government. The majority of [Turkish] people interact with [Syrian] people who are here as workers, and they cannot pay money to go to a settlement in Europe. At work, my boss told the security workers that no Syrian would use the elevator. This is only for the Turkish. In another meeting, they said, 'There is a hierarchy, and in this hierarchy, Syrians are at the bottom, and we should not talk to Syrians, not go out with Syrians, not take their phone numbers, and not give them our numbers.' They turned to me and said, 'But as a favor to you because we love you so much, we cannot apply these rules to you, but in general, we should not talk to the Syrians.' [She goes quiet for a few seconds and has unshed tears in her eyes]. All of the members of this NGO studied for only two years. They have associate degrees, but all the Syrian translators graduated from four-year colleges or are currently college students. However, they keep telling us we are at the bottom of the hierarchy. (Ahlaam)

The hierarchies are multi-layered, and refugee positionality may take away material and educational positions. Faysal was an affluent businessman in Syria. While he still had more access to material means than many Syrians in Gaziantep, his material and social status changed considerably. He compares his situation in these two places, continuously going between the past and present:

> It is really expensive for us, the Syrians who live here. Even though we [his family] are not in the middle class in society in Syria, we are more than the middle class [life is still expensive for us here too]. Also, the culture of working here is different from that of Syria. We have bad habits like bribery and many other things. The whole country was running like that, but here it is different. Many of us could not bring our money with us, and because of that, we cannot start new businesses here. There are a lot of us like that. (Faysal)

Waseem, who refused to call the conflict a "revolution" and had a very low regard for the uprising against the regime, argued that his and his family's life was "elegant and beautiful" in Syria. As a family, they were planning to expand their family business further before the war. He explains his feelings:

> We [family] were really in a good situation, but after a while, step by step, this level of society started to fall down. I thank Allah that our situation is better than the others, but we were planning a very big thing, and now we are at the bottom. (Waseem)

Fadi's feelings resonate with Waseem. Fadi argues that in pre-war Syria, "everything was amazing" because he was rich. Both blamed their loss of status on the rebels. Their financial comfort was instrumental in their satisfaction with the regime. However, a high income did not directly cause everyone to support the regime. Many who were affluent in Syrian society and had high incomes and prestigious careers supported the uprising. Alaa and her husband Salah, for example, believed in the revolution. Nevertheless, Alaa stated that the end result of leaving home and coming to Türkiye meant the loss of status and position in society. They lost everything that they built in Syria. Alaa and Salah had a strong religious identity and a political vision according to their religio-political views. Even though they had a high socioeconomic position and were at a loss in Türkiye, unlike Waseem, for them, the cause of the loss of status was not the anti-regime struggle but the regime itself.

People who had comfortable lives in Syria faced considerable challenges in Türkiye. Ziad says even the meaning of a simple lunch changed:

> Syria was very cheap. Life changed dramatically when we came here. It is more expensive. With Syrian money, if you come here, it is a big difference. 500 Turkish Liras in Syria makes you live like a king, but here, it is expensive. You cannot buy a *döner* [Turkish *kebap*] for five Liras here. (Ziad)

It is not only the affluent but also middle-class people who had a status loss as refugees. Osama, a Palestinian who was raised in Syria, was studying at the university and had a job before the uprising. He could not continue because of the conflict, and once he left Syria, he had challenging times, starting as a worker in a factory in Türkiye. He called this "starting from the zero." He narrated the challenges of the shift and how he had difficulty receiving less respect than he was used to. Therefore, loss of position is related to non-material as well as material values.

Avdel's narration points out how drastically people's life circumstances and standards of living shift when their life is interrupted and forced out of their normal:

> I am a businessman. I am originally from Qubani, but I lived in Rakka for 35 years. I was working in trade, real estate, and construction. I never joined any Kurdish or Arabic parties. I was born in 1962. When the revolution started, which we call the Syrian revolution, I was in Rakka, living with my kids. At 3.30 in the morning, three armed and masked people attacked my house. They took me and locked me for ten days in a toilet. They took whatever I owned, including my money, both dollars and Syrian money. For ten days before releasing me, they scared and tortured me and threatened to kill me. After that, we were displaced to Qubani and started our new lives. We built our life there, and then ISIS came. We ran away and came here two years ago. One of my sons was studying English, and the other Civil Engineering. Now, they are working as laborers, and there is not enough work. I cannot

> survive here. I lost whatever I owned. All of my work in Rakka for 40 years has been lost. Even what I wear now is from the support of people. I love everyone. I do not discriminate between Muslims, Christians, Arabs, Kurds, or anyone who lives peacefully. I love them. (Avdel)

Avdel kept coming back to how he found himself, from having everything to having nothing. His continuous remarks on the conditions of sons emphasized the acute awareness of the difference between their past and their present as a family. Forty years of work being lost made the future disappear. Similarly, Bagir, another Kurdish man from Aleppo, explains how his social and economic status has changed. His narrative indicates that losing their life in Raqqa made them put an effort to rebuild it in Qubani, building a pharmacy for his son, which was also destroyed. Both Avdel and Bagir built lives in Raqqa and Aleppo, respectively, and went back to Qubani, their place of origin, where they had to leave behind both. Bagir not only talks of material losses but also the loss of his family unity:

> My sons left. Two of them are in Germany, and the other one is in Lebanon, and now my old wife and I are living alone. I am now working in construction with Turkish contractors. I was born in 1955. We are not related to the Party [YPG]. I have a hope to go back to Syria. I have a lot of territory, land, and work, so I hope, inshallah, to go back one day. (Bagir)

Both men thought focusing on business and not engaging in politics would protect their livelihood, which did not materialize. Not only did people lose their livelihoods, properties, and investments, but they also could not practice their profession and had to work in much lower skill-requiring jobs. Firas points out the problem of lack of permissions for Syrian professionals, especially engineers and doctors whose licenses are not approved. Firas considers the challenge of the sheer number of Syrians, making it difficult for the Turkish government to validate people into these professions. At different levels, this problem also shows itself in professional life when educated people either cannot find a job related to their fields or pay rate and are forced to work as "volunteers" instead of paid employment. One of the female participants [the name is omitted intentionally] who had gainful professional employment as a lawyer in Syria states:

> Work is a challenge for me. I am not working for a salary here. I am not earning any salary currently. It is all about voluntary work. Sometimes I feel depressed. I am a [professional]. I have a lot of things to give, but I am not giving anything. When I first came here, I started to work with women who got arrested or violated. I finished a whole document for that now. It has been about one year and six months since I have been working as a volunteer. I am not used to sitting down, so that is why I am attending to a lot of things. However, it is difficult somehow because money is really important for us in this life here.

In order to stress the importance of work and access to economic well-being, it would be helpful to see the complete opposite of the above examples of loss of status and lack of job availability. There is a way education, work, and income potential are made upside down due to transnational needs. Amez, who was in his early 20 s, had to leave Syria before finishing his university and had to take care of his family after his father's passing. His responsibility, however, came with opportunities that increased his sense of empowerment:

> At first, I started working in tourism and was paid very badly. I did not have any experiences, no connections, no friends. They started paying me well after I started working in the NGO sector. Now, I am working for a company that pays me very well, more than I have ever dreamed of! I live at the exact social level I used to in Syria when my father was a merchant and when we were rich and had access to money. I have wonderful friends around me, and my mom and brother are with me. I did a good job of filling the gap that my father had created for my brother. I am with wonderful people, working in a sector I have dreamed of. I do whatever I want. It could only get better if I got my bachelor's degree. I start with all my current knowledge and back it up with institutional knowledge. (Amez)

While a college dropout could reach his father's rather handsome income level, pharmacists, medical doctors, academics, teachers, lawyers, and engineers may face unemployment and economic challenges in Türkiye. The "refugee" title does not capture these multiple existences even in one city. The important thing is to realize how, structurally, some people with professional degrees and experiences behind them are not recognized and face unemployment. In contrast, some others, through the use of language and NGO mobilization, are given access to wages that are considered high in Türkiye. This signals new types of fractures, tensions, and conflicts within the social segments. Even though experiences are different, as seen from the above narratives, regardless of education and professional ability, "Syrian refugee" positionality in the gaze of the receiving community dominates. Additionally, hierarchies between the citizen and the refugee, or demands of the transnational NGO sector, could ignore commonly accepted class or education-based statuses. The status people hold everywhere determines the expectations of behavior. Expectations for education level and professional knowledge do not always hold the anticipated weight as master status becomes a refugee. People who are thrown into refugee position endlessly experience structurally induced social problems.

Gendered Challenges

Gender roles and gendered challenges surfaced in different layers in refugee experiences. Fathers and their patriarchal status of being the provider were among them.[1] Some participants mentioned that their father refused to leave Syria as they were not able to survive on their own in a foreign country without the language and knowledge that is necessary to live freely in everyday life. Others mentioned the difficulty their fathers faced when they left the country. Ramez, who was deeply troubled, angry, and sad, talked about the difficulties they faced in their first six months, the lack of rooms and beds to sleep, and the family members having to take turns to sleep. Ramez, as the eldest son, while his father was with him at the beginning, became the responsible person for the entire family, including his brothers. Ramez had tears in his eyes when he talked about his father's situation:

---

[1] For studies that focus on fathers and re-shaping and challenges of patriarchal refugee families, see Papadopoulos and Gionakis (2018), Tuzi (2020), Kianpour (2019).

> After six months, I was able to find jobs for my brothers, and the situation got better. Then the problem appeared that my father was feeling sad because he was not the one who… [he stopped and tried again]; he was not the biggest one [head of the family] in the family or the one who had control. (Ramez)

Gender roles for the family patriarchs may change depending on their social position, age, and social, economic, linguistic, and physical capabilities when they become refugees. Eldest sons, regardless of their age, as in the case of Amez, were expected to shoulder family responsibility.

While there are many different gender challenges for women, such as facing sexual and gender-based violence (Papoutsi et al. 2022), the interviewees in this study mostly shared experiences of how being women made them the target of stereotyping and prejudice. Many experienced verbal abuse. The never-ending cycle of women being pitted against one another in patriarchal structures shows its ugly face in refugee and host community relations. Nour was one of the very first people I interviewed. While she loved Türkiye and had good relations with people, she remembered prejudicial treatment as one of her earlier experiences upon arriving:

> The first time [receiving adverse treatment] was in Mersin. I was with my friend. It was morning, and we were working out and doing some sports at the park. A woman came [towards me] and hit me [she shows with her hand that the other woman pushed her] in a bad way as if she was saying, 'Go away, this is my place, you are coming to our place.' Her manner was very bad. I am not used to this. I was very upset, and I went home. And the second one was also in Mersin. There is a place near the sea where everyone drinks coffee and buys corn. There was a man and a woman, and the man said to the woman, 'Give her a chair to sit on.' But her behavior was very rude and almost felt like harassment. She did not want me to get this chair. (Nour)

Nour did not bring any explanation other than these women's deep dislike of Syrians. Later, I learned about the deep-seated issues and competition-like structure created among women. I was in a hairdresser, and a young woman was chatting with me and complaining about Syrians, particularly Syrian women. I was intrigued as to why particularly Syrian women were the topic of conversation. I asked her many questions. During this conversation, I learned that Syrian women were perceived to be competition for "their men's" affections, oftentimes depicting them as "thieves" who "stole" Turkish men (also see Akyuz and Tursun 2019; Duman 2020; Narlı et al. 2020; Zadhy and Erman 2023). There was a strong belief that a considerable number of men started to prefer Syrian women for marriage. Even though officially banned by the Turkish civil code, polygyny is still practiced, and some men want Syrian women as second wives. It was circulated in informal conversations that some men divorced or separated from their home to be with a Syrian woman. The stories were creative, built on the "fantasy Syrian woman" depicted as dangerous as they were imagined to be "going out of their way to please the husband," "always took care of their hair and dressed well even when they were at home," "serviced the man in every possible way." "The fantasy Syrian woman" was something close to the orientalist depiction of Arab women (Mehdid 1993). The narrative of Syrian women about the receiving country females contextualizes two women who treated Nour badly by pushing her or refusing a chair. Just like Syrians are positioned as threats to jobs and public services, women are threatened by the existence of the othered "fantasy women." Nala also narrated an anecdote:

> On the bus, my daughter saw an empty seat next to a woman and asked if she could sit. The woman, in turn, asked her if she was Syrian. When she confirmed, the woman said, 'No, you cannot sit.' She was looking really weird to us, and my daughter started crying. She wanted to say something to her, but she could not because she was crying non-stop. (Nala)

The gaze of othering appears frequently in the narratives when women talk about their experiences as refugees. The hijab is styled differently by the receiving community women and Syrian women. Thus, it became an identity signifier. While Mariam herself does not wear hijab, she has a mixed friend group where some wear hijab, and some have a secular dress. The moment they are spotted as Syrians due to the hijab style, the gaze of the host community changes, regardless of their own secular or religious attire. Mariam said, "We always make a joke, put something on your hijab so people stop looking at us like we are Syrians. We are getting shy. Because how they are acting makes us become shy." She explained that one of her friends was stopped on the street by an old woman and was told, "Why did you come and destroy our country? Go back to your country."

The sense of competition is not the only reason that women's discrimination is remembered and pointed out. Women's cruelty is often remembered as more severe. This is because women are continuously associated with feminine characteristics of tolerance, submissiveness, and avoidance of confrontation. When women are the executors of discrimination and cruelty, it is remembered as being more severe than men's lousy treatment. Nevertheless, socially created female-to-female competition is an important matter to be examined to locate how fractures among communities are created and sustained.

When I ask Rouba about her experiences in Türkiye, she has an interesting way of combining topics that directly relate to women's gender expressions and how other women perceive them. She spent a considerable amount of her life in Saudi Arabia, and her narrative jumps back and forth between Saudi Arabia and Türkiye. Instead of telling me directly how she is perceived as a Syrian woman in Gaziantep, she is flashed back to her life before Türkiye:

> I struggled since meeting this one girl in Saudi. I was Syrian, and one of them [classmate] had a dad who got divorced from her mom and married a Syrian woman. She had this thing in her head that Syrian women could take her dad or any man, so being Syrian was a huge thing in my class. Not that I will take her dad, but because the woman who is her stepmother is a Syrian. In Türkiye, not a lot, but they feel like this as well. Also, they judge people, and the biggest problem for people in general is this judgment; they love to judge. (Rouba)

How she is perceived has much to do with the "image of the Syrian woman." The importance given to appearance is a central view of Syrian women. While the dominant society women talk about this in negative terms, some female interviewees, going from the same stereotype, emphasized it as a good attribute of Syrian women. For example, Rouba approves of women who are "in good shape." When I asked about similarities and differences between living in Syria and Türkiye, Alaa's angle is about her perception about the differences between women, creating a "general" Syrian woman where she juxtaposes them to a "general" Gaziantep women:

> Syrian women here dress up more. In Antep, of course. In Istanbul, they [Turkish women] are better. But Antep women do not take care of themselves. They learned a lot from us. They learned how we do our make-up. Also, how they deal with their children differs greatly from how we deal with ours. You know we deal with our children by giving them responsibility. I tell my son, go and get your sister from school, [while Turkish women] do not do this. Mother goes and does everything for the children. They even carry their bag. Why are you carrying your son's bag? He can do it. They treat them in a spoiled way. They care about the children more than they care about themselves. My neighbor told me, 'Once we marry, we stop caring about our relationship. We have our children, and that is it.' We have a different way. (Alaa)

Such generalizations fuel stereotypes of two groups of women, totalizing each other in their perceptions. Tasneem is direct about the extra pressure women face as Syrians due to their gender:

> It [life here] is not that bad, but it is not that good. You always feel that you are a visitor. You do not have any rights. When I have a problem, I do not like to be silent. However, I prefer to be quiet because I will face a bigger problem. *Lots of people have a terrible reputation for Syrian women* in general. I do not know why, but some of them told me because you are a Syrian, people look at you in another way, thinking of you in another way. Maybe, maybe [she stresses the word a second time], I am not sure. A few Syrian women had a bad reputation. But that does not mean that all Syrian women are badly reputed. Do you understand me? For example, they feel jealous of a Syrian woman because they [men] can get a second wife [laughing]. (Tasneem)

The wording, "People have a very bad reputation for Syrian women," forces us to think about perceptions of others and acts of labeling that come from the outside. The insecurity of women losing their husbands fuels the "fantasy women" image, which creates mutual resentment and further fragmentation. In Türkiye, through neighbor relations, women develop strong networks and are agents of creating social ties in everyday life.[2] Such fantasy creation hinders women's solidarity. Genwa's words articulate this lack of connection. Genwa works with issues related to women's social problems in an NGO and loves living in Gaziantep when she compares the lives of her sisters and some family members in Saudi Arabia and Germany. She also points out her passion for being in Gaziantep: "I can smell Syria from Gaziantep." Smell, as mentioned in previous chapters, is important for different people and is related to "corporeal knowing" (Van Manen 2016, 271). When she examines the barrier to understanding Turkish women, her answer points to a need for relational and situated knowledge of the receiving community women:

> I love Türkiye and I think when I know the language, I will love it more. I do not know how to react in their language and in their words. I want to discover how Turkish women are living here, so I want their words to understand them. (Genwa)

---

[2] Such negative views also influence the inclusion of refugees and the perception of their deservingness (Zadhy and Erman 2023; Spilda 2017).

In Genwa's words, "when people have each other's words," singular and hostile views would be broken through meaningful interaction.

Husam reports that after staying in Türkiye, his sister relocated to the Netherlands, but she often calls and tells him that "life in Türkiye was more lively" for her as she had a richer social life and activities, whereas, in the Netherlands, she found herself "sitting home all by herself doing nothing." Gaziantep has a large Syrian population, and people are mostly surrounded by others from their hometowns. Additionally, the public domain has spaces that are created for women so that they can be part of a lively social interaction. For example, because the community is large, there are "Syrian weddings," and some of these weddings are designed as "all women" celebration spaces where women get to have fun and enjoy themselves. This could signal why some Syrian women find life in Türkiye "beautiful, active, and lively" for themselves. Gender dynamics are different for differently located women. For Akila, who was living in Gaziantep with her sister as her brother had to leave them to seek a job in another city, staying alone abroad was a culture shock that took some time to get used to. When I met her, she was a confident young woman who was about to finish college and was working in an NGO. But she explains her beginnings in Türkiye:

> My brother told us [she and her sister] to go and search if we could study in Gaziantep. My sister and I, two girls, to go by ourselves! In the Middle East, girls are not like [that]. We are conservative a bit, so girls are not allowed to go abroad and stay too much. Mostly, the men do this. Some families let their girls go, but if they know the school and the university, they rent the house for you and set everything up, where you are surrounded by friends, and then you can go. But my sister and I did not know anyone when we first came to Gaziantep. We had just rented the apartment and started going to the university. We went every single day until we managed to register. My mom called us daily, telling us to watch out and not walk on the streets alone. She told us to look behind us all the time, to make sure no one was following us. She told us to buy pepper spray and ordered us not to get out of the house if we did not have the spray in our bag. If you forget, go back and take it wherever you go and be careful, she said. My sister and I are social people. We love to go out and hang out with our friends. For three months, we stayed home, did not go anywhere, only bought groceries and cooked, and that was it. We did not meet anyone. Finally, when we met our neighbors who were the same age as us, they were surprised that we had been living there for three months as they had never seen us. (Akila)

Many women like Akila are stuck between being stereotyped as "fantasy woman," which makes them the target of resentment, and women living alone in a city for the first time with the fear of sexual harassment and violence. Still, when they gained experience of operating by themselves, young women enjoyed being in Gaziantep. Some enjoyed being free, away from their family, and socializing with young people like themselves. For some, being not only in Türkiye but particularly in Gaziantep was an advantage in terms of the availability of dress choices.

Zein was one of the young women who refused the label "refugee" as she was working and relying solely on her income, positioning herself as "refreshing the economy." Zein was a secular-dressed young woman and had never been in hijab in her life. But when she talked about her life in Gaziantep, an interesting reason emerged that she was comfortable being there:

> It [life here in Gaziantep] is beautiful. At first, I had a plan to go out of Türkiye, but now I am trying to enjoy it and live with all the details in this city, and if I do not go back to Syria, I will stay here. I think Gaziantep is more open than Syria, and there is a balance. They are very close to me and to my culture, so if I wanted to pray, I would not look weird, or if I wanted to wear a hijab, they would accept it. I can go to Europe for a visit but not to live there. (Zein)

Zein's approach suggests that gendered expectations for women vary across different regions of the world. Zein wanted the freedom to have access to both secular and hijabi expressions if she so decided.

When Lina, regime-sympathizing Turkmen, talks about Syrian society and her husband, she continuously separates her experiences of girlhood from her married life. When compared, she loved the life in her father's house. She expressed that her father was an open-minded, progressive man, whereas she found her husband closer to mainstream Syrian society in terms of restrictions on women. When asked about her experiences in Türkiye, she explained the support she received from Turkish neighbors who gave her white goods and added, "Living in Gaziantep reminds me of when I was a little girl in my dad's home. It is more comfortable and more open-minded, similar to the society I was part of before I got married." It is striking how she juxtaposed herself to the Turkish community in Gaziantep, seeing them closer to the values her father's household held. She symbolically positioned Türkiye as "father's house" where she was more comfortable. How she experienced herself as a woman in her father's house, her husband's house, and Gaziantep was a determining factor in how she felt about being in Türkiye.

Social structures everywhere impose gender politics, which most of the time work against minoritized and marginalized women and men. Men, compared to their spatial advantage in their country, experience a loss of patriarchal power in the new space as they become structurally disadvantaged when they no longer have a job, property to their name, money, or retirement income in their old age. All of these make them positionally subordinate to their offspring. The gaze of the receiving community and competitive structures that pit women against one another further their exploitation and compare to their past, making the gender position even more challenging than their home country. In other instances, women may find access to work and a chance to live on their own, giving them the opportunity to feel more liberated in the refugee position. There is always a way that people experience their gender, which shifts with the structural changes in different positions people have in different spaces. The above data can be interpreted through *Gendered Geographies of Power (GGP)* (Mahler and Pessar 2001) as refugee experiences show that even though they are the same people, in different geographic scales, with changing social locations, people's experiences and ways of their agency shift from intimate to transnational levels. Class differences in the next section that position refugees differently also relate to geographic scales and how transnational experiences are different for differently located refugees.

Structural Class Injustice

Joumana, while talking about her situation as a "refugee," constantly reminded me that not all refugees are in the same situation. Comparatively, she finds it difficult to complain as she knows many others are in a more challenging situation:

> It is a beautiful life. There are a lot of locations that you can visit, including Istanbul, Mersin, and Cappadocia. I like our life here. But I think our work and wages [she works in an NGO] help us live here [this way]. If I talk about refugees, I am a refugee, but if I talk about refugees in the camps or, you know, ones without jobs, it is difficult for them, it is more difficult. For us, it is easier. There are some challenges, as I mentioned, like the visa, traveling between provinces, and permission, but it is not an issue. Now we are safe. (Joumana)

Joumana is right to think comparatively as Aisha's narrative includes striking reminders that refugee experiences are indeed multiple and vast and strongly intertwined with the class position:

> Unemployment [is the biggest problem] and it is very expensive here. Now I already have two months' rent that is not paid, and my water and electricity are not paid either. Why did I not pay for it? My son works in construction, but it is not a regular job, and my husband cannot see too well. My family is big. For example, if 1 TL bread is good enough for two people, 10 TL bread is not enough for my family. *Kizilay* [Turkish Red Crescent] is giving cards for food. I went to register my son, and they said you have two family members working. We cannot give it to you. I swear that my son's children are dying from hunger, 'no, it is not my problem. Move along-move along,' he said to me. If I did not need to, I swear I would never go and ask. People who did not need it got help. I showed them. The gold in her arm is from here to here [she points out from wrist to elbow]. They got off cars, and they live in *Karatas* [she means that Karatas is a much better neighborhood than hers]. Rich and poor are very obvious. Wealthy live in richer places. For us, they look at our neighborhood, and say, "They do not deserve it." My sister has ten kids. They also told her that she did not have the right to [a food stamp]. (Aisha)

Aisha was one of the few disadvantaged urban refugees in this study. Her narrative shows the severe lack of basic needs for lower-class refugees. While she is appreciative of good people that she met, like her landlord or her daughter's teacher, her explanation of the deep-rooted injustices in terms of poverty is apparent:

> They [Turkish authorities] never allow Syrians to work [officially]. The wage was supposed to be 100 TL, but they gave 50 TL to my son. His boss was very bad. My husband, who got injured while working] was on his back for four months. We became beggars without begging. He stayed in the intensive care. The police came and asked where this happened. My husband said don't you say that I was at work. It would not be right to tell [give away the employer], but the people opened their doors for us, let us in, and helped us. We should not cause him trouble by telling [because he was working illegally]. I have eight children, and only my son is working. After that, my son was working in a shoe shop for 80 TL per week (around 26 USD). Thank God his boss brought us coal and wood. I pray to God for him. Thankfully, now the state has given us a chance to see a doctor, and this year, they have given us an opportunity to get medication. When we first arrived, my 80-year-old mother-in-law, who was also with us, fell in the bath and broke her arm. We went from hospital to hospital, and no one accepted us. It was disgraceful. They told us it needed money, and they said it would cost 300 TL. Where can we find that kind of money? (Aisha)

Structurally forced poverty is apparent in this experience. People who came from rural areas had a severe loss of access to basic human needs as they lost their livelihood and faced the harsh conditions of city life in Gaziantep. There is no official work permit for many Syrians, and there is also no strict regulation to stop the informal economy, which leads them to be used as cheap labor and exploited. Aisha's 17-year-old son works twelve hours a day, every day, and what he earns does not even cover the rent. This, of course, is a double-edged sword. On the one hand, making people work in dangerous conditions and with the risk of never getting paid for the sums that do not prevent them from falling below the poverty line. On the other hand, it encourages employers to reduce wages in local working-class communities, which again pits workers against one another. In a different manifestation, how women are pushed to competitive structures is similar to working-class refugees and working-class locals.

Rouaa is also concerned about the inequality of work and salary conditions for Syrians:

> We need a chance to work. The salary of a Syrian is less than that of a Turkish worker. Sometimes, I hear that some people are working for 12 hours and the salary is less than half of the Turkish worker, which is not enough. We need to have a chance of a job. I worked with an organization, and the boss thought we were slaves. We have no human rights, no contract. We need a contract. When he fired me, he told me to leave the office in two days, and of course, I did not have any contract. I have no human rights, but if I was Turkish or if I had any contract, I would have privilege, but I do not have it here in Türkiye. And it is a big problem. (Rouaa)

Wage workers have a tough time during the winter as the state only provides coal for the first month of the winter, and it does not sustain for the remainder of the winter months to keep warm. People in the poverty line have better or worse times based on the good or ill faith of employers and landlords. Ayman, a student working for a Turkish man, brings a view that individual treatment is important for middle-class people as well. His boss was a supportive and even protective man. He helped Ayman to get married and continue his studies. Ayman argued that it would be challenging for a refugee to survive without a network of people and their support and work opportunities.

The challenging situation at home is also reflected in the school experience of children who do not have the means for food. Aisha's daughter Dilara is in such a condition. When she was narrating her daughter's experience, Aisha got emotional and showed a great deal of agony:

> Dilara, [my daughter] wrote a poem at school. Her teacher loved it very much. She is in the fourth grade. Her teacher is very good. My children say Turks bring food. There is food time at school here. They bring food, cheese, olives. 'We do not have any food,' she says to me. I say, 'If your father works...[she stops and cries; this is the only time she shows this kind of emotion and tears]. Then we will send food to school as well.' But the teacher divides the food and makes my kids eat as well [a long silence]. I hope she will receive her goodness in the afterlife, she will live in the mansion of heaven... I am Turkmen, and I am also a Syrian citizen. I wish all Syrians were in better condition. They need to come and see people who live in this neighborhood. Stay there for a few months, see them, and then write [about their conditions]. There is a woman there, she has four kids. Her husband was

> working all day, and suddenly he died. She lives with my mother in the same house now. My mother and sister all got food cards, and this woman is staying with them. Four children who are going to die from hunger. No one knows about them, and no one gives them anything. They give some things to the ones who fought in the war. There are women whose husbands died only 2-3 months ago, and they provide for them. This woman's husband died from a heart attack, and while they were looking for him, he was in the morgue. No one is there for them. The state buried the husband. Syrians' pain is great. (Aisha)

Author eye-camera: The singular story that is created about "the refugee" gets more varied and complex with every word of Aisha. There is a depiction of "a woman with four children who lost her husband and has no means," yet, even this depiction does not create a single story. Some, as their dead husbands belong to certain political groups, find a place to stay with their children and have at least the bare minimum, while others who have no connections suffer for years. When Aisha kept telling me, "Write this one, too," and "I am telling you all this because you asked me my story," she asked us to be aware of the multiplicities of these stories. Depictions generally are not complex but encourage us to create a mainstream understanding of "the refugee." On the one hand, we are not given stories of refugees who work in high-paying NGO jobs, were able to transfer some of their money and live middle-class lives, or active political figures, all of whom have chances to use their agency positively for their lives. On the other hand, while we are encouraged to see refugees as "weak, in need of help" we are mostly directed to see their challenges at the same level. What we are not encouraged to see, with the concealment of many different stories, is the structurally forced conditions that create advantages for some and disadvantages for others. Comparative multiple stories give us the ability to see how the existing structures function for differently positioned people.

As an NGO worker, Tasneem has been involved in distributing food stamps and faced tensions from the host community, who were also struggling with social injustice and poverty. Tasneem argues that, in terms of resource distribution, Syrians are perceived negatively:

> Especially when you are distributing food cards to a Syrian family in poor neighborhoods, if one neighbor is Syrian and the other is Turkish, the Turkish start cursing at us, "Why are you helping the Syrians? We are also poor," they say. Hey, come on! You cannot compare yourself with a Syrian. I know that the government helps poor Turkish families, so how can you compare yourself with a woman who lost her husband, who lost her children, who lost her house, but really, they feel jealous of us? If I had known Turkish more, I would not be silent, so I decided not to argue with them anymore. Just ignore it and continue your work. (Tasneem)

The situation, of course, is more complex than the depiction of Tasneem. When there are systemic structural injustices in societies, comparisons inevitably lead to tensions and fragmentation in communities. Any position of oppression has its story and experiences, and any type of suffering needs to be recognized and validated. The above observation about the poor people of the host community shows how structural injustices and inequalities create severe cases of oppression-olympics (Hancock 2011), reducing the chance for people to organize for better policies.

Rather, the oppressed of the dominant society assume the discourse of the elite, blaming "others/outsiders" for their plight (Freire 1996).[3]

Silencing, Discrimination, and Prejudice

Discrimination and prejudice are experienced in dual ways. One is institutional, as mentioned in the experiences within state institutions and the lack of poverty reduction measures. The other way is the banal, an everyday form of discrimination people face. Syrians see multiple and complex approaches from people in the receiving community, and Nazem's words capture this complexity when he sees "Turkish people having a lot of colors, like colorful fabric," not treating them as a unitary category and seeing positive attitudes as well as people who act distant or negative. While Syrian refugees are grateful and understanding about the changes in the receiving community, such as the cheapening of labor and the increase in prices of housing and property, they also know that it is not them who reduce the salaries but employers and/or property owners.

Banal, everyday prejudice and discrimination influence people in two ways when they are positioned as refugees. One is that they have to deal with continuous adverse treatment, and the other is that they feel disempowered to do anything about it. Many Syrians who are positioned as "refugees" have a sense of loss as they are part of a mass, part of a big number of people in which they are not treated as individuals anymore. Anas explains:

> The society here is very open, and there are many new people. You can make new relationships here in Türkiye, far away from the roles. It is far better compared to Syria this way. [Yet] some of the Turkish people, and I am saying some because of my respect for the Turkish people, they act with you as a Syrian, not as a human being. Maybe I learned to act as a human being with people because of them. How they act with us, they think they are giving us many more things. They are acting badly with us in the streets, on the bus, or on trams. Even in government buildings, they see us as second-level or third-level people. (Anas)

Obadiah also mentions the shift in people's attitudes when they think of him as an American because of his English accent and when they learn he is Syrian:

> At first, I get a lot of respect, but as soon as I start speaking Arabic or telling them that I am Syrian, all the respect is suddenly gone. At first, they seemed kind of interested; they wanted to know more about you. As soon as you tell them you are Syrian, it is like you are one of many, who cares? (Obadiah)

Nazem, who is involved with Syrian refugees and travels, also analyzes the negative treatments on a personal level as treatments that need to be dismissed:

[3] The opposition parties in Türkiye heavily use anti-refugee rhetoric, criticizing Erdogan's government. See Saylan and Aknur (2023), Gulmez (2019), Erdoğan (2020).

> We should look at the picture, not always from the negative side. We should look at the positive side because, in every society, they have the good and the bad. In Jordan and Türkiye, for example, [when you compare] you cannot move freely in Jordan as we are moving here, and Jordan is a country that talks in the same language. I should not look at my problem as a personal problem if a taxi driver or a bus driver has a problem with me. (Nazem)

The most important thing for Nazem was to travel back and forth to Syria. Therefore, he prioritized this aspect more than the community's negative attitude. What is important is decided by priorities in people's lives.

Haya explains the "generalizing of the Syrian refugee" from the example of renting apartments, which is a point of grievance for many:

> We are trying to change our apartment now. When I am searching for renting for apartments, I first talk on the phone. They think I am Turkish, and it goes fine, but sometimes, I get to a point where I do not know how to speak Turkish. Then, they realize I am Syrian, and they say, we do not give it [rent] to Syrians, only Turkish. It has been a month, and we are searching but cannot find any. No Syrians, they say. I cannot blame them, actually. Some Syrians unfortunately did bad things that Turkish people started to reject us. Treating all the people from one point of view may be wrong, but on the other side, I cannot blame them. This house owner gave the house, and a Syrian destroyed it. He no longer wants to give it, and I cannot blame them. (Haya)

Similarly, Rahman normalized the housing discrimination by accepting host community homeowners' generalization of all Syrians:

> Sometimes, I might get rejected when I am searching for an apartment. One time, it happened that I was talking to the guy. We saw this studio, spoke about the price and everything, and then he learned that I was Syrian. He could not recognize me all the time we were talking. He asked if I was Syrian, and I said yes, I am Syrian, and he said, 'Oh, then I am sorry I cannot give you the studio.' I told him I was a student, not a refugee, and he said, 'No, sorry. The owner of the house would not give it to Syrians.' I was annoyed the first couple of times, but then I got to know my people, what kind of people they are, how they destroy houses and all. Then, I was like ok, Syrians before showed him a sour face, and why should he give me? If I were a Turk and if I saw a couple of refugees and gave them a 2 plus 1 apartment and they moved in ten people or so and they wouldn't pay the rent, not pay the electricity, they would do this or that I would not give it to another Syrian actually. It is what's happening. It is a fact. Why would I be mad at someone for being careful of what he has? (Rahman)

Haya, Rahman, and many others who pointed out the same issue know that many individuals are different from this stereotypical image. They also know that some practices, like crowded families under one roof, reflect a shortage of meeting basic needs. Nevertheless, they find a way to normalize and accept the negative treatment of the people in the receiving community. This normalization of generalization of Syrians' behavior is a coping strategy that makes the circumstances tolerable when they face ongoing rejection and discrimination. Joumana, more than the others, focuses on the fact that "bad-behaving" people are not the majority, which makes her not accept the strongly developed prejudice and discrimination for the receiving community. Firas, knowing that it is unfair to place all Syrians under one negative stereotype, brings a rational explanation that positions himself to an impossible responsibility of being "perfect" because he is the guest who needs to "put double the effort to impress people." Being "perfect" is not attainable, yet Firas finds it a necessity to always be on his best behavior as he is situated as a "guest."

What is done to Syrians is reflected as a structural problem by few. Husam looking at the past in Syria:

> Owners judge in general. It is a societal situation because in the past, we had Iraqi people coming to Syria, especially Aleppo, and our rent prices jumped from 300 hundred to 900 [Syrian Liras]. We had the same issue before, and we used to judge Iraqi people badly because some of the people were not very good, so we used to judge them wrongly. I discovered this when I came here and saw some things. It is a societal issue. I do not blame people individually. I met a lot of people who treated me very well. (Husam)

Similar to Husam, Aykut manages to take this out of the reactions of the individuals and sees it as an inevitable result of structure that determines people's behavior:

> Negative things can happen anywhere. In Syria also. Iraqis came to Syria, and I have seen how Damascus and certain segments in Aleppo behaved towards Iraqis. Lebanese people also came before that. I have a few punch dents in my car and a few broken spots on it [car]. Sometimes, I find my tires flat just because they have a Syrian plate number [Syrians were given different plates that could identify the vehicle as owned by a Syrian individual]. But in a society, there is always a group of people who act like that. There was a group like that in Syria doing these things to the Iraqi people and the people of Jordan. Jordanian people did not have electricity. Asad gave them electricity while he cut the electricity in Damascus. And because of that, Syrians were reacting to them. (Aykut)

Husam and Aykut's words are an indication of several things. First is that there is a continuous positioning of the refugee-self in the larger community to empathize with the receiving community's feelings. Second, there are strong links between the de-regulated market economy and banal racism and discrimination. When there is no intervention in prices and employee wages, the increase in demand for jobs and housing dramatically shifts the balance in society. Such a direct and negative shift in prices, wage declines, and increase in housing prices make refugees the target of anger and resentment as they are the only people in direct interaction with the receiving community. Third, such tension among people is structural and not unique to Türkiye. Fourth, rather than political authority, people ask for responsibility from individuals and show their reactions not to policymakers but to other groups. Fifth, people can mostly relate to the root cause of the problem when they are on the receiving end of injustice but cannot have a strong voice to address the root causes as they do not hold any dominant identity position in society.

Author eye-camera: Data results of this study indicate that refugee situatedness, at least during the early years of the refugee position, is different than other minority-positioned communities in a country. Refugees hold "outsider within" position. The unitary decision of the states whether to open their doors to them or not make refugees continuously and consciously aware of the structurally forced conditions. Even though they face a lot of negative views from the community, they empathize with the host community's reaction to changing demographics and newly emerging social issues due to the sudden flow and increase of population. They are conscious of the effects of cultural differences. They do not forget the state's capacity issues or lack of preparation for facing the existence of four million refugees. At the same time, their situatedness makes them experience the negative effects of prejudice and discrimination. They are aware that they should have rights as human beings. This dual and acute consciousness makes their situatedness even more challenging. Receiving communities generally direct their frustration and anger to refugees. Nevertheless, refugee frustration, anger, or sadness cannot be easily positioned as one-directional. In a way, their camera is positioned to multiple angles simultaneously. Such simultaneity makes it difficult to channel blame in a simplistic way, as they have access to multiple seeing.

References

Akyuz S, Tursun Ö (2019) When Syrian 'girls' meet Turkish 'boys': mapping gendered stories of mixed marriages. Middle East Crit 28(1):29–49

Duman T (2020) The situation of Syrian women in Turkey. In: Carlson ED, Williams NE (eds) Comparative demography of the Syrian diaspora: European and middle eastern destinations, vol 20. Springer, Cham, pp 93–107

Erdoğan MM (2020) "Securitization from society" and "social acceptance": political party-based approaches in Turkey to Syrian refugees. Uluslararası İlişkiler Dergisi 17(68):73–92

Freire P (1996) Pedagogy of the oppressed (revised). Continuum, New York

Gulmez R (2019) The securitization of the Syrian refugee crisis through political party discourses. J Int Migr Integr 20(3):887–906

Hancock A (2011) Solidarity politics for millennials: a guide to ending the oppression Olympics. Palgrave Macmillan, New York

Kianpour S (2019) Syrian refugee fathers perceptions of identity and family dynamics in the US after displacement. Dissertation,. Virginia Tech

Mahler SJ, Pessar PR (2001) Gendered geographies of power: analyzing gender across transnational spaces. Identities 7(4):441–459. https://doi.org/10.1080/1070289X.2001.9962675

Mehdid M (1993) A Western invention of Arab womanhood: the 'oriental' female. In: Afshar H (ed) Women in the Middle East: perceptions, realities and struggles for liberation. Palgrave Macmillan, London, pp 18–58

Narlı N, Özaşçılar M, Ipek IZT (2020) Turkish daily press framing and representation of Syrian women refugees and gender-based problems: implications for social integration. J Immigr Refug Stud 18(1):1–21

Papadopoulos RK, Gionakis N (2018) The neglected complexities of refugee fathers. Psychother Polit Int 16(1):e1438

Papoutsi A, Phillimore J, Akyüz S, Bradby H, Goodson L, Vaughan C (2022) Geographies of shame: diachronic and transnational shame in forced migrants with experiences of sexual and gender-based violence. J Refug Stud 35(3):1221–1249

Saylan İ, Aknur M (2023) Discourses of Turkish opposition parties towards Syrian refugees: securitization and repatriation. Eskişehir Osmangazi Üniversitesi Sosyal Bilimler Dergisi 24(2):259–283

Spilda FU (2017) Deserving refugee or undeserving migrant? The politics of the refugee category in Turkey. Turkey's Syrians: today and tomorrow. Transnational Press, London, pp 45–59

Tuzi I (2020) Forced migration and gender relations: the impact of displacement on masculinity among Syrian refugees. Working Papers. Sapienza, University of Rome. https://phd.uniroma1.it/dottorati/cartellaDocumentiWeb/56e90468-d261-4614-9512-1a4eb732a65c.pdf

Van Manen M (2016) Phenomenology of practice: meaning-giving methods in phenomenological research and writing. Routledge, London

Zadhy AN, Erman T (2023) Confronting gendered constructions of refugee deservingness and representations: Syrian refugee women strategising for humanitarian aid in Turkey. J Ethn Migr Stud 49(9):2355–2372

Chapter 11
Conclusion

This book laid out its investigation in three intertwined layers: perceptions, experiences, and becoming of refugees. Part I employed theories of conflict analysis to examine the identities, actors, and underlying causes of the Syrian conflict, as perceived by Syrian refugees who were forced to leave their country involuntarily. Part II focused on the experiences of refugees, which shaped their comprehension of the future of Syria. Part III focused on becoming refugees in dual spatiality and multiple temporalities divided between home (Syria) and host (Türkiye). The conflict mapping in Part I is timely, as Syria is at the beginning of a new era after the Ba'ath regime was dismantled and a new regime emerged in December 2024. Perceptions presented here belong to people who have a possibility of returning or possibility of becoming Syria's diaspora. How they perceived the identities, actors, and causes shaped their experiences. Therefore, Part II connects these perceptions to multiple temporalities to examine their experiences, which shaped Syrians' projections for the future, offering insights about possibilities and challenges in the future of Syria and the role different segments could play in the newly emerging governing structure. Part III contextualizes refugees within dual spatiality and multiple temporalities to elaborate on their becoming and show how their "becoming" as refugees is interlinked with the degree of here and there along with past and future in their articulations, which informs their *present*.

The book is written with two perspectives intertwined, looking into each other. One is the eyes of the refugees, which capture how they had seen their own experiences with their own words. This perspective is the core element of the book. Of course, the refugee eye constantly operated under the gaze of the host and the international communities. Essentially, the research started as an exploratory study with a broad investigation of the remaking of the everyday Syrian refugee experience in Gaziantep by connecting it to their pasts. The other perspective is the eye of the researcher. Like any written material, this book holds an eye-camera. A perspectivalized eye functions like a camera, relieves and conceals, sees and dismisses. My

© The Author(s), under exclusive license to Springer Nature Singapore Pte Ltd. 2025
U. Ozkaleli, *De-essentializing Refugees: Perceptions, Experiences, and Becoming of Syrians in Türkiye*, https://doi.org/10.1007/978-981-96-5519-9_11

lens, as the author, aimed to capture articulations of refugees as they talked about their becoming in terms of dualities in their spatial positioning and their constant shift within multiple temporalities. The operator (I, as the researcher) in this research aspired to show her camera's position, distance, and angle. By doing so, I argue that engagement with Syrian refugee subjectivity is more possible for both the researcher and the reader. Such an attempt by no means indicates that the story is complete or includes all angles that need to be covered. While engaging it, the readers might feel that the story is incomplete or missing certain parts. Some readers may find their voice being reflected, and others may say, "Where is my story in this?" Understanding war, displacement, and "becoming" of individuals in the duration and aftermath of wars is always an incomplete story. Still, it is a story that needs to be told, reflected, and interpreted by many from various angles. Only with many different positionings and eye-cameras would we be able to reach the human experience that needs to be captured, learned, and understood.

Social research, particularly its positivist mainstream, often fails to make a necessary call for elaborate and rich stories to be told by the very people who experience war and displacement. Neither does it identify the researcher's eye-camera. Instead, the voice of the researcher becomes the voice of authority, depicting the war experience on behalf of those who lived it. The true "authority" of war experience is the people who go through with it. Social research, then, is obligated to look deeply into lived experiences through human stories. Dominant ideas, ideologies, beliefs, and experiences are constantly in the spotlight. Every time we center stories and experiences left out of this spotlight, we recognize the authorial power of the people who live, suffer, endure, and survive the pain called war.

After the first two chapters, which include methods, context, and theory, the remaining three Parts bring a detailed analysis of the data that came from Syrian people who were positioned as refugees in Gaziantep, Türkiye, during 2015–2016, which was the fifth year of the start of the war. These chapters include extensive quotes from people's narratives to show their perceptions and experiences. This work, as qualitative research based on in-depth interviews, did not intend to test theories. Rather, the theoretical explanations and conceptualizations are reached inductively through a deep engagement with field data.

The first chapter started with a methodological discussion, introducing the dialogical and intersubjective explorations (Bakhtin 2010) that ground the epistemology of the research. Methodological discussions then move to cinematographic apparatus (Baudry 1974) to position the author as the operator of the camera and the conscious effort to unconceal the existence of the operator and the lens she uses to operate it. The first section of the opening chapter introduces the methods used in the field and the approach adopted in conducting in-depth interviews. While the remainder of the book aims to reach readers outside and beyond academia, methodological presentation and discussions aspire to converse with academics who are field researchers and reviewers of such works.

The theoretical discussion and conceptual framework are densely located in the second chapter, which also shows the conceptual connection to the remaining chapters. While keeping people's narratives linked to the theories, the remaining chapters mostly focus on data-driven explorations and findings that come from the narratives of Syrian refugees. Multiple theories are connected in this work in order to capture different elements that were analyzed. "Conflict mapping" (Miall et al. 2000; Wehr 2006) was partially the foundation of preparing the interview questions along with setting my lens for analyzing protracted social/international conflicts (Azar 1985; Miall et al. 2000). I utilized conflict theories to explain how I position the state not only as an interlinked actor to the larger global political system but also as an entity that distances itself in different proximity to different identity groups. This also means that the state often competes with different identity groups within it for the loyalty of the individual (Azar and Haddad 1986; Azar 1985; Miall et al. 2000). Such competition shapes the nature of violence, whether it will be direct or structural, or it will appear as political oppression, repression, or domination toward differently positioned identities.

I diverge from the majority of the conflict theories, though, as their unit of analysis is mostly identity groups. My departure point is the individual. Because of this reason, I discussed how I position "refugee" as a social category and not as a group (Goffman 1963; Stets and Burke 2000). People who fall into the refugee category are members of multiple salient groups, and intersections of their identities create different experiences (Crenshaw 1991; Shields 2008). Such individuals holding intersectional identities are the focus of this study. To put it differently, I discussed multiple group memberships of individuals to capture how they experience themselves within the micro, meso, and macro structure (Stets 2021; Tajfel 2010; Turner 2010a, 2010b, 2012). As structure cannot be understood without power, I integrated power relations to analyze these different domains (Collins 2019). All three levels of the structure are shaped by the state's behavior toward differently located identity groups and individuals. Through their intersectional identities, individuals are treated differently by the state, and this creates various experiences. "Becoming" of an individual within multiple group memberships can only be understood if their agency is articulated. This work brings relational pragmatics analysis of agency, which focuses on past, future, and present (Emirbayer and Mische 1998), to explain refugees' agency as it understands agentic capabilities through seeing the multiplicity of temporality and effects of spatial positioning. By focusing on capturing the agency of individual refugees within dual spatiality and multiple temporalities, I argue that elaborating on the agency of Syrian refugees could be effectively done by locating them within relationships and life episodes through stories (Somers 1994). Their narratives are particularly useful for reaching multiple representations of refugees' agentic selves and recognition of their subjectivity. It should be emphasized, however, that the majority of the participants in this study were against the regime. While there were few participants who showed sympathy or support for the Asad regime, the general positionality of the refugees in Gaziantep was one that felt victimized by it. Therefore, the refugee eye that is prevalent in the book is anti-Asad and anti-Ba'ath regime.

Part I, Chaps. 3–6, investigated the identities, actors, and causes of the conflict in the perception of refugees. The way in which study participants perceive international actors and their religious extensions, such as ISIS, is analyzed in Chap. 3.

How international actors are perceived by people who are located in different identity groups fits with Azar's (1985) interlinked view of the international and domestic aspects of conflicts. The chapter showed the Sykes-Picot Agreement of 1916 as a common, important historical reference to Syria's colonial past shared by Syrians from different ethnic groups. The emphasis on Sykes-Picot, along with contemporary actions of Western states, showed the continuation of colonial legacies over Syria, people's awareness of these policies, and increasing skepticism toward Western human rights discourse. The chapter continued with discussions of people's views on ascriptive identities such as religion and ethnicity as primordial and the source of the conflict, while others see these identities as being used for political purposes to divide people in a conflictual manner. An important finding is that not all people are locked into ethnic-religious-sectarian identity differences, and they do not view the world from a rigid identity conflict angle. However, what emerged from the field analysis was that armed conflict intensified the perception of primordial identities, making people believe that the root cause of the conflict was the inherent differences in people's identities. Even if people had experienced friendships and interactions with other identity groups earlier, observation of the contagious nature of intergroup violence during the war led them to believe that enmities were primordial, buried, waiting for a spark to ignite. Even though identity clashes are all politically induced in their perception, resentments were now too real to move away from the "us" versus "them" binary. What also emerged was that at the time of the study, rather than an overarching "Syrian" identity, ethnic, religious, or local identities were used more for people to self-identify, indicating the richness that may not fit into the "nation-state" discourses.

Chapter 4 focused on internal actors, analyzing the Asad Government and the Free Syrian Army (FSA) as the main conflicting parties. Even though no actor was depicted as an idealized entity, the regime and/or Asad were seen as mainly responsible for the violent conflicts and war. The Asad regime included and blended both the father and the son and generally depicted the forty-year-long Ba'ath regime under the family control of the Asads. The Hama Massacre of 1982 remains the most dominant historical memory, explaining both the Hafez Asad era and as a symbol of the regime's general approach toward its citizens, which also reflects current events. The Hama 1982 massacre and the brutalities that were experienced during this time caused a collective and transgenerational trauma (Kaufman 2023; Volkan 2001) not only among the members of the Muslim Brotherhood, the direct target of the massacre, but Syrian society at large. Hama became the graveyard of dissent for many different segments and ideologies that challenged the regime. Commonly, Asad and the regime were merged into a singular embodiment to the extent that when people were talking about "the regime," they constructed their sentences as "he" rather than "it." The blend of the man into the government as a singular entity mainly was the foundation of opposition to the existing governing structure. Intertwined usage of "regime" and "he" also signals the patriarchal nature of the governance embodied in Asad, the man. It is so embedded in the thinking of many participants, both men and women, that they referred to a future leader in their envisioned Syria as a "he."

What emerged from the people's accounts is that the regime systematically used violence to provoke further violence from the protestors, knowing that the regime had superior firepower. This became most evident in the refugees' narratives in their common belief that just like *Shabiha* (militia) or ISIS was either created or supported by the Syrian state/regime. In other words, refugees in Gaziantep commonly believed that turning peaceful demonstrations for democratic opening into a total civil war was the regime's deliberate strategy to suppress the democratic demands of the initial protests. Another common view was that promoting the radical Islamist groups was a strategy of the Asad regime, as many moderate opposition members were eventually consolidated under regime loyalty, for they did not want to be governed by the radical Islamists. In refugees' words, therefore, their peaceful revolution was "stolen" or hijacked by the regime by turning it into a bloody civil war. Such a strategy ensured that Asad and Ba'ath stayed in power despite their lack of legitimacy.

Given that they were refugees located in Gaziantep, a city bordering Aleppo, the majority of the participants were supportive of the FSA. Unlike the later developments and depictions of FSA as formed by jihadists, participants of this study who were secular or opposed to Islamic governments were also supporters of FSA in the early years of armed struggle. Another important finding of this chapter is that not all refugees who fled to Türkiye were affiliated with the opposition groups who fought against the regime. Among the people who fled were villagers who neither supported the regime nor the FSA. This made them vulnerable to the violence exerted on them by both sides, as the dominant ethos was "You are either from us or against us." Refugee narratives show that many people, initially displaced to save their lives from regime bombing, attempted to build a life within Syria. However, when they encountered violence and insecurity from other fighting groups, most notably from ISIS, they were ultimately forced out of the country. Accounts show that the FSA also became a source of insecurity for people who did not want to be part of the violence. Some refugees who had fighting-age sons fled to save them as they did not want their children to die either for the regime or the FSA, as they did not believe in armed struggle or that the results would be beneficial for the ordinary people.

Chapters 5 and 6 focused on how participants of the study explained the causes of the conflict in Syria, particularly the role of coercive state politics and economic instability, respectively. In Chap. 5, many participants gave rich accounts and depictions of their lives and relations with other identity groups. The analysis showed that the state had divisive policies toward individuals in various identity groups. Consequently, on a micro level, individuals from different religious and linguistic groups lived parallel lives that largely lacked cross-cutting ties. Such policies nurtured stereotypes and prejudices, which weakened community spirit at the macro-Syrian level. Field analysis detailed how these stereotypes and prejudices developed in individuals' experiences and minds, reflecting their everyday experiences during the Asads' era. Fear was the driving emotion that the regime used for all groups through silencing, repression, and persecution. This was probably the main reason for the immediate dissolution of Syrian society. For many study participants, during pre-war Syria, people were mostly identified with localities, e.g., Aleppian and Damascene. "Syrian" was never made an over-arching identity with political cohesion even though Arabness or being (Sunni) Muslim was prevalent in self-identification. The majority of the interviewees met, interacted, and learned about people from other places in Syria after becoming refugees in Gaziantep, where they mostly experienced being called Syrian out of Syria. Silencing and repression were experienced differently by participants under the Syrian government.

Chapter 6 distinguished poverty and class discrimination from economic oppression as diverse participant voices emerged, revealing individuals with varying income levels experienced discrimination and oppression in distinct ways. For the poor and lower classes, basic needs and higher life standards were systemically denied by the regime, while the middle classes experienced drawbacks at the meso and macro levels as the Asad government either favored a certain number of people for the detriment of others or did not allow economic openings and opportunities. This chapter also discussed how class-based divisions strongly shaped the views of individuals. Many participants who supported the revolution found inequality and systemic lack of basic needs for the majority of the population as a reason for the initial protests, along with the corruption and attacks on dignity. The analysis indicated that many participants, especially from the younger generation, were optimistic about Bashar Asad coming to power, as he was viewed as young and open to reform. Thus, many were shocked by his endorsement of violence against pre-teens at Dar'aa. At the point of the Dar'aa incident, the participant accounts showed that parents broke their silence about the historical events, which was influential in changing the younger generations' overall view of Bashar Asad when parents' accounts were enforced by his lack of initiative to take measures against violence toward children.

Few participants who were against the uprising argued that the "poor" were the cause of the conflict, blaming the lower classes for the war and arguing that they did not know the meaning of freedom or equality, which were empty words. Gender inequality and the patriarchal view toward women, for example, fathers not sending daughters to school, was given as an indicator for this claim. The chapter argued that men who are expected to be protectors and providers of the family who suffer from poverty need to be evaluated from a class dimension as "tradition," "religion," and "mentality" become strong shields against appearing "weak," giving men in poverty a sense of control and power over the education decision. Participants' views on economic capabilities surface the hidden aspects of how rural or urban poor are treated. It also shows the role and contribution of small business owners as regime action became detrimental to their business, which made them act against it.

Chapter 6 also pointed out the gap between the needs of people at the starting point and the progress of the protracted conflict. At the beginning of the conflict, some segments of society demanded access to basic needs such as health care, education, and meaningful and gainful employment. Others with more means demanded dignity, political expression, representation, and access to decision-making structures. For both groups, once the conflict reached a destructive endpoint, the scale of the needs dramatically dropped to worse levels, depriving people of the most basic needs, such as shelter, food, electricity, and clean water. Additionally, people faced constant insecurity, which included daily engagement with bombs and bullets. Many are pushed to believe that going after dignity, rights, and equal enjoyment from development would lead to destructive wars, and life without these demands would have been better. In other words, wars become tools against the masses to stop them from asking their fair share from the state elites. Furthermore, individual refugee experiences make it apparent how colonized states can turn the struggle between haves and have-nots into civil wars. In other words, colonizing structures through wars prevent countries and regions from transforming into democracies. The chapter concluded that Syria today, instead of fulfilling its human potential, is facing political and economic setbacks and growing generations that are cut off from formal education. The last thing anybody is talking about anymore is "dignity, freedom, representation, and a system that articulates everyone's rights."

Part II of the book includes Chaps. 7 and 8, which move from experiences in the home country to experiences of the self as a refugee in the receiving community. Chapter 7 scrutinized identity and belonging. How people identify themselves and their sense of belonging is no longer based on their life in Syria but after the experience of displacement. The chapter articulated how refugees spatially live through dual experiences continuously, always negotiating "here" and "there." They also exist within multiple time frames: "before" and "after." That is, their experiences of leaving home, before becoming a refugee, and after it. The meaning of today is always in relation to the bleakness of the future or the disappearance of the past as they know it. The chapter deals with the complexity of dual spatiality and multiple temporalities of identity and belonging in terms of proximity to the lost home, the idea of return in terms of security and memory, and how they feel displaced both in the home country and in the host. Chapter findings show that relationality to time differs. Loss of home is traumatic to many, but for some, it manifests as living in the past and waiting to regain it. For others, it manifests as a refusal to think about the past due to losses. How the past is located influences future projections differently, which, in effect, decides who they will be in the present moment. For example, refugees who are driven to focus on regaining the past refuse to adjust to present circumstances. People who refuse to think about the past and their losses may have difficulty envisioning a future and may feel a lack of belonging in the present.

Chapter 8 analyzed how participants envision the future of Syria in a post-war moment. They take different angles, some connecting the future to the scriptural past or the historical past, while others focus on the enmity of today shaping relations of the future. Many saw a bleak future in connection to the lack of schooling of new generations. Participants also had different views about the political system that awaited Syria. Some were sure of the division of the land on ethnic, religious, or other identity differences and perceived this as a weakness, while others considered it an inevitable necessity. The analysis showed that there were four streams of ideas regarding the political governance of Syria. First, people who believe in the religious-based rule where Sunni Islam is the base of the society as it represents the majority of the population in a system that is not democracy. Second, people who believe in democracy but are firm in their conviction that without a transitional benevolent dictatorship to prepare people for many facets of institutionalization for democracy, Syria would not be able to practice it. Third, people who believe in democracy but do not see it possible in the foreseeable future as conflict continues and there is no clear and acceptable leadership to represent society. Fourth, people who believe that Syria needs to start building an institutional structure for a democratic future, and with all the experiences, it is possible for Syria to have free, fair elections and a democratic system where freedom and justice are prominent. Democracy versus authoritarian rule was a complex matter, as some thought representative democracy was possible and attainable as it was experienced through the Local Councils, while others, even if they believed in democracy, argued that the "ripe" moment for democracy could come only after a benevolent dictatorship that could establish governance institutions. Some of the arguments reflected the Western liberal debates on "institutionalization before democratization" (Paris 2004).

Regardless of their belief in democracy or authoritarianism, the majority believed in the necessity of a strong leader who was Sunni because they were the majority. Similar to the previous chapter's findings about people demanding more advanced rights and falling back to needing basic subsistence, their view of governance followed a similar trajectory. Analysis of different temporalities in terms of governance showed that Syrians, at the beginning of the peaceful demonstrations in 2011, were ready for democracy. At that particular moment, Syrian people from all religious, ethnic, and linguistic segments had a common demand for more progressive change. Particularly, younger generations demanded change for the betterment of their social, economic, and political rights. It was a moment of flourishing homegrown progress stolen by the war. Some participants argued that the step taken back in terms of material conditions and armed engagement makes it difficult for Syria's immediate future to nurture a democratic regime. They emphasized that along with regress in education levels and material conditions, having armed groups managing the areas under the control of rebel factions eliminated the homegrown practice of democratic evolvement of Local Councils.

Part III, composed of Chaps. 9 and 10, focused on people "becoming" refugees. While previous sections focused on the Syrian context, Chapters 9 and 10 investigated the experiences at the micro, meso, and macro levels by taking the structure of the receiving community at the center. Chapter 9 followed the participants in their journey of learning to be refugees in the receiving community of Gaziantep, Türkiye. Through the gaze of the receiving community and the conditions that they faced, refugees experienced what it is to become a refugee. By crossing the physical border, their self-identity also passes through the mental gate between being a citizen (Aleppian or Damascene, etc.) and being Syrian to become a refugee. In order to locate their challenges, Chapter 9 focused on leaving home and transitioning from home to the receiving community and existing under the gaze of the new community and the state. The chapter, through the examples presented by the participants, argued that people who are hired to jobs that directly work with refugees, as officers or managers in public offices, influence the implementation of the policies (meso level). Refugees problematized such people's behavior more than the ordinary person on the street (micro level). If the people who worked in public offices were against the existence of refugees in the receiving country, continuous dealing with such individuals would change the everyday experiences of people who are positioned as refugees. The chapter also focused on the ambivalence of being a guest or a refugee and how self is negotiated when coming face to face with a different language and a school system. Participants with children cared most about school decisions. People who plan to leave Türkiye and people who hold on to the hope of returning home in a few years refrained from sending their children to Turkish schools, which showed that their future projections influenced their present decisions. The ones who focused on the past and home country's culture and native language, regardless of future expectations, wanted their children to stay in Syrian schools. Two groups of participants targeted to send their children to Turkish schools where they could master the Turkish language and learn to be part of the dominant culture. People who were certain that they were to stay in Türkiye for many years, and people who could not envision what their future was going to be like. Their reasoning for the decision was different, though. For the former, the motivation was to prepare the children for the future and equip them to survive in their new home. For the latter, the focus was on the "now," surviving at the moment regardless of what the unknown, unclear future held.

Chapter 10 analyzed the social and structural problems that refugees face in terms of their status, their gendered experiences, class positions, and issues of prejudice and discrimination. Displacement and war experience are challenging for all refugees, yet, experience in the new setting is not identical for individuals who are pushed to a singular "refugee" positionality. Chapter 10 looked at the differences between middle- and upper-middle-class refugees and refugees who came from either lower classes or rural areas. The stark class differences are presented, but some unexpected advantages and disadvantages also appear. For example, educated professional people experienced a dramatic loss of social status and unemployment, and younger people with language access without much formal higher education were presented in Türkiye with opportunities through international NGOs, which tilted the social hierarchies. The chapter also showed how refugees remarkably distinguish between prejudice and discrimination at the micro level, individual interaction, and discrimination at the meso level within formal organizations, particularly official institutions of the host state. The refugee-self is continuously positioned in the larger community to empathize with the receiving community's feelings. There are strong links between the de-regulated market economy and banal racism and discrimination. When there is no intervention in rents, prices, and employee wages, the increase in demand for jobs and housing dramatically shifts the balance in the receiving community. Such a direct and negative shift in prices, wage declines, and rise in housing prices make refugees the recipient of the anger and resentment as they are the only people in direct interaction with the receiving community. Refugees are aware of the reasons why receiving community people show discrimination. It is because such tension among people is structural and not unique to Türkiye, and also some compared Syrians' attitudes to others when they came to Syria like Iraqis. People mostly can relate to the root cause of the problem when they are on the receiving end of injustice but do not hold any dominant identity position in society to change it.

This book aspired not to reduce people to "the refugee" where they can be treated as a singular group with one definition. It emphasizes that even within similar social locations, singularizing experiences reduce our understanding of the consequences of war displacement on individuals' becoming. The study also revealed a strong class-based dynamic at work in terms of root causes of the conflict and experience of displacement. Still, not all that are disadvantaged are disadvantaged in the same way, and not all refugees are disadvantaged.

When I was starting this research, someone asked me "if I was sure that I was ready to 'deal' with war traumas and stories." Another advised me to keep as far away as possible from such "depressive" topics. Listening to the war experiences and loss of loved ones, homes, and pasts is not easy. Neither is it easy to work on, think about, analyze, and write about it extensively. It is also difficult for the readers. Reading about war is indeed difficult. However, as authors and readers of war texts, we should not have a choice of listening, writing, thinking, and reading about war experiences. We should not have a choice because people who face, endure, and live in war, people who lose their loved ones and themselves to wars, are not given a choice whether to go through with it or not. It comes unplanned, unhinged, and without permission. That is why listening, writing, and reading war stories is not the same as living it.

Choice is the most precious freedom we all should have. Unless we all are free to choose not to have war, our engagement with it, even if it is only about listening, writing, reading, and thinking about it, should not be a choice. A frustrated participant told me, "You do not understand what it is to be a refugee unless you lived it!" I could not agree more. I promised him that every time I wrote, I would never forget that. Nevertheless, I also asked him if I should not at least aspire to empathize and stay connected to the pain that was created. We agreed that disinterest would not only be a worse alternative but also a grave mistake. I hope the readers engage with the experiences of refugees with such an interest. You, reader, like I, unless you have experienced it, will not understand what it means to leave home abruptly, to be separated from loved ones for an unclear period, not to be able to go to your room and rest your head on your pillow even for a minute. You will not know what it means to leave your library and your trees behind; you will not understand why four o'clock was the time that the day was meaningful as it was the lunch hour with the entire family that could never be attained at that very table. You will not understand unless you have lived through such an experience. You will not understand why the color of that sea is not like looking at another sea, and no place could give you the same feeling as that particular park bench at the entrance of the bazaar. You may never understand the feeling of seeing a city that is thousands of years old in the rubble. You may never fathom some other place on this earth as you went as a "refugee" that did not mean much to you, suddenly becoming an inseparable part of you as you buried your parent there. Still, you may aspire to find an empathic connection. Until the day our future generations consider war unfathomable, we should stay engaged and disturbed by the pain of war.

References

Azar EE (1985) Protracted international conflicts: ten propositions. Int Interact 12(1):59–70. https://doi.org/10.1080/03050628508434647

Azar EE, Haddad RF (1986) Lebanon: an anomalous conflict? Third World Q 8(4):1337–1350

Bakhtin MM (2010) The dialogic imagination: four essays. University of Texas Press, Austin

Baudry JL (1974) Ideological effects of the basic cinematographic apparatus. Film Q 28(2):39–47

Collins PH (2019) The difference that power makes: intersectionality and participatory democracy. In: Hankivsky O, Jordan-Zachery JS (eds) The Palgrave handbook of intersectionality in public policy. Palgrave Macmillan, Cham, pp 167–192

Crenshaw K (1991) Mapping the margins: intersectionality, identity politics, and violence against women of color. Stanford Law Rev 43(6):1241–1299

Emirbayer M, Mische A (1998) What is agency? Am J Sociol 103(4):962–1023

Goffman E (1963) Stigma: notes on the management of spoiled identity. Penguin Books, New York

Kaufman S (2023) The roots of ethnopolitical conflict. In: Byrne S, Matyók T, Scott IM, Senehi J (eds) Routledge companion to peace and conflict studies. Routledge, New York, pp 17–27

Miall H, Ramsbotham O, Woodhoulse T (2000) Contemporary conflict resolution. Polity Press, Oxford

Paris R (2004) At war's end: building peace after civil conflict. Cambridge University Press, Cambridge

Shields S (2008) Gender: an intersectionality perspective. Sex Roles 59(5):301–311

Somers MR (1994) The narrative constitution of identity: a relational and network approach. Theory Soc 23(5):605–649

Stets JE (2021) Micro, meso, and macro processes in identity change: the 2020 Cooley-Mead award address. Soc Psychol Q 84(4):286–308

Stets JE, Burke PJ (2000) Identity theory and social identity theory. Soc Psychol Q 63(3):224–237

Tajfel H (2010) Introduction. In: Tajfel H (ed) Social identity and intergroup relations, vol 7. Cambridge University Press, Cambridge, pp 1–12

Turner JH (2010a) Theoretical principles of sociology, volume 1: Macrodynamics. Springer, New York

Turner JH (2010b) Theoretical principles of sociology, volume 2: Microdynamics. Springer, New York

Turner JH (2012) Theoretical principles of sociology, volume 3: Mesodynamics. Springer, New York

Volkan VD (2001) Transgenerational transmissions and chosen traumas: an aspect of large-group identity. Group Anal 34(1):79–97

Wehr P (2006) Conflict mapping. https://www.beyondintractability.org/essay/conflict_mapping

The manufacturer's authorised representative in the EU is Springer Nature Customer Service Centre GmbH, Europaplatz 3, 69115 Heidelberg, Germany. If you have any concerns regarding our products, please contact ProductSafety@springernature.com

Printed and bound by CPI Group (UK) Ltd, Croydon, CR0 4YY
01/10/2026
02225925-0008